Meeting Disability

A European Response

Patrick Daunt

CASSELL

For François and Patrice

Cassell Educational Limited
Villiers House
41/47 Strand
London WC2N 5JE

© Patrick Daunt 1991

1666843

First published 1991

British Library Cataloguing in Publication Data
A catalogue record for this book is available from the British Library.

ISBN 0 304 32482 5 (hardback)
0 304 32386 1 (paperback)

Phototypeset by Intype, London
Printed and bound in Great Britain by
Dotesios Ltd, Trowbridge, Wilts

Contents

Preface

The balance of material in this book reflects the actual evolution of the response so far of the European Community to the challenge of disability; it does not represent a view of the intrinsic relative importance of the various topics which are covered.

The references given at the end of each chapter are confined to European and international documents. Even so, they do not claim to be a complete bibliography, except as far as concerns policy documents and published studies of the European Community institutions. Virtually all the documents listed are available in English. Policy documents of the European Community exist in all the other European Community languages also. As to studies and conference reports produced by the European Commission I have indicated (in brackets at the end of each entry) the languages in which they exist, using the official two-letter code to be found in *Social Europe* supplement 7/86 (for which see References to Chapter 2). These are: DA = Danish, DE = German, GR = Greek, EN = English, ES = Spanish, FR = French, IT = Italian, NL = Dutch, PT = Portuguese. In the few instances where no English language version exists, I have given the title of the document in the original language, followed by an English translation in square brackets; I have used the same procedure for the names of associations, establishments, etc. in Appendixes 1 and 2. Subject to stock, all the Community documents referenced are available on request from the Division for Measures in Favour of Disabled People, Directorate-General V, Commission of the European Communities, 200 rue de la Loi, B-1049 Brussels. Documents of the international organizations (the United Nations and its agencies, OECD, Council of Europe, etc.) always exist in English but must be asked for at the organization concerned.

I wish to acknowledge above all the support and advice of Professor Peter Mittler of the University of Manchester, without whom this book would not have been published in its present form. The kindness of Professor Klaus Wedell of the London University Institute of Education in arranging for me to be a visiting fellow of the Institute has also been a great help to me.

Since I returned to England from Brussels in 1987 I have received much encouragement too from Dr Seamus Hegarty of the National Foundation for Educational Research, and Professor Mary John of the University of Exeter.

Of those disabled people, professionals and family members with whom I worked in Brussels, and to whose inspiration any merit this book may have is entirely due, the number is too great for me to list them here. For many of them, the contribution which they are making to improving the quality of life for 'Europeans with a disability' is mentioned in the text and indexed. I only regret that it has not been possible to do this for all.

Part I

Disability and Europe

Chapter 1

The Background to Action

INTRODUCING THE BOOK

The purpose and character of the book

The aim of this book is to explore policy issues at the intersection of two themes which are evidently of great public interest but which have not, it seems, been brought together in a book before — disability and Europe.

This aim is served by four objectives:

1. To present to the reader *the reality of the disabled people of Europe* — who they are, and their difficulties, achievements and aspirations; also to illustrate how, throughout the European Community, society at large and government in particular have succeeded or failed in understanding and responding to that reality.
2. To describe *the contribution to this response which has been and is being made by the European Community as such*, and by other European or international activity; also to demonstrate the unique potential of the Community as promoter of a better quality of life for disabled people.
3. To frame *guidelines for future action*. Specifically this will include the needs for comprehensive and coherent policies which cover all aspects of autonomous life; for increased participation by disabled people in the preparation and implementation of measures that affect them; and for advances in professional training and co-operation.
4. To lay down a *theoretical basis* on which a framework of policy can be built. Central to this will be three beliefs which I have derived from my professional experience in the fields of education and disability:

- that we should found all our initiatives and programmes on a *principle of equal value*, the determination, that is to say, that all people (including therefore all disabled people) are to be valued equally by society and in society;
- that the aim of all policy should be to ensure the *highest possible quality of life* for all disabled people;

– that all measures in pursuit of that aim should be based on a recognition and formulation of *the rights of disabled people*.

By 'disability' I mean all kinds of disability and resulting handicaps. For those who have not explored the realm of disability to any great extent it may present itself as both confined and specialized, and therefore of limited interest even if developed on a European scale. Yet I believe that we do not have to venture far into the subject before it is brought home to us that its component issues together comprehend every aspect of human aspiration and activity and are individually of immediate and compelling interest to every one of us.

Since it is now generally acknowledged that at least 10 per cent of all people experience a significant degree of physical or mental impairment, there can be no pretence that disability is merely the concern of some trivial minority. When we add to that number all those family members and workers in the medical, social, educational and other fields whose lives are more or less involved with those of disabled children and adults it is evident that the 'constituency' of the subject is enormous.

Not so long ago, it is true, common knowledge of disability was obscured by medical vocabulary, and its reality sheltered within the privacy of nuclear families or hidden behind the walls of hospitals and asylums. Much of this barrier of concealment has now been demolished — for a number of reasons, among them the policy operating in all European countries to reduce or close long-stay residential institutions and enable many more disabled people to live in the open community. With it has gone the legitimacy of ignorance and disinterest: disability is now undeniably and irreversibly in the public domain.

What is presented here is not the result of academic or objective study, but something much more personal. It might be supposed that someone working as a European civil servant, as I was until 1987, would be engaged in 'pure administration' and inevitably distant from the daily realities both of disabled people and of those who work with and for them. In fact the reality of setting up and managing for five years the Bureau for Action in favour of Disabled People of the European Commission was not at all like that. Apart from all the other things which could be said about it, it was for me personally a profoundly rewarding, enlightening and moving experience. It not only helped me to understand something about a great number of particular issues about which I knew little or nothing before; it offered me a coherent mass of new impressions and evidences, which both corroborated and helped me to clarify the values which I had been trying to establish throughout my professional life. In this way it carried my beliefs forward in the direction in which, so to speak, they wanted to go.

I stress this personal character of the book here first of all because it gives the most pressing reason for my having wanted to write it, but also because I hope this affective aspect of what I have written may make it more interesting to Europeans who either themselves experience disability or have other good reasons for caring about it.

This explains too why, although the book has a rather firm structure, I have drawn on all sorts of material, including 'hard' facts about legislation or statistics and so on, but also reported opinion and anecdote as well as my own judgements of problems and of solutions to them. At various points in the book and particularly towards the end of it, I have entered into theoretical discussion.

The scope and structure of the book

Since the experiences on which this book is based belong almost entirely to the twelve countries of the Community as it is at present, it is the European Community that I generally mean when I refer to 'Europe'. I hope however that the book's messages will be relevant to all European situations, in the central and eastern regions as well as in the west, and indeed beyond Europe too.

The book is in three parts:

- The two chapters constituting *Part I* aim at establishing the context and foundations of what the European Community has done and is doing in the realm of disability. For the rest of this chapter I shall be giving a brief sketch of the historical background and establishing the context of the subject as I propose to treat it. The next chapter will consist of a summary account and evaluation of the Commission's first action programme to promote the social integration of disabled people which was inspired by the 1981 International Year of Disabled People and came to completion in 1987.
- The four chapters of *Part II* will focus on issues. The first will present the salient problems and potential of disabled people in Europe, and highlight some of the responses to this challenge made in the public and private sectors at international, European and national levels. There then follow three chapters which illustrate and comment on measures which have been undertaken in the three broad domains of employment, the environment and education.
- The first chapter of *Part III* starts from an account of what the Community is doing now by means of its second action programme concerning disabled people (known as Helios), and then addresses the immediate prospects for further action. Finally in the last chapter I go on to set out my suggestions for action in the future and my beliefs about the principles and values which should underlie this.

Before leaving this Introduction, there is something about the book's content and scope which I need to explain. As I have just said, in the most detailed part of the book I have divided the content into three fields — employment, environment and education. This is not therefore a book exclusively concerned with education, and it may seem strange that it appears as one in a series of books which are.

There are three reasons for this. First, as we shall see, although education is not the only sector considered here, its prime importance in relation to the whole clearly emerges. Secondly it is, I am convinced, a good thing, above all when we are thinking about people with disabilities, if education is not treated in isolation from the other main functions of life. The fact that, after several years of failure and frustration of the endeavour, the European Community has succeeded in developing one programme which comprehends educational, social and economic integration is something which deserves to be celebrated.

Thirdly, my own background is in education. Before coming to Brussels I was headmaster of the Thomas Bennett Community School, a somewhat radical comprehensive school in the New Town of Crawley. I was also national chairman of the Campaign for Comprehensive Education and author of a book in which I first set out the 'equal-value principle' which figures also in this one.[1] When in 1974 I first joined the service of the European Commission in Brussels I worked in the Education Division, and it was my concern for equal opportunity in the education systems and in particular for the problems of children with special needs that led to my being asked in 1981 to design the first action programme of the Community to promote the social and economic integration of disabled people.

For me therefore extension from a concern for the education of children with special needs to a consideration of the social and economic realities of disabled persons of all ages is something quite natural, indeed inevitable.

THE HISTORICAL CONTEXT

The specialist tradition and the post-war boom

During the nineteenth and earlier part of the twentieth century the main lines of progress in responding to disability consisted of improvements in medical treatment and the creation of specialized institutions of education and residential care. Over this period the foundations of what later has come to be known as the 'medical model' of disability were firmly laid down; a person with a serious disability of any kind was perceived as a patient, and disabled children thought of as special cases. For them life could never offer more than limited opportunities. The task of the professional was to reduce the consequences of a tragic infliction as far as possible and the chief requirements of friends and family were protection and compassion.

It is easy now to look back with disapproval at this period when paternalism was dominant, but it would be fairer to acknowledge that the progress that we have seen in both attitude and achievement since the last war would have been impossible without that foundation of specialized systems of care. Technical advances, such as the use of braille, hearing aids and wheelchairs, made it possible to begin to think of the lives of people with motor or sensory disabilities in more active and independent terms. No less important was the precious gift of objectivity contributed by the medical tradition. The sense of guilt felt by disabled people themselves and their parents was, if not eliminated, at least greatly diminished and dramatic advances were made in the understanding and treatment of mental illness.

The large number of young disabled soldiers returning from the First World War led to a quite new sense of responsibility in Europe to find means for reconciling disablement with the chance of an active and productive life; hence the creation of special workshops, reserved occupations and reserved places in public transport. The situation after the Second World War was somewhat different, but the effects on the conception of disability and the services needed to respond to it were even more striking. There were relatively fewer disabled veterans but the economic situation, so far from being one of imminent depression, promised a prolonged boom with a consequent severe shortage of labour.

This 'market-driven' impulse to find a means for employing disabled people previously supposed to be unemployable was reinforced by two other factors. For one thing, the post-war development of the notion of the Welfare State implied improvements in provision for the victims of industrial accidents; compensation costs provided an incentive to rehabilitation aimed at active resettlement. Again, the motive may have been economic but the effect was both to reinforce positive attitudes towards disabled people as workers and to encourage increased investment in vocational rehabilitation. Secondly, the work of often voluntary bodies was leading to a more positive perception of the potential of mentally handicapped people, for whom a graded series of active options was devised, rising from day centres through so-called training centres and sheltered employment to full employment on the open labour market.

The 1940s, 1950s and 1960s, then, are the years in which we see a dramatic development of legislation in European countries aimed at promoting the training and employment of disabled people. Early examples are the United Kingdom's Disabled Persons (Employment) Act of 1944 and the 1947 regulation on the placement of the less able-bodied work-force in the Netherlands. There followed the French law of 1957 on the vocational and social rehabilitation of the handicapped and Luxembourg's 1959 law on the retraining and placement of the disabled. Belgium legislated for the social resettlement of the physically handicapped in 1963, and in 1968 Italy established its regulations for the obligatory employment of disabled workers. Discussion of the evolution and effectiveness of all these initiatives belongs to Chapter 4; here we need only observe that by the end of the 1960s the notion that there should be positive action for the employment of disabled people was firmly established almost throughout western Europe.

The militant movement

As the boom calmed down it became clear to those closely involved, including many disabled people themselves, that this set of initiatives, important as they were, did not go nearly far enough to meet the demands of disabled people for equal opportunity in society and on the labour market — demands which the legislation had itself helped to stimulate. What was sought for now was not simply the wooing of disabled workers when that happened to be economically convenient, but a recognition of the right of disabled people, however severe their functional loss, to the same chances for self-improvement as anyone else.

The origin of this movement was not in Europe but the United States. Although professionals played an important part in the development of these ideas, they are above all associated with the efforts of motor disabled people, many of them centred on universities, of which Illinois and Berkeley in California were especially prominent. For these mostly young people, independent living (IL) was the primary aim; this, as opposed to rehabilitation with all its paternalistic associations, became the hallmark of the movement. Instead of being an irremediable misfortune calling for charity, handicap had to be seen as an intolerable injustice which could be eliminated.[2] Owing much to contemporary movements such as civil rights, consumerism and the drive to close down long-stay institutions, the promoters of IL enhanced their own credibility by founding their political campaign on the provision of effective services, such as the Center for Independent Living established at Berkeley in 1972. A major political success followed soon after, with the adoption of the 1973 Rehabilitation Act, including the celebrated Article 504 which banned discrimination on the grounds of disability in any programme or activity receiving federal financial support.

Militancy in the same spirit lay behind the decision of a number of physically disabled people, dissatisfied with the dominance (as they saw it) of the prestigious Rehabilitation International (RI) by professionals rather than people with disabilities, to lead a breakaway movement at the 1980 world congress of RI in Winnipeg, and to found the following year in Singapore a world organization 'of' rather than 'for' disabled people, to be known as DPI, Disabled People's International.

There were moreover comparable initiatives in Europe at this stage. Founded in Nancy as early as 1964, the GIHP was originally the Groupement des intellectuels handicapés physiques, a title which tells a lot about the inspiration, characteristic of the period, which made its creation possible. Under a new name, Groupement pour l'insertion des personnes handicapées physiques (but the same acronym), it has, as we shall see, developed into one of the most dynamic organizations run by and for disabled people in Europe; as with the IL movement in the United States, its political pretensions have been based on effective service provision.

In Italy meanwhile things were happening which were very different in character but had equally wide and deep implications. Inspired above all by the ideas and work of Professor F. Basaglia in Trieste, a nation-wide movement took place to close the psychiatric hospitals and integrate their former patients — some of whom were mentally handicapped, others with a history of mental illness — as fully recognized citizens in the open community. This bold and, some would say, hazardous initiative was paralleled by innovation in schools, widespread throughout the western world and pioneered within Europe in Italy and Scandinavia, which aimed at the integration of children with disabilities into the normal educational system. As early as 1969 the Danish parliament recommended educational 'mainstreaming' to local authorities, and only two years later came the Italian law establishing the right of disabled children to education in the same schools as all other children.

Quite as important as the mainstreaming of children with various levels and kinds of disability into ordinary schools, was the trend, not yet fulfilled throughout Europe, to enable children with moderate or severe mental handicaps to participate at all in the education system. A good example was the Education (Handicapped Children) Act passed in the United Kingdom in 1970. The power of health authorities to provide training for these children was removed, and the staff and buildings of junior training centres were transferred to the education service. Many thousands of children were thus entitled to special provision within the normal education system for the first time.

First steps by the European Community

The 1970s also saw the first initiative of the European Community to act in support of national efforts to improve the services and opportunities for disabled people.[3] Given the economic preoccupations of the Community at that stage of its development, it was inevitable that this early action in the field of disability was concentrated on the promotion of vocational rehabilitation and training and so of open employment. Yet it was not restricted to this: of the four principal activities, two were outside these limits. All four have survived in one form or another to the present day. They were:

1. *The initial action programme to promote the vocational rehabilitation of disabled persons.* Operated from Luxembourg by Umberto Vidali, this activity had to make do with a small budget. It was none the less the first action undertaken by the Community for disabled people alone, and therefore established a vital precedent. It also took the first essential steps in enabling the Commission both to find means for co-operation with national ministries and to make direct contact with the professionals and disabled people in all the Community countries. At the practical level, the principal achievement was the launching in 1975 of the Community's network of rehabilitation centres. Comprising some 30 establishments or groups of these, concerned originally with physical disability but before long also with mental handicaps, the network quite soon developed into the most active means for professional co-operation between a number of units of functional and vocational rehabilitation to be found in Europe, possibly in the world. It has moreover passed the test of time, having been continued and developed, as we shall see, throughout the succeeding action programmes.[4]

2. *The European Social Fund.* Although, in spite of its name, the Fund's activity is restricted to the support of vocational training projects aimed at the open employment market, it has since the inception of the Social Action Programme in 1974 held a position of unique importance as being the Community's only financial instrument in the social domain. Moreover from early on 'the handicapped' were recognized as a priority category, and for a number of years about 10 per cent of all Fund expenditure was devoted to projects in their favour. Built into the Fund's regulations has been a permanent priority for the poorer regions of the Community, and for this reason, for disabled people as well as for others, the good effects of its interventions during the 1970s were seen above all in Ireland and the Mezzogiorno of Italy. Where significant innovation was involved, however, important projects related to disability were supported in more favoured regions also, as came to light in the Mulhouse seminar referred to in my next section.

3. *The scheme to support housing projects for disabled people.* Within its Social Action Programme the Commission was engaged in the promotion of better living and working conditions for workers, and for this purpose decided to give a priority to migrant workers, workers in the coal and steel industries and workers with disabilities. In 1975 the Commission presented to the Council a report on the elimination of architectural barriers to the mobility of disabled persons. Since this was however an area where, at least at that stage of its development, the Community would have had difficulty in framing legislation, it was agreed that future policy work on this topic should be left to the Council of Europe in the framework of what is called the Partial Agreement in the Social and Public Health Field, while the Commission would concentrate its effort on the institution of a modest scheme of grants to support practical housing projects for disabled people in the member states. A number of excellent individual projects were

supported with grants in the first five years or so of the scheme; these are described in a Commission report of 1980. By the end of the initial action programme in 1981 the annual amount available for the scheme had more than doubled from 450,000 ECUs to about 1 millon ECUs, but the relationship of the activity to the main programme on the social and vocational integration of disabled people remained undetermined.

4. *Activities in the research field.* Towards the end of the 1970s the then Directorate-General for New Technology and the Information Market in Luxembourg (DG XIII of the Commission) had begun to explore the need for the creation of a Community data base of technical aids for disabled and elderly people; as we shall see, this initiative was to have important consequences in the future. At the same time a programme of concerted medical research operated by the Directorate-General for Science and Research (DG XII) had already included topics relevant to disability, again with positive implications for future development and interdepartmental co-operation. Moreover, the Commission's concern (particularly in the context of free movement policy) with social security and other benefit systems had led to the preparation of a study, not published until 1981, on the financial provision for 'the longer-term disabled' in eight of the Community countries, another issue bound to be of increasing importance as work in the disability field developed.

I have now brought my account to the point where the Community's initial programme to promote the vocational rehabilitation of handicapped people was about to be superseded by new developments. In summary, I need to say on the negative side that the range of relevant service sectors under active consideration was distinctly limited, that (apart from the Social Fund) the amount of funds available was evidently modest, and that no progress had been made or even envisaged by means of Community legislation. On the positive side however we can see that by the beginning of 1981 significant and continuing activity was there where not long before nothing had existed at all. The all-important principle that the Community could be active in a field such as housing as well as in more strictly vocational areas was firmly established. Major interventions of the European Social Fund in favour of training activities for disabled workers were regularly approved and, particularly in Italy and Ireland, were having a dramatic impact. A tradition which favoured high aspirations and genuinely sought for quality at the point of service delivery was establishing itself. And any ambiguity about the Community's concern for those with mental as well as for those with physical disability had been once and for all eliminated.

LAUNCHING A NEW COMMUNITY INITIATIVE

Education — attempts and set-backs

In spite of the fact that education is not mentioned in the Treaty of Rome, the new sense of progress and confidence associated with the accession of Denmark, Ireland and the United Kingdom in 1973 offered a favourable climate for the creation of a Community programme of co-operation in the educational field. Under

Commissioner Ralf Dahrendorf, a new Directorate was set up in the Directorate-General for Science and Research with the task, among other things, of preparing and operating this activity.[5] I was recruited to the Division responsible for this in 1974.

On arriving in Brussels I was engaged, with more enthusiasm than success, in the development of co-operative actions at the secondary school level on such diverse topics as language learning, the study of European themes, environmental education, exchange of experience between administrators and teacher training. More interestingly for our immediate purpose, I was asked to explore some of the problems of educational equality of opportunity, the promotion of which had been happily identified as one of the priorities of the programme. Chief among these was the topic of children with special educational needs as a result of disability — 'handicapped children' as we would then have called them.

It might be supposed that the programme as a whole, and my bits of it in particular, would have had difficulty in getting going and that they picked up speed as they went along. What happened was the opposite: we started off famously, and in the first two years or so made plenty of progress — so much indeed that our member states took fright. The Danish authorities above all, alarmed at that time by new interventions on the part of the Community in a number of fields, imposed and maintained a successful veto on all the admittedly somewhat ambitious proposals of the Commission over roughly the three-year period 1978–81.[6] Of course, as far as the main education activities are concerned, this is all past history; later the political climate became very much more favourable again and substantial progress has been made in many areas. What concerns us here is the effect at the time on the efforts of the Commission to initiate work on the education of children with special needs.

Work on this topic in the Commission's Education Division began in 1977 when I asked I. Skov Jørgensen, at that time head of the Special Education Department of the Danish Ministry of Education and Danish secretary of Rehabilitation International, to prepare a study on the education of children with disabilities in the Community countries. Finally published in 1980 as No. 11 in the Commission's Education Series under the title 'Special Education in the European Community', the report, as well as bringing together basic up-to-date information on the subject for the first time, identified ten convergent policy trends, a list which has been influential in establishing the foundations of the Commission's own policy.

The same publication contained also selected papers of a first conference on special education in the European Community organized by the Commission in Rome in December 1978, with the co-operation of the Italian Ministry of Education and the Accademia dei Lincei. This conference, for which Jørgensen provided the working paper, highlighted the radical approach of the Italian authorities to school integration and the contrast between this and the relatively cautious measures being adopted in the majority of member states. It also brought into contact with the Commission a number of the experts engaged in the already well developed programme of the Paris-based Centre for Educational Research and Innovation (CERI) of the OECD concerning the 'education of the handicapped adolescent'. This set off a period of collaboration between the Commission and CERI which was to prove fruitful.

Following on from this, I was able to convoke an informal group of national experts nominated by Ministries to help me frame an action proposal for submission to the Community's Education Committee of senior national civil servants and so to the Council of Education Ministers. Experience of the operation of the programme to improve the transition from school to working life for all pupils had led me to believe that a network of local innovatory projects located in all the Community countries should form one of the principal components of such a programme. This idea was refined at an intensive seminar held at the Ifaplan research centre in Cologne; an experts' report arising from this gave the Commission all it needed in order to complete its programme proposals.[7]

My presentation to the Education Committee of the Commission's proposals for an action programme to promote the education of children with special needs took place early in 1981 and was a complete failure. The fact that the International Year of Disabled People had already begun weighed for nothing compared to the negative atmosphere created by the fear of a Danish veto. All that the Dutch president of the Committee could offer the Commission was a programme of further studies and experts' meetings. Since this evidently would have been a waste of time and money, the whole topic was effectively dead and buried.

Yet the idea of a Community network of local projects lived on, adapted however to serve a programme concerned with social and economic rather than educational integration. The idea had caught the attention of the cabinet of the British Commissioner, Ivor Richard, responsible for employment, social affairs and education. In the autumn of 1981 I organized a conference on the transition of young disabled people from school to working life in Noordwijkerhout in the Netherlands, with the collaboration of the European Centre for Work and Society in Maastricht. At this event Ivor Richard presented what came to be known as the 'district projects network' as one of the most important initiatives which the Commission was about to take to promote a better life for disabled people.

We need now to consider how it was that 1981, while a year of failure for the Commission as far as concerned the education of children with special needs, saw dramatic progress in the Community's response to the social and economic needs of disabled adults.

The International Year (1981) and the Community response

The United Nations declared 1981 to be the International Year of Disabled People. One can sometimes hear it said that the Year was a failure. It may be that there were those who, in their own situation, found the Year a disappointment; many on the other hand believe that it had a real influence on the level of public awareness of the reality of disability and on the promotion of more positive attitudes. Henry Enns, chairman of Disabled People's International, in an article which is critical of the follow-up during the decade since the International Year, yet says of the Year itself: 'That year, 1981, ushered in a new era for disabled people . . . the year also ushered in a new global social movement of disabled people.'[8]

It is certainly true that the International Year was a critical source of inspiration to disabled people themselves throughout the world, stimulating them to become aware of each other and of the need to work together in a common cause. I am also convinced that its impact on the public, on professionals and on local and national authorities was, at least in the western world, profound, going well beyond a merely vague modification of attitudes to express itself in many practical measures, above all (as we shall see) in relation to the accessibility of the physical environment. Apart from the United Nations Centre for Social Development and Humanitarian Affairs in Vienna which undertook direct responsibility for the Year and its aftermath, 1981 was also influential within specialized United Nations agencies, notably the World Health Organization (WHO), the International Labour Organization (ILO) and the United Nations Educational, Scientific and Cultural Organization (UNESCO). Among European and International Organizations outside the United Nations, on the other hand, the impact of the Year is harder to perceive.

However, the European Community — which is not an International Organization in the strict sense, but an extension of government — proved its capacity for auto-nomous action by its response to the Year. In a most welcome example of the various organs of the Community operating in a coherent and complementary way, all the consultative and decision-making institutions were involved in bringing about an agreement to launch before the end of the Year a new action programme far wider and deeper in its scope than anything that had been attempted before. As to timing, it was a close thing: the programme was not finally adopted until 21 December 1981 and the official document recording this is rather dramatically dated 31 December. But, provided it manifested the Community's recognition of the Year by being adopted within its duration, that the decision came at the very end of it was no disadvantage. On the contrary, in this way the Community signalled that the Year was not to be used as the occasion for some merely symbolic or cosmetic gesture, but as the springboard for an entirely new level of Community action, planned to last for the next four years but certain (as could already be confidently foreseen) to extend a long way beyond that.

It was the European Parliament which, appropriately enough, acted first, by adopt-ing on its own initiative, as early as March 1981, a wide-ranging Resolution on the Economic, Social and Vocational Integration of Disabled People. The title is impor-tant for three reasons, adherence to all of which is maintained throughout the text. First, the aim now is not merely rehabilitation but integration. Next, the social aspect is unambiguously promoted to equality with the economic one. And thirdly, the Parliament recognized the need to speak, in general terms, no longer of 'handicapped persons' let alone of 'the handicapped', but of 'disabled people'.

Before the end of the summer, the Economic and Social Committee, an important element in the Community's formal consultative structure, had presented, also on its own initiative, an Opinion on the Situation and Problems of the Handicapped, a far more enlightened document than its title might lead one to suppose.

It was now the turn of the European Commission to make a formal proposal, without which nothing new could actually happen. The preparation of this was entrusted to Umberto Vidali, in that part of the Commission's Directorate-General for Social Affairs which was located in Luxembourg, and myself. Vidali had been operating since 1974 the initial action programme on vocational rehabilitation I have described above. As he was due to retire from the Commission's service at the end of 1981, it was likely that the implementation of whatever programme the Com-mission put forward would fall to me, as it in fact turned out.

Entitled 'The Social Integration of Disabled People — a Framework for Community Action', the Commission's document did not appear till early in November; this gave us time to take the ideas of the other institutions into full consideration when formulating our own, but was dangerously late if a Council decision was to be reached by the end of the year.

However, the United Kingdom, which held the presidency of the Council of Ministers for that half-year, being determined to succeed in this, ensured that the proposal was taken through the various levels of the elaborate Council procedure with commendable speed. And this was in spite of a number of difficulties. The Germans insisted on a reform of the constitution of the network of rehabilitation centres as the price of their support for the new programme; the Commission had not annexed a draft Council Resolution to its proposal, so this had to be freshly drafted; nor was it at all clear how the new action was to be financed. Moreover, the determination of the Danes to defend their national sovereignty entailed an acrimonious discussion of the status of the Resolution which was to be adopted by the Council in order to empower the programme.[9]

Fortunately, in the event these difficulties did not affect the Commission's freedom to develop all aspects of the action programme with equal facility and to devote appropriate resources to each of them impartially. Indeed the apparent weakness of the Council's enabling instrument had no practical effect of any kind, and during the course of the programme no objection was raised to its full implementation by the Danes or anyone else.

In one respect the Council had gone a step further than even the Commission had proposed. In the light of the experience I have described in the last section, the Commission had carefully avoided any mention of education in its proposal. Yet at the insistence of several national delegations, education did after all figure in the text of the final instrument: the member states were invited to 'promote measures to prepare handicapped people for an active life, in particular by integrating them in normal education and training wherever possible'. It is an interesting example of how, given a fluid political context such as that of the Community institutions, failure can be succeeded quite rapidly by success.

Introducing the Community's first action programme (1982–7)

The first action programme to promote the social and economic integration of disabled people was composed of three interdependent activities:

1. The development of *Community policy instruments*, with these objectives:

    – directly, to establish Community policy and influence national policies
    – indirectly, to influence practice by being applied in the other components of the action programme.

2. The operation of a diverse programme of *co-operation and support*, involving the active encouragement of innovation, of exchange of experience and of the dissemination of good practice, with these objectives:

    – directly, to improve the quality of all aspects of the promotion of social and economic integration in the member states

– indirectly, to influence national and Community policies, by providing the raw material out of which Community instruments could be fashioned.

3.   The servicing of both the above actions by means of *information initiatives and systems*.

It is now time to give an account of how we set about operating this first action programme. Although I shall also give my view of the extent to which what we did was successful or not, the true value of what could be learned from the experience will not be apparent until I address the issues in the four chapters of Part II.

NOTES

1   *Comprehensive Values* was published in Heinemann's Organisation in Schools series in 1975.
2   For this brief account I have drawn on Gerben de Jong, 'Defining and implementing the "independent living" concept', in N. M. Crewe and I. K. Zola (eds), *Independent Living for Disabled People*, London 1983.
3   For readers not familiar with the operations of the Community institutions, a brief explanation of their processes and responsibilities is given in Appendix 3.
4   For the membership of this rehabilitation network during the various programmes see Appendix 2C.
5   In 1981 the educational action was transferred to Directorate-General V (Employment and Social Affairs). The new Directorate included also Vocational Training, previously in DG V, linked to Employment. The DG added Education to its title. More recently Education and its associated sectors have broken off as a separate Task Force on Human Resources, Education, Training and Youth. See further Appendix 3.
6   Had Denmark not vetoed progress at this time, it is quite possible that another member state, either France or the United Kingdom for example, would have done so.
7   The results of the seminar were presented in a report (unpublished) prepared by Nora Ferro, Edwin Sims and Werner Berndt. Although there was no follow up in the educational field at that time, the report made a useful contribution to the preparation of the district projects in the first action programme.
8   The quotation is from the editorial in the 1990 No. 1 issue of the DPI journal *Vox Nostra*.
9   As a result of Danish insistence, the Resolution was formally adopted not by the Council only but by the 'Council and Representatives of the Governments of the Member States', in recognition of the fact that a number of the activities (for example, those concerned with access and housing or with welfare) fell outside the scope of the Treaty of Rome.

REFERENCES

Community policy documents
Council Resolution of 21 Jan. 1974 concerning a social action programme (O.J. No. C 13/1 of 12 Feb. 1974).
Council Resolution of 27 June 1974 establishing the initial Community action programme for the vocational rehabilitation of handicapped persons (O.J. No. C 80/30 of 9 July 1974).
Communication of the Commission to the Council: Rehabilitation of handicapped persons — Elimination of architectural barriers to their mobility (COM (75) 432 of 25 July 1975).
Report from the Commission to the Council on the initial Community action programme on

the vocational rehabilitation of handicapped persons, 1974–9 (COM (79) 572 of 26 Oct. 1979).
Council Conclusions concerning the further implementation of the initial action programme for the vocational rehabilitation of handicapped persons, 9 June 1980 (7334/80 Annex I).
Communication of the Commission to the Council: Information on pilot housing actions to promote the social integration of handicapped persons and migrant workers (COM (80) 491 of 9 Sept. 1980).
Resolution of the Parliament of 11 Mar. 1981 concerning the economic, social and vocational integration of disabled people in the European Community (O.J. No. C 77/27 of 6 Apr. 1981).
Opinion of the Economic and Social Committee of 18 Apr. 1981 on the situation and problems of the handicapped (O.J. No. C 230/38 of 10 Sept. 1981).
Communication of the Commission to the Council of 14 Nov. 1981: The social integration of disabled people — A framework for the development of Community action (O.J. No. C 347/14 of 31 Dec. 1981).
Resolution of the Council and Representatives of the Governments of the Member States of the European Communities of 21 Dec. 1981 on the social integration of disabled people (O.J. No. C 347/1 of 31 Dec. 1981).

Commission studies and conference reports

J. Albers, J. Boisseau and J. G. Somerville, *Comparative Study on the Rehabilitation of Handicapped Persons in the Countries of the Community* (3 vols), Brussels 1974. (DE, EN, FR)
I. Skov Jørgensen, *Special Education in the European Community*, Brussels 1978 (Education Series No. 11). (DA, DE, EN, FR, IT, NL)
Oliver Hegarty, *Interventions of the European Social Fund in Favour of Disabled People in Ireland and Italy*, Brussels 1982. (EN)
Séminaire sur l'aide du Fonds Social Européen en faveur des personnes handicapées — rapport final [Seminar on aid of the European Social Fund in favour of disabled people], held at Mulhouse, 5–8 Oct. 1981, Mulhouse 1982. (FR)
Gabriel Fragnière (European Centre for Work and Society), report of CEC Conference on 'The preparation of handicapped children and young people for active adult life', held at Noordwijkerhout, 19–23 Oct. 1981, Maastricht 1983. (EN)
Brian Abel-Smith, *Social Security Provision for the Longer-term Disabled in Eight Countries of the European Community — a case study*, Brussels 1981. (DE, EN, FR)

International organizations

United Nations, *World Programme of Action concerning Disabled Persons*, New York 1983.
World Health Organization, *International Classification of Impairments, Disabilities and Handicaps*, Geneva 1980.
Council of Europe (Partial Agreement in the Social and Public Health Field), *A Coherent Policy for the Rehabilitation of Disabled People*, Strasbourg 1984.
Council of Europe (Partial Agreement in the Social and Public Health Field), *Legislation on the Rehabilitation of Disabled People*, 3rd edn, Strasbourg 1988.

Chapter 2

The Community at Work: The First Action Programme (1982-7)

In this chapter I shall set out the basic facts about the first action programme which we launched in 1982, and then give a brief account of the activities by means of which it was implemented. Finally I shall explain how, before this action programme to promote social and economic integration was completed, the education of children with special needs was after all, and against all expectation, accepted as a topic which the Community could and should address.

THE BASIS OF THE FIRST ACTION PROGRAMME

The scope and structure of the programme

The range of disability

We started our programme with a determination that it should be inclusive. From the beginning we were determined not only that when we spoke of disabilities the term 'physical' should include sensory as well as motor, but also that for us people with mental disabilities included all those with mental illnesses (or a history of mental illness) as well as those with intellectual impairments. As the programme developed we came to realize that we needed also to be unambiguous about including all those who experience disability as a result of internal and invisible impairments (which might be, for example, cardiac or pulmonary, or might involve special conditions such as arthritis, diabetes or cystic fibrosis), and those whose disability is associated with ageing.

From the beginning of the programme we based our terminology on the International Classification of Impairments, Disabilities and Handicaps (ICIDH) of the World Health Organization (WHO). This not only meant that we were supported in our inclusive approach when anyone was inclined to undermine this, but also that we had to learn, and try to teach others, to use 'disabled' and 'disability' as the general descriptive terms rather than 'handicapped' and 'handicap'. The reason is of course that, if we follow the WHO definition, 'disability' is a relatively objective term, indicating a loss of function resulting from an impairment of whatever kind, whereas 'handicap' is the disadvantageous consequence of the interaction between the disability and an environment which has failed to respond or adapt to it. Since therefore it is the aim of disability policies to reduce or if possible eliminate handicaps, being handicapped is a merely contingent state and it is incorrect to describe the long-term condition of someone experiencing the consequences of an impairment as that of being handicapped rather than disabled.

It did not however prove possible to be altogether consistent in this. For one thing, even among English-language speakers the term 'mental disability' has never really caught on, and 'mental handicap' is still often used as the general term even by those closely involved.[1] There are also numerous difficulties in other languages, notably in French where an acceptable equivalent to 'disabled' does not exist. In the Community, where even when the original language of a document is English the French version is often taken to be the official one, the word 'disabled' used by an author may emerge in the published document, via the French word 'handicapé', as 'handicapped'.

The content of the programme

The programme focused on two broad areas:

– employment, including vocational training and rehabilitation
– the environment to independent living, comprising mobility (including public transport), access to public buildings and facilities, and housing together with services to the home.

The range of activities available to the Commission was relatively wide. At policy level there was the choice between the preparation of constraining instruments such as Directives or Regulations which would have legal force over and above national law, and more gentle expressions of political will such as Recommendations. In the area of technical co-operation there was the possibility of operating networks by means of study visit schemes, seminars, training sessions and so forth. Direct grant aid would be severely limited by the financial constraints of the programme, which was never intended to perform a major financial function; however, there was already the scheme to support housing projects and there were good prospects for creating a programme of support to the European co-operation of non-governmental organizations.

As for information, there was every possibility of being able to finance the research and development costs of European data bases, as well as setting up a limited but respectable documentation service of selected political and technical items, and establishing newsletters. Finally, there would always be the chance for an annual programme of studies, whether in preparation of policy initiatives or as a support to the programme's own operations.

Having defined our target population, our sectors and our range of activities, I can now list the seven principal elements of which the programme was composed:

Policy
– the preparation of a series of policy instruments
Co-operation and support
– development of the network of rehabilitation centres
– setting up of a network of local projects to promote social integration (the 'district projects')
– continuation of the scheme to support housing projects
– supporting the European activities of non-governmental organizations
Information
– the development of a system of European data bases
– the establishment of a documentation and newsletter service

The duration and resources of the programme

The duration

The action programme was intended to last for four years. In the event, the Commission had not set up the unit to run it until the middle of 1982 and an enhanced budget was not voted until 1983. There was however no difficulty in extending the programme into 1987, seen as a hinge year between the first and second programmes.

Staff resources

Staff resources were from the start and continued to be minimal. Umberto Vidali retired at the end of 1981 and I was appointed head of the new division responsible, to be located in Brussels and known as the Bureau for Action in Favour of Disabled People. The term 'Bureau' was intended to indicate a relatively open, informal, even perhaps militant style, after the manner of the Commission's already established Bureaux for relations with the social partners and for women's questions. So far so good; it must however be admitted that the words 'in favour' have been unpopular with militant disabled people, at least among anglophones.

I remained the only administrative grade official in the unit until the programme was nearly half completed, when I was joined by a new recruit to the Commission's service, Bernard Vanderhaeghen. Strength at this level was also reinforced for a period by the secondment to us of Louis Van Amelsvoort from the Dutch Ministry of Social Affairs. At executive level we had from the beginning the services of Jean-Claude Limpach, responsible for documentation and much organizational support. Gerhard Leussink joined the team later in the programme when the scheme of grants for housing projects was finally integrated into the main activity.

It was obviously going to be essential to find a way of including disabled people in the central team. It is to the credit of the authorities of the Commission that they arranged for a blind telephonist, an accomplished linguist, to be transferred to my division as a secretary, and for a young Belgian man with tetraplegia who had come to the Commission on a 6-month traineeship to be able to stay on under contract.[2]

Yet it would have been quite impossible to carry out the whole programme, including the maintenance of direct contact with a network of local projects, without the additional help of at least a small team of experts working under contract for the duration of the programme and located in Brussels close to the Commission's own offices. Overall co-ordination of the group, which took the name of Interact, was undertaken by Professor Dr André Storm of the University of Louvain la Neuve, who also represented the Charleroi rehabilitation centre on the centres network and was responsible for liaison between Rehabilitation International and the European Community. Claudine Van Lierde, a consumer economist who had completed for Vidali a valuable study on door-to-door transport systems for disabled people, took on the task of animating, co-ordinating and evaluating the network of district projects.[3] Lieven Joniaux, who had worked as an expert on the housing programme for disabled people, edited the district project newsletter and undertook the practical organization of the numerous district seminars and conferences. Danielle Rimbert, the expert who had initiated the practical work on the idea of a data base of technical aids, moved from Luxembourg to Brussels to be co-ordinator of the information system development.

Financial resources

The credits voted for the programme grew over five years from one quarter of a million ECUs at the outset to about sixteen times that; this does not include the support given by the Social Fund to vocational training activities in the district projects. Every year the support given by the European Parliament to the Commission's budget proposal was dependable and crucial. Equally important was the flexibility enjoyed by the Commission in the deployment of credits among the various activities according to annual need.

Managing the action programme: consultation and liaison

Consultation

Obviously it would have been impossible to carry out a programme of this kind without regular means of consultation. On the unofficial side, I constituted a Dialogue Group of representatives of some 25 European or international organizations of or for disabled people. The Group met once a year for two days of discussion covering all aspects of the programme. Similarly, we arranged for annual meetings with the secretaries of Rehabilitation International in the Community countries; these represented key organizations in each member state, a few governmental, the majority paragovernmental or voluntary.[4]

For official contact a Liaison Group of representatives from relevant Ministries in each country met for two days under my chairmanship about four times a year. The Ministries typically represented were those of Employment, Social Affairs or Health. For special purposes it was always possible to elicit facts or opinions from any of these groups by means of written response to questionnaires. Since however the effectiveness of this procedure is well known to be limited, I instituted the method of consultation workshops, held in Brussels after the Commission had completed its programme of studies in preparation for a policy initiative and before the proposal itself was finally formulated. These workshops brought together for three days experts on the particular topic, members of the governmental Liaison Group and representatives of all the Commission's co-operative networks — the district projects, the rehabilitation centres, the European non-governmental organizations and the Rehabilitation International secretariats. In this way we were able to ensure that all the main participants in the programme contributed to the development of policy at the most crucial stage in its formation, and that the Commission's proposals were widely and deeply based.

Liaison

The large number of policy sectors which the programme involved clearly entailed the need to keep contact with many other units in the Commission's services. In our own Directorate-General, this meant the European Social Fund among others. Elsewhere, among the most important links were those with the programme for concerted medical research, the Directorate-General for Transport and the many proliferating programmes concerned with new technology.

Turning to the Parliament, regular formal contact had to be kept up with the parliamentary Committee on Social Affairs which meets in Brussels, and, whenever a Commission proposal was going through, with the full assembly in Strasbourg. Of considerable informal value also was the Parliament's All-Party Group on Disablement, created on the British model and convened by Derek Prag, the Member of the European Parliament for Hertfordshire. Although it was not always easy to get a sufficient number of non-British parliamentarians to attend these meetings, the character of which was not familiar to everyone, their contribution was a unique one, above all when I was able to accompany the Commissioner responsible for social affairs for discussions there. The work of the Group certainly fostered the invariable support of the Parliament which our programme enjoyed.

Among the International Organizations our principal contacts were with the United Nations Global Decade programme centred in Vienna, the International Labour Organization (particularly during the establishment of the Convention and Recommendation described in Chapter 4), the OECD (CERI) programme on the Handicapped Adolescent and the Partial Agreement within the Council of Europe, which was invited to send an observer to our Liaison Group.

IMPLEMENTATION OF THE PROGRAMME

The preparation of policy instruments

Employment was the obvious choice of content for the first in the series of policy initiatives which the Commission was to bring forward. At the beginning, the hope was to have carried through two or three of these within the four years allotted to the action programme, the instrument on employment being followed by others in the environmental field. This conception of a continuing effort at the level of direct policy intervention, and of the direction which it should take, proved useful and, I believe, is continuing to do so. But the timing foreseen was over-optimistic: by 1987, only the instrument on employment had been adopted, although preparatory work on environmental issues was well advanced.

The Recommendation on employment

After some discussion, and against the advice of its legal service, the Commission decided to bring forward not a constraining instrument — a Directive — but something very much weaker, a Recommendation. The argument put forward by the political advisers of Commissioner Ivor Richard was that a draft Directive on the employment of disabled people, brought forward at a time of high unemployment throughout the Community, would encounter insuperable difficulties in the Council, so that either it would never get through or it would be adopted after considerable delay and in such a truncated form as to be virtually useless. A Recommendation on the other hand would have a fair chance of being adopted within a reasonable time, its weakness of form being also compensated by a relative richness of content; moreover, it would always be possible to bring forward a draft Directive at a later stage, which by focusing on points where the member states had evidently failed to carry out the terms of the Recommendation would have a much better chance of success.

The presentation of the Commission's proposal was preceded by a careful period of preparation.[5] Two earlier studies on the statistical aspects of the employment of disabled people had been completed by the Commission's Statistical Office, but had not succeeded in overcoming the formidable difficulties which attend any statistical review of this topic, let alone an attempt to do this at a European level. We determined therefore to take a more qualitative approach. The first study we undertook was prepared, from a point of view of social psychology, by Mary Croxen John of the Open University[6] and published under the title 'An Overview: Disability and Employment'; the report is distinguished by the vigour of its presentation of the need for a consumer model rather than an administrative one and for the invention and elaboration of the concept of an 'ideal rehabilitation route'.

A second report was established for us by Eliane Vogel-Polsky and her colleagues of the Centre de sociologie du droit social in the Free University of Brussels. Published by the Commission as 'The Economic Integration of the Disabled: an Analysis of Measures and Trends in Member States', it consists of a valuable analysis of legislation in the field, as well as containing some penetrating thinking on such issues as paternalism and marginalization. In its concluding guidelines, Vogel-Polsky comes down strongly in favour of a Community Directive on the employment of disabled people.

Lastly, we invited the former Dutch Minister of Social Affairs, Wil Albeda, with the co-operation of the European Centre for Work and Society,[7] to present a report on 'Disabled People and their Employment' which brought together the results of previous work on the subject, added more on the contribution of the new technologies, and ended with a set of recommendations for action at European and national levels.

Finally, the experts responsible for these studies were invited to present their conclusions at a consultation workshop which was held in Brussels, the first of these events described on pp. 20–1 above.

The content of the Recommendation as it was finally adopted in July 1986 will be presented and discussed in Chapter 4. Here I shall mention only two significant factors in the political process preceding its adoption. The first of these concerns the Council which, in spite of the Commission's having opted for the least menacing form of instrument possible, did all it could at all stages of the process to weaken its content, especially on the question of employment quotas. The second is the action of the European Parliament which, while giving unanimous support to the Commission's initiative in principle, was critical of the fact that the proposal was too weak both in its form (that is, not a Directive) and in its content — particularly on the question of employment quotas.[8]

This polarization of approach between Council and Parliament in response to the Community's first-ever policy instrument solely concerned with disability is instructive. It surely foreshadows a conflict about the nature of Community 'competence' and responsibility of which we shall hear a lot more in the future.

In some ways the outcome of our employment initiative, so meticulously prepared, was disappointing. At least, however, we had shown that it was possible for the Community to receive the practical problems of disabled people into its policy framework, and had established a platform on which other initiatives could be built. I shall describe the follow-up to the Recommendation in Chapter 7.

Preparatory work on the environment for independent living

Meanwhile, within the first action programme we were able to make considerable headway in the preparation of the intended series of policy initiatives in the environmental field. Policy studies were completed and consultation workshops held on transport and public accessibility, and a policy study on housing commissioned.[9] The knowledge acquired in these fields will be presented in Chapter 5 and recent progress described in Chapter 7.

Co-operation and support

The network of rehabilitation centres

At the start of our programme this network had already been running for six years. There were nearly 30 members, all the then ten member states except Greece being represented, and a programme of study visits and other activities was in operation.[10]

During the course of the action programme progress in the effectiveness of the network was made in a number of respects:

- a regular budget was established and the work of co-ordinating the activities contracted out to one of the network members
- the fundamental programme of seminars, exchange group study visits, and intensive professional training sessions was increased and diversified

– Greece was integrated into the network and a special programme of exchanges and seminars instituted to support this; Spain and Portugal, on their entry in 1986, were very quickly brought into full participation
– direct contribution to the development of Community policy was ensured by means of ad hoc working parties and the participation of members in consultation workshops
– dissemination of the results of network activity was improved by the establishment of a network journal (published in three languages) and the institution of an 'outer network' of centres with which members undertook to communicate.

By the end of the programme on the other hand there remained two difficulties which needed more radical solutions than we had been able to bring about. For one thing, though we had made some headway with the problem of dissemination of the experience gained, there was still a lot more that needed to be done. The 'outer network' did not operate equally well in all countries, and the form and targeting of the journal needed review. In some member states the national representatives on the Liaison Group did not play a significant part in the dissemination process.[11]

Secondly, the needs of the main categories of disability were unevenly represented among the various member states, and some barely at all. There were for example, no centres specializing in the needs of those with hearing impairments, nor, until the accession to the network of the Spanish National Association of the Blind (ONCE, Organización nacional de ciegos) Centre in Barcelona, of those with disabilities of sight. In some countries the centres dealt only with mental handicaps, in others mental handicaps were not included at all. Although the regulation of the network had from the beginning been that members were appointed by the Commission on the recommendation of the member state concerned, there was not a great deal of interest in the Liaison Group in addressing this question.

Thirdly, although both functional and vocational rehabilitation were well represented, the great majority of the activities were in specialized contexts, and developments in the direction of integrated training were inadequately involved.

In Chapter 7 we shall see how some of these deficiencies have been addressed since 1988 in the second action programme (Helios). The unique opportunity which the network affords for the advancement of quality in rehabilitation by means of the exchange of experience more than justifies its modest cost, and its continuation into the second action programme was something over which the Commission never had doubts.

The network of district projects

The idea of a European Community network of local activities, aimed at the social integration of all disabled people within that locality, was something entirely new, arising as we have seen from a proposal conceived in 1981 when we were working on the education of children with special needs.[12] Selecting and co-ordinating local communities was evidently more difficult than doing this with rehabilitation centres, but even more important given the wider objectives of the new programme: local communities are obviously closer to the day-to-day realities of social integration and independent living. They also involve disabled people themselves more actively, as well as engaging not only professionals but also local politicians and administrators, the two sides of industry and the voluntary sector.

In addition to the costs of the networking activities which were met from the programme's own budget, we were able from 1983 on to arrange for very substantial contributions from the European Social Fund towards the basic costs of training activities in each of the districts selected to take part in the network. In spite of the administrative and financial complications which this relationship with the Fund entailed — so massive that the whole project almost sank beneath their weight at the moment of launch — all the projects were selected and ready to participate by the end of 1983. Rather simple criteria were used: districts were to comprise a population of about 300,000; they should not represent an extreme of economic wealth or poverty; and there should be the guarantee of a public or voluntary body willing and able to take on the role of local co-ordination. Each of the large member states, and Belgium and the Netherlands, nominated two participating districts, the other countries one. This gave us initially a network of 16 districts, 19 after the accession of Spain and Portugal in 1986.[13]

Thanks largely to the work of the Interact team, without whom very little could have been done, this first network of its kind recorded these achievements:

- an ambitious annual programme of theme seminars and plenary conferences, located in the districts by rotation, was designed and successfully carried out; this ensured a great deal of effective exchange of experience, as well as often having a major impact in the region and country hosting the event
- the programme was also able to finance a scheme of group study visits; this enabled districts which had identified common interests to intensify their co-operation
- as a result of this programme, reinforced by advisory visits on the part of the Commission's Interact experts and by means of national evaluators appointed by the authorities in each member state, all districts were able to make significant progress on at least some of the aspects of social integration, and some districts over a wide range of needs
- an attractive project newsletter was instituted and widely distributed in all nine Community languages
- through their own seminar programme and by participating in consultation work-shops, the districts were very quickly able to make a valuable contribution to the development of Community policy.

On the negative side it must be said that the link with the Social Fund created more difficulties and limitations than it was worth and my hope that this would establish a precedent for an entirely new level of co-operation between the Fund and the policy departments proved vain.

The expectation that all the districts should effectively promote the integration of all categories of disabled people over all the relevant life functions proved to be excessive. Evidently, a network, or more than one network, with many more district members but with fewer demands made on each would be more acceptable locally and therefore more effective globally. As we shall see in Chapter 7, this point was fully met in the design of the next action programme.

As with the network of rehabilitation centres, the problem of the effective exploitation and dissemination of the network experience within the member states was addressed but not solved. National evaluators made a contribution to this, no doubt, but the Commission had little opportunity to assess how well this was done. The Commission's own evaluation of the product of this whole activity has never reached the light of day. The contribution made by national official representatives to discussion of the dissemination problem was insignificant.

In spite of this element of disappointment, the total account of this true innovation was positive, and there was, again, no doubt for the Commission about the value of incorporating a similar, though significantly modified, element in the second action programme to start in 1988.

The grants to support housing projects

We have seen how this scheme had been operating since 1976 under separate administration from that of the main rehabilitation programme. This separation continued until 1984 when the responsibility for the scheme was passed to the Bureau; from then on it was fully integrated into the social integration programme where it clearly belonged.

The purpose of the scheme continued to be the support of model innovatory projects rather than large-scale building programmes; grants rarely exceeded 100,000 ECUs or 15 per cent of project costs. By the time our action programme was drawing to a close, 147 projects had received grant aid, the support often extending over a number of years; in 1985, 19 projects in seven member states were supported, 20 in eight countries in 1986. As with the network of rehabilitation centres, a special effort was made to integrate into the scheme the new member states, Greece and later Spain and Portugal.

The incorporation of this activity into the main action programme offered the opportunity to apply the experience of good practice which it had brought to light to Community and national policy. A report was prepared which described some of the best examples of good practice carried out with the aid of the scheme,[14] and dissemination within member states was encouraged by extending the criteria to include projects for the setting up of advisory, information and resource centres on independent living. Most important of all, the lessons derivable from the supported projects were to form one of the principal sources of knowledge and ideas for the Commission's main policy initiative on housing and services to the home which it was planned to bring forward after those on transport and public access.

It is impossible to say how many projects would never have been successfully completed without the Commission's financial help. What is certain is that our support was useful not only in itself but as a sign of recognition which made it easier for promoters to win financial or political backing at home. In spite of its modest budget, the scheme derived a unique value from its ability to give direct support to grass-roots developments without all the restraints and complications of the vastly larger Social Fund, and to do this in an area such as housing which is by no means an easy one for the Community to intervene in.

Yet there remained the problem of the isolation of the scheme from the Ministries of Housing and Environment in the member states, and the consequent severe limitation in the extent to which it was able to have an impact on national policies. Another difficulty, equally serious, was that the existence of a scheme of direct grants to housing projects alone was out of step with the Commission's vision of the environment for independent living as comprising three essential elements, not only housing but also transport and public access. Ideally, what was needed was a tripling of the credits under this budget line to enable the scheme to be developed so to cover all three of the environmental essentials.

How I tried to tackle these two problems when preparing the next action programme to follow after 1987, and what happened to that endeavour, I shall describe in Chapter 7.

The non-governmental organizations: co-operation, and support for their work

The Commission's practical co-operation with many of the international and European non-governmental organizations (NGOs) of and for disabled people developed rapidly during the course of the action programme and soon established itself as one of the most important and successful elements of the whole of the Community's action. The character and potential of these bodies is of such interest that I shall describe this activity in a little more detail. It was also above all through collaboration with them that I and my colleagues came into direct and regular contact with disabled people. The success of this co-operation owes much to the personal attention given to it by Bernard Vanderhaeghen from the time he joined the Commission's core team, and also to the enterprise and ingenuity shown by the NGOs themselves.

From small beginnings, the Commission's relations with NGOs blossomed by means of the Dialogue Group and the consultation workshops which I have mentioned above (pp. 20–1). But the unique strength of the relationship depended on the combination of this consultative role with the scheme to give financial support to the NGOs' European activities. This began with the European section of what was in 1981 the World Federation of the Blind, but became, after union with the Association for the Welfare of the Blind, the World Blind Union (WBU). The European secretary, Jean-Paul Herbecq, was conveniently located in Brussels, and it was in discussion with him that I developed the idea of the presentation to the Commission by an NGO of an annual programme of encounters and other events involving the European membership, to which the Commission would endeavour to give financial support which could amount (subject to a ceiling) to 50 per cent of the total eligible costs of the programme. Soon the WBU set up a committee responsible for relations with the European Community, of which the blind Welshman Tom Parker was president, himself already deeply experienced in international co-operation. Latterly responsibility for day-to-day liaison with us was shared between Tom and Leonard de Wolf who, being in Antwerp, could visit the Commission much more easily and more cheaply.

Still in the early days of the action programme, I was visited by a representative of the Breakthrough Trust, a British organization concerned with services to deaf people and with promoting relations between those who can hear and those who cannot. This led to the first visit to Brussels of Andrew Kenyon, who was to prove one of the outstandingly creative figures emerging on the European scene as a result of the action programme. Through his efforts and with our support the first encounter of deaf people from a number of different countries took place in Brussels, and real progress in the nature of our work could be seen when for the first time a meeting was held with the concurrent aid of interpretation in both spoken and sign languages.

The Commission was indeed fortunate in finding so early in the action programme partners in associations run entirely by disabled people as well as for them. Later on there was a further even more important initiative on the part of the community of deaf people, the foundation of the European Community Secretariat of the World Federation of the Deaf (WFD). The Commission was able to give special support to the first successful endeavours to get this venture off the ground, having persuaded our financial control to permit grants of over 50 per cent during the first year or two when a new European organization is trying to build up its programme and its membership at the same time and is obviously vulnerable.

Moreover, I instituted the arrangement that, contrary to the normal rules of what facilities are permitted, we should once a year offer to the European groups both of the WBU and of the WFD one of the Commission's meeting rooms with full spoken-language interpretation, without the cost of this being deducted from their annual activity grant; this specific act of recognition of the need to compensate the difficulties of communication which sensory disabilities imply was, at least tacitly, accepted by the Commission. Before long we were also able to persuade the Commission to pay first the travel costs and later the professional fees of the sign-language interpreters required at the main annual WFD meeting. With signing in full flow in all or virtually all the gestural languages of the Community, these meetings became one of the most inspiring events of our year, both for the sheer physical grace of the signing itself and for the intense feeling of cultural richness and solidarity which it expressed. How effective the contribution of the WFD's European group has been we shall see in the next chapter.

In the first section of this chapter I have mentioned our annual consultative meetings with the secretariats of Rehabilitation International. In addition to these we were able to sponsor an annual theme-based seminar hosted by RI secretaries in different countries by rotation. Relations with RI were also cemented by many personal interactions: one of RI's world vice-presidents, John Bermingham, and the chairman of its World-level Vocational Committee, Ib Nielsen, were members of the network of rehabilitation centres, while the chairman of RI's International Commission on Technical Aids (ICTA) when our programme started was Paul Dolfuss, the medical director of the Mulhouse rehabilitation centre, also a leading member of our network.

Two of the regular beneficiaries of our scheme of support were themselves managers of activity networks. Early on we set up a close working relationship with Mobility International (MI), which runs a highly innovatory and enterprising exchange programme for young people with every kind and level of disability; very often the activities involve integration of disabled and able-bodied youngsters, and MI gives particular attention to involving countries where resources are not abundant and to outlying regions of the Community. After a time, MI was able to expand its annual programme of about twelve events to comprise two elements, the Europrogramme for disabled and other young people, and the Euroteam Programme for professionals.

Later in our action programme, François Vittecoq, the chairman of the Committee on Handicapped People of the Confederation of Family Organizations in the European Community (COFACE, Confédération des organisations familiales de la Communauté européenne), set up a network of co-operation between parents and professionals working on the problems of mental handicap. Known as Euramis, this activity soon established itself in localities in a number of member states; without our support I do not suppose it would have been possible to do this at all.

As our action programme continued, so inevitably the number of our partners increased, including entirely new European associations which owed their existence to our scheme. How hazardous the early days can be was shown by the history of the Association internationale autisme Europe, which after an enormously successful opening conference in 1983 which overflowed one of the main halls of the Paris Congress Centre, very nearly petered out before being revived some years later.

For us another priority was to encourage the European efforts of already well established bodies, such as the International League of Societies for Persons with Mental Handicaps (ILSMH), the World Federation for Mental Health (WFMH), the Fédération internationale des mutilés invalides de travail et invalides civils (FIMI-TIC), the European Alliance of Muscular Dystrophy Associations (EAMDA) and the International Cerebral Palsy Society (ICPS). And at the same time as establishing new regular clients and keeping faith with old ones, we needed to leave some resources for one-off European events which deserved support, some of these initiated by national organizations of disabled people, parents or professionals.

By the end of the first action programme in 1987, it was clear that the only problem with this element in the programme was a growth in the demand which would very soon exceed our financial resource, and the possible need therefore to devise more stringent criteria during the next action programme.

Information: Handynet and other services

The Handynet project

At the outset of the action programme, Danielle Rimbert, the expert who in Luxembourg had initiated work on the possibility of a European data base of technical aids, moved to Brussels to work for us alongside the Interact team. I was then able to give her a mandate to design and prepare a Community information system on disability which was to be computerized, multilingual and widely accessible. Since both the gathering and the distribution of information would involve networking, Rimbert christened the project 'Handynet'.

Handynet was not to be a data base only of technical aids, but a system made up of a number of data bases, or modules, which would be built up over several years and eventually embrace information on all the issues of which the Commission's actions in the field of disability are composed. Of these modules, the data base on technical aids, Handyaids, was to be the first. There were good reasons for this. The particularity of technical aids lends itself to systematic treatment, while their complexity and multiplicity require it. Moreover we had inherited from our Luxembourg colleagues the conviction that comprehensive, accurate and up-to-date information at a European level was an essential prerequisite of the development of a free Community market in technical aids, something which clearly did not exist and which it was essential to achieve — not for merely doctrinaire reasons so much as for the benefit both of producers and consumers, above all of the clients themselves.

Fortunately we had a helpful mandate from the Council: the 1981 action programme Resolution invited the Commission to 'pool the information, taking into account the existing national systems, and ensuring an exchange of information between the services involved . . . including the representatives of handicapped people'. Earlier in the Resolution, the member states themselves were invited to 'promote the development and availability of technical aids, the pooling of information and experience in the field and the application of new technologies, so as to facilitate the communication, mobility and employment of disabled people'.

By means of two seminars, and a number of studies and operational contracts,[15] the Handynet project moved forward steadily throughout the course of the action programme, though it cannot be said that the regular information about its progress which we afforded to the representatives of the member states on the Liaison Group was always understood let alone perceived as requiring some active response. By the end of the programme in 1987 the project could record these achievements:

- the Nordic classification of terms concerning technical aids already established by co-operation between the Nordic countries and existing in English as well as Danish, Norwegian and Swedish was translated into the other Community languages
- a common format for the profile of each technical aid to be recorded in the Handyaids data base was drawn up by a team of three experts, all of them responsible for operational technical aids data bases in their own countries[16]
- a contract was established with the European Space Agency to provide the main computer host facility for the data base, and the first steps taken to make this operational
- a design for the development of other modules and services of Handynet was prepared, and studies of information needs completed, covering a number of topics, including employment, training, mobility and access
- specialized working parties were set up to ensure that the Handyaids module took full account of the needs of people with visual disabilities,[17] and the first examples of Handyaids were tested for consumer friendliness by a co-operative of disabled people in Rome.

Yet by the end of the first action programme it was still evident that a number of member states were holding Handynet at arm's length, if not actually hoping it would go away. There could be little doubt that the future of Handynet was assured: not one argument had been produced to show that it was unnecessary or impracticable, or that its objectives could be achieved by any other means. But there could be no doubt either that some tough negotiations lay ahead.

Other information services

Apart from the Handynet project, the first action programme confined its information activity to services which could reliably and regularly be carried out from the resources available. The most substantial of these were the documentation service of study reports and political texts operated by Jean-Claude Limpach in the Commission's core team, and the two publications, one a journal and the other a newsletter,[18] distributed by the networks of rehabilitation centres and district projects. In addition our blind secretary, Jeanne-Françoise Crahay, initiated a scheme for the production and distribution of key Community documents in braille and on tape for visually disabled people. Regular information notes on the progress of the programme were also sent to the Commission's information offices in all the member states. This left a great deal which we were unable to do without the provision of a full-time information officer.

EDUCATION – AFTER ALL

In Chapter 1, I explained how my early endeavours to launch a European action on the education of children with special needs had come to nothing owing to the political problems, and in particular the Danish objections, which were affecting the whole education programme in the late 1970s and early 1980s. As a result the action programme started in 1982 was concerned with the social and economic integration of adult disabled people, but not with the educational integration of children and young people with disabilities.

At the beginning of 1984 France held the presidency of the Council of Ministers and therefore of all the Council committees, including the Education Committee. It was a period when the French government was engaged in a new set of initiatives to promote the integration of children with special needs into ordinary schools, and the French took the opportunity to propose to the Education Committee that there should be a Community activity on this topic. Needless to say, although we had some reservations as to the wisdom of restricting the programme to the notion of integration instead of including all aspects of the education of children with special needs, we in the Commission welcomed the French initiative.[19]

That the proposal came from a member state, and especially from the country holding the presidency, and not – as so many proposals did – from the Commission, was I believe vital to its success. School integration was not a specially easy topic for the Germans, for example, to address at the European level, still less for the Dutch. Objection to a Commission proposal concerning this topic might well have been strong and fatal. As it was, everyone wanted to please the French and the proposal got through with very little difficulty, apart from some rather delicate negotiations as to what should and what should not be said about special schools in the document to be put before the Ministers.

What emerged was not a programme but a pre-programme. This was quite good enough – indeed anything more would have been impossible to cope with. For one thing there was no budget; for another there was no way in which so important a new element could be grafted on to an action programme which was already half way through its course. Besides, time was needed to reflect together with national experts as to what the objectives and make-up of a programme on this topic should be.

It was agreed therefore to set up a Working Group on Educational Integration, made up of delegations of not more than two people from each country, composed of officials or professionals from Education Ministries, and chaired by the Commission. The main task of this Group would be to help the Commission first to prepare a report for the Education Committee on the situation of integration in the member states, with a focus on any evidence for a convergence of approaches and measures among them, and following that to present a Communication to the Council with a proposal for an action programme on educational integration. Such a proposal could be timed to coincide more or less with that for the next action programme on social and economic integration, so that the whole could be planned together and the goal of a comprehensive 'cradle to grave' approach to the needs of those with disabilities at last achieved.

The Educational Integration Working Group got quickly under way and the report 'Progress with regard to the Implementation of the Policy of Integrating Handicapped Children into Ordinary Schools'[20] was published in October 1986, the sections on the situation in Spain and Portugal following three months later. The Group was fortunate in containing a number of members with considerable previous experience of international work, such as Auguste Dens from the Flemish part of Belgium, Jørgen Hansen from Denmark, Klaus Hasemann from Germany and Sean Hunt from Ireland.

In addition to this main strategy, one or two preliminary actions could already be attempted which would help the future programme to get off to a good start, provided these did not make significant demands on resources. For one thing we were able to boost considerably the participation by educationists concerned with children with special needs in the scheme of study visits abroad for educational professionals run by the Commission's Education Division.

Immediate interest was also shown by the Group in the contribution which new technology could make to the education of children with disabilities. Even when education was in the doldrums I had managed to arrange for Jørgen Hansen to produce a European study on 'Teaching and Training the Handicapped through the New Information Technology', which was published in 1984 and established a firm conceptual framework for our future treatment of the subject. Interest in the topic was further roused by a European conference on 'The New Information Technology and the Education and Training of Disabled Persons' which I organized near Manchester in 1985 with the help of Rhys Gwyn of the Centre for Information Technology and Education of Manchester Polytechnic, whose report was published the same year.

Following this Jørgen Hansen was able to set up an informal development group of experts concerned with new technology and special education in different countries with the understanding that the Commission would be able to find some modest resources to enable it to start its work. It was in this context that we were able to envisage a European data base of computer softwares relevant to special needs education as one of the possible early modules of Handynet. A working party was set up to prepare this, under the chairmanship of Philippe Lamoral, the chairman of the European Association for Special Education (EASE). It was evident that the topic of new technology in its educational application would need to be given a certain priority in the action programme on educational integration which we could now foresee as being adopted in 1986 and launched in 1987 at the latest.

NOTES

1   Especially in an educational context, the term 'learning difficulty' is now often preferred to 'mental handicap'. In educational discussion, too, the expression 'children with special needs' is conveniently used to cover all disabilities; a disadvantage is however that it could equally well be used to refer to the requirements of children with exceptional talents, a very different issue. Many difficulties of nomenclature occur also in the field of mental illness. Here the French have an advantage as they can speak of 'handicapés psychiques', for which there is no English equivalent.

2   It was sad for us that Charles Humblet, after initiating important work on the media and autonomous living, left us to set up independently in Australia. For Jeanne-Françoise Crahay, our blind secretary, see p. 31 above.

3   Later in the programme Van Lierde was joined by Mary Kyriasopoulou and Clemens Russel from the teams of the Ahaia and Berlin (Spandau) district projects respectively.

4   For the membership of the Dialogue Group and of the RI secretariats during this and the succeeding programmes, see Appendixes 2A and 2D.

5   For these studies, see References to Chapter 4.

6   Dr John is now Professor of Education at the University of Exeter.

7   The director of this Centre, Gabriel Fragnière, was one of the leading figures in the setting up of the Association for Teacher Education in Europe and the Association internationale autisme Europe; see also under Handynet studies in References below. Dr Albeda was assisted in the preparation of the report by Stefanos Grammenos, now director of the Centre for European Social and Economic Policy in Brussels and the Commission's principal consultant on employment and disability.

8   The European Parliament wanted the Commission to engage to bring forward a Directive if member states failed to introduce a precise quota system within a given time. This proposal was carried by a vast majority, only the British Conservatives with their few allies, and those to the right of them, dissenting.

9   For details of this preparatory work in the environmental field, see References to Chapter 5.

10 For the membership of this network during this and the following programme, see Appendix 2C.

11 There was, for example, no evidence that the then Manpower Services Commission regarded this European co-operation as of any value.

12 See Chapter 1, p. 12.

13 For the districts which participated in this network, see Appendix 2B.

14 For this report, see under References to Chapter 5.

15 For convenience, details of the Handynet studies and seminar reports completed during the first action programme are grouped together in the References to this chapter below.

16 The three experts were Theo Bougie of the Lucas Stichting voor Revalidatie at Hoensbroek, Josiane Pierre of the Centre de réadaptation of Mulhouse, and Renzo Andrich of the Servizio informazione e valutazione ausili in Milan (SIVA). Of these institutions, the first two were members of the network of rehabilitation centres. The director of SIVA, Antonio Pedotti, was leader of a Community concerted medical research project on the evaluation of assistive devices; SIVA is also associated with the Fondazione pro juventute, another rehabilitation network member.

17 The working party on technical aids for visual handicap was convened by Pier-Luigi Emiliani of the University of Florence who was also leader of a Community concerted medical research project on new technology and visual disability.

18   The *Journal of the Network of Rehabilitation Centres* was first published (in German, English and French) in December 1984, and the *Interact News*, in all the Community languages, at the same time. With the new programme in 1988, the two were amalgamated in the *Helios Newsletter*.
19   'We' included Hywel Jones, formerly head of the Education Division and by then director for Education, Training and Youth, and his successor as head of the Education Division, Domenico Lenarduzzi.
20   For study and conference report details, see References to Chapter 6.

REFERENCES

Commission studies and conference reports

Note For studies etc. on employment, the environment and education see References to Chapters 4, 5 and 6 respectively.

Handynet conference report and studies:

Antonio Pedotti and Renzo Andrich, *European Co-ordination of Information concerning Disabled Persons*, Proceedings of a European workshop held at SIVA, Milan, 25–27 Sept. 1984, Milan 1985. (EN)
Thibault Lambert, *Information Needs regarding the Employment of Disabled People*, Centre technique d'études et de recherche sur les handicaps et les inadaptations, Vanves 1985. (EN, FR)
Wolfgang Ettel *et al.*, *Information Needs on the Rehabilitation and Training of Disabled Persons*, Gesellschaft für Information, Frankfurt am Main 1985. (EN)
Gabriel Fragnière, *Les besoins d'information des familles de personnes handicapées* [Information needs of the families of disabled people], Maastricht 1985. (FR)
Klaus Blach, *Need for Information on Access to Buildings for Disabled People*, Lyngby 1986. (EN)
Hans Aengenendt, *Information Needed regarding the Mobility of Disabled Persons*, Gruppe Hardtberg, Bonn 1987. (EN)

Other conference and study:

Bernard Kitous, *Communication Facilities for the Disabled — technical aids*, Paris 1982. (DE, GR, EN, FR, IT, NL)
Antonio Pedotti and Renzo Andrich, *Evaluation of Assistive Devices for Paralysed Persons*, Proceedings of a European workshop held at SIVA, Milan, 27–29 Apr. 1983, Milan 1984. (EN)

Other Commission publication:

The Social Integration of Disabled People, Social Europe Supplement 7/86, Commission of the European Communities, Luxembourg 1987. (DE, EN, FR)

Part II

Needs and Responses

Chapter 3

An Overview

THE QUANTITY AND QUALITY OF NEED

The quantity of disability

In the study of 'The Handicapped and their Employment' which he completed for the European Commission's Statistical Office in 1983, Guy Mangin concluded that the chief use of the estimates achieved was to 'illustrate the overall policies of a given country' and to help in 'comparing national policies', rather than in having any strictly 'statistical value', either for clarifying the effectiveness of measures or for fixing the number of people with disabilities throughout the Community.[1]

The problem with statistics concerning disability is of course that the great majority of figures available are administratively derived and specific to the operation of a particular service or benefit: they tell us, for example, how many disabled people are registered as eligible under an employment scheme, or are in receipt of a particular social security or welfare benefit, or are accommodated in a certain kind of institution. Even at national level, such figures may be difficult to disaggregate (in terms of age, sex or type of disability), and virtually impossible to aggregate, both because the various administrations apply different criteria of disability and cover different disabilities, and because it could be impossible to discover either who had not been included in the final count or who had been counted twice.

It is obvious that these problems are magnified if we attempt any comparison between different national figures, since for whatever cultural or other reasons we very soon come across discrepancies that look insuperable. The scale of the problem is well illustrated by the study on special education which Skov Jørgensen prepared for the Commission in 1978. Jørgensen's official sources reported the existence of some 1,400 deaf children in Italy and over 7,000 in France, of about 72,500 mentally retarded children in Germany and in France again over 300,000; the category of children identified in Belgium as 'atteints de troubles instrumentaux' did not appear to have any equivalent in English.[2]

For its part the Commission decided to assume that about 10 per cent of the whole population had some significant physical, mental or psychological disability; throughout the Community of 12 member states this would give a total of over 30 million disabled people. Certainly there has been no reason to suppose that there is any real significant difference among the Community countries as far as concerns the size of these three broad categories.[3] The validity of this working figure was corroborated by the World Health Organization.

This estimate received considerable support from what was perhaps the most convincing set of figures obtained by Mangin, the percentage prevalence of people with 'physical handicaps' in the Netherlands. Since this gave a figure of 8.7 per cent of the population (8.3 per cent of all males and 9.0 per cent of all females), and since this excluded all those (known to be numerous) with only mental or psychological disabilities, the working figure of 10 per cent for all disabilities would appear to be, if anything, a conservative one. If the assumption that the real prevalence of disability does not vary significantly among member states is valid, and given that as a rule reliable approximations not precisions are what is needed for policy purposes, to extrapolate from one country whose figures are likely to be dependable to the Community as a whole should give as useful a result as trying to compare non-comparable data from all the countries.

More recently the practice of taking 10 per cent as the working figure has received from the United Kingdom a corroboration which is virtually conclusive. In September 1988 the Office of Population Censuses and Surveys (OPCS) published a report which is especially valuable and influential for a number of reasons. Like the earlier Dutch figures referred to, the OPCS data include details of age and sex, but, unlike them, they cover mental and psychological as well as physical disabilities; on the other hand, whereas the Dutch calculation starts at age five, the British one comprises adults only (16 years and over), prevalence of disability among children being the subject of a separate report. They also include an important innovation, consisting of a scale of ten levels of severity of disability.

The results of the survey are startling, showing a total prevalence of disability as affecting 14.2 per cent of the adult population if all ten categories of severity are included. Even if the lowest of the ten categories is discounted, the figure is still 11.4 per cent; if the second lowest is also not considered, it is 9.5 per cent. These figures amount to more than double those which had previously been used for policy purposes by the British government. Breakdowns of the figures according to kinds rather than levels of disability are also interesting (9.9 per cent of adults have a locomotive disability, 5.9 per cent a hearing one, and 5.5 per cent one affecting personal care), as also are ethnic differences (the rates for whites are higher than for Asians, and the rates for West Indians higher still).

An important factor, and one which is of increasing concern to professionals and policy makers, is the relation between disability and ageing. On no criteria do current estimates of the proportion of disabled people who are over 60 years of age fall below 70 per cent. What is more, that this percentage will increase significantly in the next 30 years is a certain implication both of the general rise in the percentage of elderly people (and especially of the older elderly) who will incur disability in association with ageing, and of the increasing participation in that greater longevity of people with long-standing disabilities which are not age-related.

If we look at the converse question, the percentage of elderly people who are disabled, we find figures which are less high but hardly less serious in their impli-cations. Estimates in France, using criteria which reveal a disability prevalence of 12 per cent in the population as a whole, give figures of 35 per cent for those in their 70s and 50 per cent for those over 80; prevalence of severe disability is twelve times higher among the over 80s than it is generally. The recent United Kingdom survey just cited as giving a significant disability prevalence of 14.2 per cent for the whole adult population has 24 per cent for those aged 60–69, 40.8 per cent for those 70–79 and 71.4 per cent for those over 80; the respective percentages for severe disability (fifth level and above) over those three age-ranges are 8.4, 16.9 and 43.8, compared with 6.2 for all adults. The same survey shows that the chance that someone over 80 will be profoundly disabled is eleven times greater than for the population as a whole.

For the policy-maker the large and increasing number of people who are both disabled and elderly is of particular importance in its implications for the provision of personal care services and for the planning of a physical environment favourable to independent living — transport and other means to personal mobility, the accessi-bility of public facilities, housing and services to the home. But the availability of desirable and accessible educational opportunities for elderly people, including elderly disabled people, is also an important need and one which is often overlooked. And, at least among the less aged members of the elderly community, there will be an increasing demand for retraining, flexible retirement schemes and new full- or part-time employment.[4]

Two important facts concerning childhood disability emerge from the United King-dom survey of disabled children under the age of 16, which appeared in 1989, the year after the adult survey. First, whereas there are nearly six times as many adults in category 1 (least severe disabilities) as there are in category 10 (the most severe), the number of children estimated to be in category 10 is actually higher than that in category 1.[5] Secondly, 70 per cent of disabilities affecting children are of mental or behavioural origin; of the children in category 10, no fewer than 96 per cent have a mental disability.

It is good to know that the European Commission is maintaining its concern for Community statistics on disability. Yet while we must not underrate the intransigence of the difficulties in this area, we should not either overestimate their effect. Much can be done by means of collecting data locally about the realities of disabled people and their day-to-day needs; such information may be both more accurate and more relevant to the planning and delivery of service provision than national statistics however sophisticated. Local data gathering of this kind proved useful to the partici-pants in the district projects network in the Commission's first action programme; in the United Kingdom, valuable work of this kind has been done by the Greater London Action on Disability (GLAD) and, for Northern Ireland and elsewhere, by the organization Outset.[6]

Moreover, whenever for policy purposes we are trying to reach a realistic overview of the 'world of disability', we need to remember that this comprises, as well as disabled people themselves, not only all the family members and life partners who are closely involved in disability as part of the reality of their daily lives, but also all those professionals, of many different kinds, who work for all or part of their time with or for people with disabilities. It is necessary to stress this point again and again in order to rebut the persistent false assumption that, as far as concerns mere magnitude, disability is a marginal domain.

Before leaving this purely quantitative aspect of disability, there are two general observations which I need to make. First I must mention and welcome the tendency to present data in terms of actual functional disability rather than of impairment as medically defined. Though I am convinced of the need for a new synthesis, and indeed alliance, between the medical and socio-political approaches to disability problems, there can be no doubt that purely medical categorizations, however useful as a starting point, can be unhelpful if they continue to dominate our language, and so our thinking, in the social and educational domains.

Secondly, some general reflection is needed about the probable trends which will characterize the prevalence of disability over the next two decades or so. By far the most certain and very probably the most important of these is that which relates to ageing, already referred to: there will be a steady increase in the percentage of the whole population which is elderly, and this rise will be especially steep among those who are very old (the 'fourth' rather than the 'third' age); since people with long-term disabilities will share in this extension of longevity, and since also there will be an increased incidence of new disabilities associated with ageing among the larger percentage of people living beyond the age of 75, there will be a substantial increase in the prevalence of disability among elderly people and this will of course affect the disability figures for the population as a whole.

When it comes to children and those of the adult population who are not elderly it is not possible to be so certain about the future. The most that can be said is that in the short term it is unlikely that the increase in the prevalence of disability among elderly people will be balanced by an equivalent decrease among other age groups. As to the disabling effects of disease or trauma incurred during childhood or later, there is little that can be said except that advances in prevention, cure and treatment will be countered at least to some degree by the extent to which, also owing to improved medical intervention, people who would have died in the past survive but with a long-term disability.

When on the other hand we consider congenital impairments, it is indeed true that prenatal screening leading to induced termination of pregnancy is already having an effect in reducing prevalence which can be dramatic for some congenital disorders.[7] The prevention or avoidance of pregnancy, and the selection of those live infants to whom life-saving interventions will or will not be offered,[8] are other factors at work in the congenital sphere. While it would not appear likely that these developments will have a significant effect on global prevalence figures within the next decade, it must be supposed that before very long their impact, enhanced by the contribution of research on live human embryos, will be considerable. At some point down this path a new, and from various points of view possibly disturbing, phenomenon may begin to present itself — a significant difference between the prevalence of congenital disabilities in Catholic and non-Catholic cultures.

The quality of handicap

I want now to attempt some general assessment of the extent to which and the ways in which people with disabilities are in fact handicapped in the development of their individual potential and the achievement of a full and autonomous life. The issues raised now will be treated in more detail in the following three chapters; what I am trying to achieve here is an overview.

Some positive factors

Where so many difficult problems exist, a completely unbalanced picture would result if some account were not first given of the many salient positive features in the situation of disabled people in Europe. As well as the advances in medical treatment which we have just referred to, considerable progress has been made in the theory and practice of pedagogy, opening up new learning possibilities for mentally retarded as well as physically disabled people at all levels of education and training. In some cases this effect has been highlighted by the consequences of the 'mainstreaming' tendency to integrate disabled children or young people into ordinary schools or colleges.

Equally important has been the contribution which technology has made and is making to the reduction or even elimination of handicaps however severe. The range and quality of technical aids, and of information about them, are in general advancing all the time, and there is no form of disability whose potential handicapping consequences cannot be reduced in one way or another by their means; the present contribution, let alone the future potential, of aids using new informatic or telematic technologies is especially important. The benefits offered extend over every phase and almost every aspect of life — basic functioning, education, training, employment, leisure, communication, environmental control, mobility, security. Increasingly it is no exaggeration to say that the blind can read, the deaf can use the telephone, people with motor impairments can move with considerable freedom, the mentally handicapped can learn. With the aid of a computer, even a person so severely paralysed from birth that he can only nod his head or blow is able to communicate and to control his environment.[9]

The combination of technical advances with changing attitudes and a developing sense of public responsibility has brought a number of wider ranging benefits. Tetraplegic people may be able to drive cars which have been specially adapted for them; in a number of cities public transport systems have been adapted or door-to-door transport provision established. There have been many imaginative and flexible housing schemes which enable independent living, without loss of the necessary professional support and without the creation of ghettoes. Mobility in the street has been improved by the provision in some cities of ramps for wheelchair users and of tactile or audible aids for blind pedestrians. Much has also been done to make public buildings — offices, hotels, shops, educational establishments, cultural and leisure facilities — physically accessible, and to adapt work-places to the needs of disabled employees. It is true that in all these areas the record of achievement throughout the Community is extremely variable, but the achievements are real and the basis of good practice firmly laid down.

Much of this practical achievement has resulted from (and, in its turn, further encouraged) changes of attitudes — among employers, for example, trade union officials, administrators and case-work professionals; to some extent also among the general public. At times, indeed, it is hard not to be impressed rather by the darker side: the persistence of apathy, ignorance and ill-disguised fear towards many forms of disability can be a depressing phenomenon. Yet, on the positive side, there is a growing concern, for example, to break down the barriers which have traditionally existed between the practitioners of different professions and either administrators or, even more important, their clients. In some countries at least, magazine programmes or documentary films broadcast on radio or television are having an important impact. There is a widespread and increasingly effective will to be rid of the debilitating effect of an undue paternalism which has characterized much well-intentioned activity in the past. Though reservations and prejudices persist, it is encouraging that many employers have completely changed their attitude when they have learned in practice what a disabled worker has to offer. Indeed there is a mass of evidence from every walk of life and every level of society that this is a domain where anything is possible once the ice is broken.

Not rapidly, at least in Europe, yet perceptibly and increasingly, disabled people themselves are responding actively to this complex of predicament and opportunity. Individuals, of course, have always done this; more and more it is now being realized that, apart from the heroic few, disabled people need organization and solidarity if the challenge is to be met. In all Community countries the associations of parents and families of disabled people, and of disabled people themselves, are more or less influential, and the trend is for their influence to grow; at European level also it is being felt, and the Commission is encouraging this development. The truth is that the goodwill of the non-disabled is essential but is not enough; it cannot alone be relied on to produce effective results, least of all when (as is the case now) there is powerful political pressure against public spending. Disabled people need therefore the support of well directed self-advocacy too. This will nowhere be more effective than where linked to active self-help initiatives — a point I shall develop a little later on in this chapter.

In summary, the positive factors affecting the general situation of disabled people in the Community can be seen as a combination of somewhat slow and sporadic but distinct progress as far as concerns environmental questions, supporting systems, the attitudes of others towards disabled people, and the self-image and aspirations of disabled people themselves, with very much more rapid advances in the scientific and technological fields. What matters most of all is that this combination is changing and will continue to change the threshold of capability in respect of independent living. The reality now is that to speak of incurability, ineducability or unemployability, in an absolute sense, is no longer possible. The worst that can be said is that in some situations we cannot perceive how this or that person can make significant progress towards enhanced autonomy and independence in the foreseeable future — and even then, quite often and probably more and more frequently, we shall be proved wrong.

Negative factors

Yet for very many of the disabled people of Europe the positive developments just described are a mere dream and the overall picture given by the preceding paragraphs would seem to be totally unrealistic. We must therefore now look at the principal general problems which act as barriers to the achievement of a full and satisfying life for many thousands of people with disabilities. Among these difficulties we can distinguish those which derive from the nature of disability itself, those which are an effect of the complexity and priorities of modern life and those which are centred in the response which society makes to disability.

One group of problems concerns the very diversity of disabilities. On the side of the disabled people themselves, this factor has acted as an understandable brake on the development of a sense of comprehensive solidarity, and therefore has in practice tended to impede the formation of effectively powerful structures of self-help and advocacy. For administrators and providers of services the diversity also constitutes an intractable difficulty; they are perpetually either trying to find a narrow path between over-specialization and over-generalization in their definition of the problems to be confronted, or they are having to make a series of discrete decisions to take comparatively narrow or broad approaches to specific situations or needs.

Disability also entails, both for the disabled person and the policy-maker or service-provider, the dilemma of stigma. In order both to plan services and to deliver them, the provider must know what or where the needs are, and be able to make at least some assessment of trends. So the provider needs to identify disabled people, collect detailed information about them, perhaps for certain purposes invite or require them to register themselves as disabled persons. The pursuit even of an active policy of integration depends on first identifying and distinguishing those who are to be integrated. And for the disabled people themselves the dilemma is clear enough: to qualify for a benefit, they must accept a categorization which may diminish their self-image or damage the way others perceive them. For them too, therefore, the public route to integration may appear irksome and over-exposed.

Whatever might be the best solution to these difficulties, I am convinced that endeavours to diminish or disguise the realities of disability make little contribution towards finding it. While we must respect the Danish inclination to include measures for disabled people within broader legislation covering the needs of all those who are disadvantaged in society, I have no doubt that any attempt to apply that principle over the Community as a whole would have detrimental consequences for disabled people. Also, while there is no question that the concept of 'normalization' has made an important contribution to the development of positive attitudes to disabled people in Scandinavia and to the institution of generally excellent services for them there, I have very serious doubts of its transferability to other cultures.[10]

Nor should policy-makers be timid about spelling out the fact that disability measures are designed for the benefit of people who are (for example) blind, deaf, paralysed, mentally handicapped or mentally ill, and that measures that fail to take account of the needs specific to these diverse disabilities fail altogether. It is absurd at one moment to proclaim that we are going to 'love the difference' and then to proceed to do everything possible to hide the differences away. We must beware too of those in positions of authority who may use slogans about the avoidance of discrimination and stigma as an excuse for complacency or as a convenient way of avoiding the expenditure of money and effort which practical measures aimed at solving real problems inevitably entail.[11]

We need next to reflect on the problems for disabled people which arise from the general character of the society in which they live. There are two aspects to this question. The first is objective, and concerns the instability, complexity and technicality of modern life as it affects all of us. In order to take part to a merely average extent and to avoid isolation from the majority of the benefits of modern life, we need to be able to communicate widely and quickly, to learn new procedures, to acquire, store and access information, to be freely mobile. Coping with the totality of these demands may entail physical responses which are beyond the possibility of those with sensory or motor disabilities, are not intelligible to mentally handicapped people and can only inspire fear in those with histories of mental illness. Many of these difficulties are likely to be heightened in urban situations, but they are by no means confined to these — indeed, as far as mobility is concerned, disabled people living in rural environments may well be worse off than they would have been fifty years ago. In many different ways disabled people may find that the technical demands of modern daily living put them at a disadvantage compared to other people and therefore result in an accumulation of handicap.

But there is another complication of contemporary life which is more subjective and may (for all we know) be no more than temporary, since it is a question of political climate. Whatever one may think of the constellation of political values which have infiltrated Europe from across the Atlantic over the last decade or so, there is surely no doubt that they elevate the importance of individual success in a world not merely perceived as competitive but admired for being that. I do not mean to suggest that these ideas are essentially, let alone deliberately, unsympathetic to disability as such, or that every sustained effort to reduce public expenditure is against the interest of disabled people. But, whatever the intentions, it is inevitable that a highly competitive environment will create difficulties for those who have to struggle for equality of opportunity; above all for the most severely disabled, the chance for a fair start in life may never present itself. Moreover, where public budgets are perpetually under severe scrutiny, the service needs of minorities with special problems are always likely to be at risk. It must be remembered too that service expenditure by properly elected local authorities is commonly spoken of in certain quarters as 'spending other people's money', a notion which, like all populist ideas, receives more respect than it deserves.

Coming now to the problems arising from the response of society to disability, these can be seen as being of three kinds: those which manifest themselves in legislation and more generally at the political level, those which affect the provision of services and those which relate to attitudes of the public at large.

If we consider legislation in favour of disabled people, we find that although there are many useful measures in force in the Community countries, the total picture is unsatisfactory for four reasons. The basis of past legislation naturally reflects the vision of the time, a vision which may now appear limited or distorted; nor have modifications generally kept up with changes in the situation or in attitudes. Legislation has also often been piecemeal, so that the various elements do not cohere. Thirdly, implementation is not always effective, and monitoring often not provided for. The detrimental effect of these inadequacies is, finally, aggravated by financial constraint.

Underlying these rather practical deficiencies there are two influences at work which are more deeply seated and which affect the whole political process. The first of these is what we may call political snobbery. In a world which does not (in spite of the Beatitudes) regard the meek as deserving to inherit anything, let alone the earth, those who devote their political or administrative lives to the problems of disability will not be seen as having taken the high road to fame and fortune. For one thing, such do-gooders proclaim their own 'wetness'; for another, they are in danger of becoming permanently identified with one domain, the complex world of disability which it is extremely convenient, for reasons of political cosmetics, to have covered without those who have serious personal ambitions having to bother their heads with it.

Now this might not matter very much if it did not affect the degree of priority which is given to disability issues by those who are really engaged in the game of power. But it does: the strategy of the serious political players will be, first, to make sure that they distance themselves from disability (since one's image must not be tainted with anything which smacks either of charity or of failure), and second, to make sure that sufficient gestures are made to keep the disability lobby reasonably quiet without any fundamental commitment ever being made to meet the problems by means of comprehensive action.

The second underlying problem at the political level while not, for sure, confined to the United Kingdom would seem to be especially characteristic of the British view of democracy, that it is something to be regarded with considerable suspicion unless decently presented in one of the forms hallowed by tradition. According to this view, while it is, at least in theory, permissible for an individual disabled person to speak up for himself in his own cause, there is something foreign and odious about the idea that disabled people should elect disabled people to represent them and to battle for places on decision-making bodies for this purpose. A common trick of champions of this particular form of resistance to power-sharing is to sneer at the idea of including one disabled person on a committee to represent disabled people as an example of 'tokenism', as if it were not obvious that to have one such representative is very much better than to have none at all.[12]

We need now to look at typical problems affecting the provision of services, of which I can distinguish three that stand out. The first of these is that of fragmentation and the lack of co-ordination. Services are organized in relation to specific needs so that at the same time a disabled person has to relate to a number of professionals or agencies, none of which is capable of looking at his or her problems as a whole or concerned to consider the impact of one intervention on other aspects of the client's life. The professionals themselves tend to be over-specialized and to have little or, at best, inadequate contact with each other; activities of co-ordination are often left to chance. In the field of interprofessional co-operation, although there are striking examples of good practice, the general standard falls far short of what is needed. Evidently this fragmentation effect can be especially acute during a transitional process when the disabled person passes in time from one agency or establishment to another,[13] but all rehabilitation is a process in this sense and therefore subject to the dangers of discontinuity.

One of the chief genuine difficulties in this area arises from the number and diversity of bodies and individuals whose work, even at local level, needs to be co-ordinated if disabled people are to be offered an overall service which is comprehensive and user-friendly. For one thing, public institutions, voluntary organizations and the private commercial sector have all to be involved. For another, responsibility for co-ordination, if it is assigned anywhere, is almost inevitably lodged with one of the specialized services whose vision of the total need may be limited by its own professional preoccupation. A clear example of this can be seen in the recent growth of the concept of 'care in the community' which we can perceive in the context of deinstitutionalization policies in the United Kingdom and elsewhere. The disabled person leaving a residential institution is attributed almost exclusively passive roles, as the client of social services, a patient of the health service and a resident in some form of semi-sheltered accommodation; his or her active life as worker in need of employment, as student in need of education or training, and as consumer requiring the means for mobility and access to facilities is generally afforded far less attention. Essential as care evidently is, if it is all the open community has to offer it is by no means clear that the closing of long-stay institutions will work to the benefit either of the service-providers or their clients.

A second problem affecting services and facilities is that of standardization and the need for the administrators to simplify their problems if they are not to become unmanageable. There is nothing new or remarkable in the assertion that bureaucrats and even the providers of primary services tend to categorize and so simplify the problems of groups of clients, and thus (at least in the eye of the clients themselves) tend to underestimate the importance of factors specific to the individual. Up to a point, this may be inevitable, and therefore best accepted; but for many disabled people the consequences may be too serious to be tolerable. For them the complex particularity of the effects of their impairment is the very essence of their life, all day and every day; either solutions take this singularity into account or they are no use at all. It is no comfort to know that most wheelchairs can get through a door if your wheelchair cannot.

A recurrent problem therefore is that of the agent — administrator, professional, employer, hotel-keeper, whatever — who will adapt what is on offer so far and no further. To be told that what you are providing is inadequate is annoying to the professionals, who naturally like to believe that they know their own business; when a budget which allows for adaptations has been set, the discovery that they have been undercosted is a lot less than welcome. All forms of individualization are expensive in one way or another, and for that reason alone compromises will sometimes have to be made. What matters is the encouragement of professional attitudes which actually welcome the particularity of individual need instead of regarding it as a mere inconvenience. This will ensure that the best is always done within the limits of available resources, that cost is not falsely used as an excuse for not taking the extra trouble that individualization of services demands, and that skills are developed in assigning relative priorities to various individual requirements.

The third outstanding problem affecting the quality of services to which, to my knowledge, disabled people draw attention is that of paternalism. If inadequate in some respects, services may offer or impose too much in others. It would be quite wrong to exaggerate this point; when we listen to some militants on this subject we may receive the impression that all protection and security is intrinsically evil, all parents tyrants and all care professionals engaged in some kind of therapy on behalf not of their clients but themselves. Yet it must also be said that many disabled people and professionals are convinced that care in the family or in institutions can be over-protective, inhibiting the disabled person from developing his or her individuality or active potential. The effects of this may be extremely serious if the accustomed protection is suddenly removed, for example on the death of parents or the closure of an establishment. Problems of this kind, it seems, may affect those with physical disabilities and histories of mental illness as well as people with mental handicaps.

Even if living in semi-independence in the open community, the disabled person can still be the victim of a paternalistic approach on the part of professionals who underestimate his or her potential for autonomy, personal development and active involvement in social or occupational life. Certain professions have established a reputation for being patronizing; from a given point of view, all disabled people can be perceived as chronic patients, and traditionally patients must be given only that amount of information about their own condition which is judged good for them by the professionals.

Certainly, general changes in our social behaviour in the direction of a more informal, less deferential style, combined with specific efforts of organizations of disabled people and of the parents of disabled children aimed at emancipation from their traditional position of dependence and inferiority, have led to the development of many situations where disabled people and their families are free to relate to professionals on equal terms, and to a growing realization among caring parents of the dangers if children with disabilities are over-protected. But it would be a great mistake to suppose that the problem of paternalism is virtually solved and only needs a short passage of time to have vanished totally. Only recently I read in the brochure of an English nursing home that among its provisions there would be 'a facility to care for persons classed as young disabled, many of whom will die without ever returning home'. Copies of this document were freely and openly available in the main entrance of the building, where they were no doubt read by the residents and their relatives with great interest. Caring and well-trained professionals can only exhibit such massive insensitivity as this when they are prisoners of a tradition that simply does not perceive the clients as fellow human beings in the full sense.

This rather pessimistic reflection brings me to the last of the barriers to progress in our field which I shall describe here — the problems which relate to the attitudes of the general public to disability. No one appears to disagree that the situation in this regard is, in spite of the efforts which have been made to improve it, still a long way from being satisfactory throughout our culture. Often the origin of the problem is not any kind of ill will but simply ignorance or embarrassment or a combination of these. This was well illustrated in a series of cartoons produced by the district project of Liège in our first action programme. In one, for example, a blundering non-disabled person is asking an evidently blind man: 'Now what is your disease — I mean handicap?' and receives the reply 'I'm blind. How about you?' In another a mother is explaining to a neighbour that her little boy is deaf; 'But it's not infectious, is it?' is the response.

The difficulties are much more severe with some disabilities than with others. Yet (for example) wheelchair users who have no impairments other than their paralysis have to contend with realities which are far worse than mere pinpricks of irritation. Even if one can get hardened to being stared at it must be almost impossibly difficult to accept without at least occasional anger or distress the frequent examples of total ignorance either of one's needs on the one hand or of one's capabilities on the other. Worst of all, perhaps, is evidence of a suspicion that a motor disability must imply some kind of mental defect, and the tendency to suppose that the wheelchair user cannot speak for himself but only through the medium of some non-disabled helper — the 'Does he take sugar?' phenomenon.

The difficulties are likely to be worse where the disability includes uncontrolled movements (especially of the face) or distortions of speech. Here we must I suppose recognize the operation of a more or less deep-seated aversion of an atavistic kind. If that is correct, then we can hope that if society continues on its present pluralistic course this effect will in time simply disappear altogether. Meanwhile (though some of us may, for whatever reason, be better at this than others) most of us can only overcome this impulse to shrink away if we have had the opportunity to learn to do this by means of sufficient direct personal contact and communication for us to be able, as it were, to penetrate 'below' the initially difficult surface to the real interesting person underneath — after which we can return to a full awareness of our new friend's physical appearance to find that the problem of aversion has miraculously been annihilated.

This phenomenon among others is most sensitively and movingly explored in a French film in the production of which my predecessor Umberto Vidali was involved.[14] Here an intelligent well-qualified girl with cerebral palsy is given a job by a bank but is only allowed to work in isolation away from the area of day-to-day business since the customers would not like to see her face. In a long interview the bank manager defends his action and indeed proclaims his confidence in his own benevolence and indignation at the idea that anyone should call this in question; yet the more he protests the more clearly the filming reveals the waning of his own faith in the position he is holding — a position which however he cannot abandon either. We are left with the disturbing question for ourselves: 'I, of course would not behave in the cowardly fashion of that employer . . . or is it just possible that I might?'

Different problems again occur in the relations between hearing and deaf people. Being an invisible disability, a person's deafness may first of all simply not be perceived, so that difficulties of comprehension are assigned quite different causes; even when deafness is recognized the severity of the handicaps which it entails may be greatly underestimated. Most difficult of all for those hearing people who do not happen to have acquired any experience of deafness in their normal life is the problem of how to communicate with a deaf person when one is encountered. Ignorance here of what to do and what not to do is very often total. The hearing person, without one single idea of how to proceed, is almost inevitably inclined to get away from the situation as soon as possible, and if he finds that he cannot do that may experience many of the feelings of fear and revulsion of someone caught in a trap.

It is true that hearing persons as individuals cannot be altogether blamed for this, since it would be quite normal for them to have received no help or information of any kind, at any time in their lives, which might make it easier for them to cope with the situation. But for society at large there can be no excuse; it is a typical example of the non-violent but relentless tyranny exerted by a majority over a minority of whatever kind. Just as immigrants are expected to assimilate to the host society, any attempt on their part to preserve and foster their original language and culture being obstructed in every possible way by the politics of national populism, so deaf people are expected to assimilate to the majority of hearing people by learning to speak and to lip-read; if there are any remaining difficulties of communication the onus is on them and them alone to remedy them. Information about the reality of sign languages as true languages, let alone any recognition of their beauty and cultural richness, are rarely to be found because people do not want to know about these things.

Still less do people want to be told how difficult it is for a person who has been profoundly deaf from birth or infancy to learn the spoken language, not only, that is, to speak it but even (a problem of which the general public is quite unaware) to read it. Yet it would only require a small act of imagination in reflecting about what it must really be like to be deaf for anyone to perceive that the notion of simple assimilation is both inhumane and unworkable, and that what is needed is a completely new approach, hearing and deaf people sharing the effort and coming to meet each other on common ground, each from the secure basis of a community and language in which they are fully privileged members.[15]

The difficulties which society as a whole has in relating to any kind of mental impairment are if anything even more serious than these. The problems start with the confusions which are constantly made between mental handicap or retardation and mental illness. The International League of Societies for People with Mental Handicaps has published an excellent brochure which sets out the distinction in clear and simple terms.[16] Too often however a very simple and obvious difference is confused by people who ought to know better: it is a common experience to read a report in the so-called intellectual press which confounds the two classes of disability radically from beginning to end.

Sometimes the confusion is deliberate. When the recent Convention of the International Labour Organization was being framed, the Germans fought successfully among the European Community delegations to have any distinction between mental handicap and mental illness excluded. Belgian officials did the same, but unsuccessfully, when the second action programme of the Community (Helios) was being discussed in the Council. Sometimes, I dare say, the official motive may be benevolent: it may be thought easier to get politicians to agree to a vague formulation whereas they might make difficulties with a more precise one. Not every politician anxious to be seen as a champion of disabled people would be sure of the unambiguous advantage in having his name associated with the cause of people who are mentally ill.

More often than not, however, the motive behind deliberate confusion is a less noble one. In spite of the clear lead given by the World Health Organization in including mental illness unambiguously as a form of disability, the whole subject is one which inspires terror in the hearts of many administrators. Mental illness is associated in the public mind with deviant behaviour; to include it openly in what should be 'good news' programmes is to open the way to phenomena which may be too dreadful for officialdom to contemplate — alcoholism, drug-abuse, sexual deviance and so forth.

It would be easy merely to sneer at official pusillanimity in the face of the diverse reality of mental illness in our society but to do only this would hardly be fair and would certainly not be helpful. The problem exists, after all, for organizations of disabled people too. Indeed it exists for all of us, and can only be seriously addressed at a level which I shall not attempt to explore until near the end of this book.

In European discourse, the difficulty of discussing mental illness is made harder by linguistic difficulties whose importance derives from the extent to which they inhibit our progress in the search for open, truthful and acceptable ways of referring to people with disabilities — ways too that can be made to work at European and international levels. That these linguistic problems affect other disabilities too has already been mentioned in Chapter 2 (pp. 17–18). The subject is too complex for detailed discussion here. Practice is so diverse and subject to change of fashion that it is generally inappropriate to criticize severely people of goodwill who use the 'wrong' term. However, we should recognize that in a world where mass communication and information are dominant functions, we should do well to endeavour to play our part in the search for terms in all languages which are both objectively correct in distinguishing different realities and subjectively welcome in respecting the feelings of disabled people towards their own disability.

Before leaving this discussion of the problems which arise in the response of society to disability, there is an important phenomenon which appears to apply largely if not only to mental handicap. My experience of the European scene suggests strongly to me that there is a marked difference in the response to people with mental handicaps among the different cultures in our Community countries. My firm impression is that some countries, of which Italy is perhaps the most obvious example, are much better than others at accepting people with mental handicaps, readily and with true sympathy, into the mainstream of child or adult life. I remember, at the very first bringing together in 1983 of representatives from our district projects in the first action programme, one of the German members of our network saying 'I can see we have a lot to learn from Italy about what to do about mentally handicapped people'. At first sight, it might look like a typical north–south difference and that this splendid openness is a Mediterranean quality. But I am not sure that that will work as an explanation, since I believe the Irish have this quality while I am not convinced that the Greeks do. The question is therefore worth asking whether it is an effect of Catholic culture.

In summary, we may say that the alienation effect which is such a common factor in the relations between those who have disabilities and those who do not would appear to be a compound of a more or less rational apprehension that disabled people are likely to make inconvenient demands on us with quite irrational fears derived from an ignorance which has itself been fed by the system — the past tendency to set up segregated establishments and separate services which isolate people with disabilities from the rest of society. Moreover the development of special services, as well as tending to segregate disabled people, has encouraged the belief that their needs are in fact being well met by specialists, and that therefore nothing more is required of the individual citizen in this regard than the payment of his taxes. Deinstitutionalization in particular, and the whole movement of which it is a part, require a totally different approach, making a quite new demand on the local community to be aware of its disabled people and to take responsibility for them. There is therefore a vicious circle to be broken: the essential visibility of disabled people — on the street, in the theatre, at the pub — both depends on new attitudes and is a prerequisite of them.

RESPONSES TO THE NEEDS

The non-governmental response

My aim in this section is not to give a systematic account of the contribution to the development of policies aimed to meet the problems of disabled people which has been made by organizations of or for disabled people, still less of the multitude of vital services which they provide.[17] There are hundreds of such organizations in the European Community and it would be quite impossible to do any kind of justice to their work in a book of this kind. What I shall try to do here is to focus on the issues which disabled people themselves and families of disabled people have concentrated on in their efforts to promote equality of opportunity and to indicate some of the chief successes and difficulties which they have encountered in this endeavour.

In the first chapter of this book I drew attention to the importance of the Independent Living movement of the 1960s and 1970s in the United States as the inspiration of much that has been achieved in Europe. Not long ago one would easily have supposed that this element of American leadership was finished for ever and that henceforth the Europeans would have to carry the torch of militancy on their own. When I attended the annual conference of the President's Committee on Employment in Washington in 1982 I had a strong impression that the show was really for the benefit of those who had succeeded in life rather than for those who still needed help. Reaganomics was in the ascendant and 'Business not Rehab is what matters now' was the slogan most often heard. Outside the White House the old champions of the Movement chanted their campaign cry: '"What do we want?" "Five-O-Four!" "When do we want it?" "Now!".' Section 504 of the Rehabilitation Act had been passed almost a decade before. There did not seem to be a new cry.

What has happened since is interesting evidence of the way a dynamic movement can experience a period of apparent stagnation only to revive again with new vigour. On 26 July 1990 President Bush signed the Americans with Disabilities Act (ADA) which comprises sweeping provisions promising progress on a scale as yet unimagined in Europe. As well as outlawing discrimination in employment, the Act requires all employers of more than 15 people, restaurants, theatres, offices and shops to adapt their premises so as to be fully accessible on pain of prosecution; public transport is made subject to the same requirements. What is more, the anti-discriminatory force of the legislation will extend to AIDS sufferers, alcoholics and drug abusers. The achievement is a magnificent tribute both to the efforts of the active organizations of disabled people in the United States and to the quality of American 'civil society'. As the title of the Act is intended to reveal, the principle is reinforced that simply to be an American citizen implies the possession of rights that are inalienable.

The issues that have been identified as crucial by the American champions of Independent Living and the causes they have fought for have been taken up by the international movement of disabled people, notably by Disabled People's International. For all militants it is natural that questions of terminology should be important. I have already referred in Chapter 2 (p. 18) to their rightful insistence that we should refer to 'disabled people' or 'people with disabilities' rather than to 'the handicapped'. Also reasonable is the claim of active representatives of disabled people that they should be the ones to determine their own terminology. The right-ness of this principle is reinforced by the evidence of what happens when they themselves infringe it by presuming to designate those who are not disabled as 'temporarily able-bodied', a term which, quite apart from its minatory flavour, is evidently inept given that the vast majority of people who are 'able-bodied' are this for the greater portion of their lives.

As well as words, the active representatives of disabled people are much concerned with models, and in particular with an attack on traditional ways of thinking of and behaving towards disabled people typified by the 'medical' and 'administrative' models. Attacks on these lines have a powerful basic justification founded on the unacceptable paternalism and oppression which may still survive from the past; they form a valid element of the campaign for equality, provided they are not exaggerated. That the purely medical way of regarding disabled people should not be allowed to dominate is not the same thing as the elimination of it altogether; confusion between these two things is not made excusable by the fact that it is an example of a kind of muddled thinking which is particularly commonplace. The argument that because disabled people are not 'sick' they do not in any way come within the medical sphere is invalid. We all come within the medical sphere to some extent.

Also under attack from militant disabled people is the 'disability model', by which is meant the tendency to think of a person's disability as *the* problem in a given situation rather than perceiving the injustices inherent in the environment itself, and to define the person in terms of his or her disability rather than of his or her capacities. Both critiques are surely correct and fertile. Whether down the line there will be some collision between the notion that a 'disability model' is bad but the use of the term 'person with a disability' is good I am not sure. What is already a problem is the choice of a word to indicate the model which is to be commended. In an educational context I have heard the term 'curriculum model' used. To me that sounds quite unhelpful and, when applied even to employment situations, actually absurd.[18]

The principal causes for which militant disabled people have fought, apart from the obvious demands for improvements in services, benefits, accessibility and employment, include freedom from institutional care, empowerment, control of one's own organizations and services of advice or assistance, and the perception of equality of opportunity as the central aim. They have also stressed the need to promote and support self-advocacy, peer counselling and specific training opportunities in independent living. Among these many fruitful ideas I believe that those of control and empowerment need some discussion.

As we saw in Chapter 1, the Independent Living movement has from the first concerned itself not only with political action but also with the provision of services by disabled people for disabled people. As well as the GIHP in France, this kind of development has been pioneered, for example, by August Ruggerberg in Munich and the Independent Living Centres in the United Kingdom. The GIHP of Languedoc-Roussillon centred on Montpellier runs a door-to-door transport service, a hostel for disabled students, a service of assistants for care at home, a bureau of technical advice on accessibility and the adaptation of dwellings, and a system of support to those making claims or involved with administrative problems. There could be no better basis than this for the development of good employment opportunities for disabled people, for the demonstration of their active capacity, initiative and versatility and for the enhancement of their political power.

Control in another sense, the direct employment of their own care assistants by disabled people themselves, using an allowance of money granted to them personally by the state for this purpose, is also a prominent part of the militant programme (see Chapter 5, p. 109). Linked to this are campaigns to replace fragmented systems made up of numerous specific benefits and services based on varying criteria of eligibility by a unified substantial independent living allowance which would offer the disabled person the maximum personal freedom in choosing how to spend his or her benefit. Supposing that the amount of benefit awarded could be determined by a points system which reflected individual needs reasonably accurately, this kind of personal control of one's own finances could make a valuable contribution to autonomy for people with physical or sensory disabilities; whether it would work for those with mental handicaps is less obvious. It should be borne in mind too that a total substitution of cash benefit for services mediated by voluntary or statutory bodies would leave disabled people at the mercy of budget cutting or freezing imposed by central government.

Turning now to the notion of empowerment, we can observe that while national organizations of disabled people can base their development of political influence on the provision of essential services to their members, this option is for obvious reasons not one which is readily available to such associations operating at the European or international level. Yet that it is possible for a European grouping both to develop a service function and to create a strategy to influence decision-making had already been proved by the leadership of the blind and deaf communities in Europe before the end of the first action programme of the European Community.

How this empowerment has progressed during the second action programme (Helios), and what is needed if its full potential is to be realized in the future are questions I shall address in Chapters 7 and 8 respectively. I need only say here that during the first programme the initiatives taken by those representing the sensory disabilities were not equalled in the sphere of motor impairment. A chief cause of this was the relative weakness of Disabled People's International in the countries of the Community, heightened by the unwillingness or inability of the representatives of DPI to commit themselves to the modes of European co-operation actually on offer. DPI's stance also raised questions about the form under which the various associations of and for disabled people should come together to create a united front whenever that is needed; this issue too remained unresolved until the Helios phase.

Official responses

The national level

In this brief review of the responses of national, European and international authorities to the needs of disabled people, I shall not (again) be looking at specific measures, since consideration of these will occupy the next three chapters, but concentrating on the efforts that are made to co-ordinate policy and to promote the extent to which disabled people themselves are able to participate in framing it.

Within the member states a number of efforts have been made to increase the influence within government of those who are promoting the social and economic integration of disabled people and to facilitate the co-ordination of measures for this purpose, notably by the appointment of a minister with special responsibility for disability policy. In France the choice of a disabled person to occupy this position has proved both a valuable symbol and effective in practice. In spite of this example, the fact that ministers of the disabled are normally junior ministers within one of the big established departments tends to link disability with one or another of the main policy sectors and so limit the effectiveness of co-ordination over the whole field; in particular the gulf between education and other sectors seems never easy to bridge. It could be interesting to see whether it would not be more effective to attach the ministers for the disabled directly to the office of the head of government, giving them their own civil service made up of officials seconded from all the relevant departments — not only social affairs and health but also employment, education, transport, environment, communications, culture and so on — together with a powerful mandate to co-ordinate and monitor the activities of those ministries relevant to disability. This idea is taken up in Chapter 8.

At national level too it is possible to detect a convergent trend to pay more attention to the organizations *of* disabled people, some of them rather recently launched, as opposed to the organizations *for* disabled people whose influence is often more firmly established but in which disabled people are normally outnumbered by professionals and family members. There is a danger that rivalry or even hostility may develop between the two kinds of organization. To a limited extent such tension may be inevitable and not necessarily unhealthy, but if carried too far it is bound to weaken the influence which the totality of those closely concerned with disability can have on government and on society; in Greece the conflict has even developed on classical political lines, a matter of considerable concern.

A good example of successful development in this direction, on the other hand, has been the evolution in recent years of the Dutch Council of the Disabled (Gehandicaptenraad), which has acquired a high reputation both for the extent to which it represents the aspirations of disabled people and the respect it commands in governmental circles. Its mandate however only covers the needs of physically disabled people, so that the questions of how the needs of non-physically disabled people should be represented and of how a single forum for all disabled people should be constituted remains unanswered. The equivalent Council in Denmark represents all the associations of and for people with every kind of disability, and to my mind comes closer to the ideal model for representation at European as well as national levels.

International and European levels

It would not be reasonable to expect a lead in this matter from either the Council of Europe or the OECD (Organization for Economic Co-operation and Development). The OECD's work, though its high quality is reinforced by inputs from non-governmental organizations, is largely a matter of the interaction between experts and ministry representatives. In the Council of Europe's activity in the disability field most of the work of the secretariat derives from the servicing of its governmental committee.

Of great interest are recent developments affecting the participation of organizations of disabled people in the United Nations. The UN Centre for Social Development and Human Affairs in Vienna, which is responsible for the Decade of follow-up to the 1981 International Year, has given priority to Disabled People's International in its consultation procedures and by this means has established a completely new level of regular participation on the part of disabled people in international decision-making on issues that affect them. To have given such a prominent role to an organization which is both militant and relatively strongly representative of Third World problems has obvious value. Yet there are disadvantages too: at the global 'Mid-Term Review of the Decade' which was held in Stockholm in 1987 the opinions of the representatives of deaf and mentally handicapped people, for example, were swamped by the predominance of the experts group, largely drawn from DPI. Moreover of the three themes with which the Decade is officially concerned, Prevention, Rehabilitation and Equal Opportunity, the majority of the principal experts convoked were only interested in the third — and said so.

This problem of the themes has been overcome by the United Nations in the arrangements they have made for the Global Project which is intended to contribute vital activities of public awareness and fundraising to the end of the Decade. For this the United Nations has found a neat solution by appointing as co-ordinators leaders of DPI, Rehabilitation International and Impact (the world-wide action, based in the United Nations Development Programme in Geneva, aimed at the prevention of avoidable disabilities); in this way the three themes of Equal Opportunity, Rehabilitation and Prevention are equitably represented. But the problem of the representation of all the main kinds of disability in a common framework with a clear mandate remains unresolved.

Although within the same limitation implied by the representation of disability as a whole by physically disabled people alone, recent events in another of the United Nations agencies, the International Labour Organization, have also made an important, indeed dramatic, contribution to the development of true participation in policy formation at the international level. In 1982 the ILO addressed itself, in the spirit of the Decade, to the adoption of an Instrument which would complement and update its 1955 Recommendation No. 99 on the Vocational Adaptation and Rehabilitation of the Handicapped. According to normal procedures, the text for plenary adoption would be prepared during the course of two annual conferences by a tripartite committee consisting of large sections representing governments, trade unions and employers' organizations in a considerable number of member countries.

During the first year, the draft of a new Recommendation was prepared, the proposal, eloquently put by the trade union group, that there should be, not a new Recommendation, but a Convention — a legally constraining instrument, once ratified — having met with little support from the governmental side[19] and total opposition from the employers. In a gentle way, too, the admirable ILO secretariat had felt constrained to speak against the idea of a Convention on the simple grounds that it was beyond the Committee's mandate.

But a seminal decision was also made at this point, which was to start the second year's work by hearing opinion from representatives of organizations of disabled people. The major presentations which I remember were made by DPI, RI and the World Blind Union. The core argument was that to adopt only another Recommendation at that stage would be to give an unmistakable signal to disabled people throughout the world that in nearly thirty years no significant progress had been made in the awareness of the problems of disability or in the priority that was to be accorded to them. To this point there was and could be no answer; it was at that moment that one could enjoy the spectacle of the governmental group beginning to swing. It was like a great ship answering the helm — slow at first, then a movement of seemingly irresistible power. First the Canadians showed their conviction that there must be a Convention as well as a Recommendation, then the socialists, the Scandinavians, the other western Europeans — with the one predictable exception[20] — then before long virtually the whole governmental group had simply changed their minds. Though the employers used every procedural trick they could devise to head off what was for them an unthinkable result which had come from nowhere, the secretariat and the Hungarian chairman were too strong for them and the Convention was safely carried, a triumph of empowerment limited only by the refusal of certain governments to take international co-operation of this kind seriously.

The enlightened approach of the United Nations in Vienna and the International Labour Organization in Geneva has made a precious contribution to the advancement of the status of disabled people throughout the world. Nevertheless, I believe that the structure adopted by the European Community, whereby a forum is created on which all disabilities are represented, will prove in the long run to be the right one. I believe too that this structure can and should be established in the development of policy participation within countries as well as for European and international purposes. Certainly, it requires acceptance of the probability that, at least for the foreseeable future, not all the organizations will be represented in the same way. This will very likely be unpopular with the militant representatives of physically disabled people, but, in my view, if there is a likelihood of conflict there, it is one which has to be engaged. As far as non-physical disabilities are concerned, we must recognize that in the development of participation and so of empowerment, professionals or parents (or other family members or equivalents) will have an active ongoing part to play without which lasting, solid progress will not be made. Getting the right solution will depend on devising parental and professional roles that are both realistic and acceptable. A means for bringing this about is proposed in the last chapter.

NOTES

1 For Mangin's report, see References to Chapter 4.
2 For Jørgensen's report, see References to Chapter 1.
3 I am thinking here of the development of European policies; for some other purposes, no doubt, such things as regional or socio-economic variation may be important.
4 For disability and ageing in general, see Patrick Daunt, *Age and Disability — a challenge for Europe* (with French parallel text: La Vieillesse et l'invalidité — un défi pour l'Europe), report of a Eurolink Age seminar held at Florence, Mar. 1990, London 1990.
5 There is however the probability that a significant number of children in category 1 were not identified.
6 Two Outset units in London are involved in the second action programme (Helios) as local model activities on independent living.
7 Often wrongly referred to as 'prevention'.
8 As is the case of children born with spina bifida.
9 The examples of Christy Brown and Christy Nolan in Ireland come to mind.
10 There are other difficulties about normalization. In a lecture delivered to the Royal Society of Arts in May 1987, for example, Professor J.K. Wing of the Institute of Psychiatry finds it 'arrogant' (*Journal of the Royal Society of Arts*, Jan. 1988).
11 For recent discussions see references to Brahm Norwich on p. 142 and Tony Booth on p. 143.
12 That I am not exaggerating this point was well illustrated by the recent answer of a British junior minister to a parliamentary question about the inclusion of disabled people or people with a knowledge of disability on local committees concerned with community care. This would not, she replied, be 'in the interests of disabled people'; besides, 'there was nothing to prevent' such representation.
13 This point was stressed in the study prepared for the Commission by the National Bureau for Handicapped Students (see References below).
14 'Le Regard des autres'created by Vidali, Monique Saladin and Alain Casanova (Starfilm International) as the first item of a 'vidéothèque internationale' (1982). See the publication *Le Regard des autres* by Vidali, Saladin and Casanova, Paris 1990.
15 For the educational implications of these points concerning deaf people, see Chapter 6.
16 See Henry V. Cobb and Peter Mittler, *Significant Differences between Retardation and Mental Illness*, a position paper of the International League, Brussels 1980, reissued 1989.
17 See the Koeditz study, in References below.
18 The idea of a 'curriculum model' of employment was put forward by British academics at the Commission's 1989 Rotterdam conference on educational integration, for which see Chapters 6 and 7.
19 Belgium, alone of the Community countries, supported the idea of a Convention from the outset.
20 The United Kingdom, also one of the few countries to speak against the Convention in the plenary session. The value attributed by the United Kingdom to the ILO's work was accurately reflected in the level of its representation and the quality of its contribution.

REFERENCES

Note For the ILO Convention and Recommendation, see References for Chapter 4.

Commission studies

Boris Ford, *Interprofessional Support for Younger Handicapped People*, Bristol 1983. (EN)

Volker Koeditz, *The Role of Independent Bodies and Organizations in relation to the Transition of Handicapped Persons from School to Working Life*, Heidelberg 1985. (DE, EN, FR)

Richard Stowell and Deborah Cooper, *The Access of Disabled Students to and within Establishments and Programmes of Post-compulsory Education*, London 1986. (DE, EN, ES, FR, IT, NL)

Philip Waddington, *Local Services for Disabled People — a European Community guide*, Amsterdam 1986. (DA, DE, GR, EN, FR, IT, NL)

Other reports

J. Martin, H. Meltzer and D. Elliot, *The Prevalence of Disability among Adults*, *OPCS Surveys of Disabilities in Great Britain, Report 1*, Office of Population Censuses and Surveys, Social Survey Division, HMSO, London 1988.

J. Martin, H. Meltzer and D. Elliot, *The Prevalence of Disability among Children*, *OPCS Surveys of Disabilities in Great Britain, Report 3*, Office of Population Censuses and Surveys, Social Survey Division, HMSO, London 1989.

Chapter 4

Employment and Vocational Training

CONTEXT AND PRINCIPLES

The importance of employment

Disabled people and their representatives, supported in this by those who are working to promote improvement in their quality of life, insist on the importance of paid employment as one of the chief components of equal opportunity if not the most important of all. Employment is therefore often treated as the 'flagship' policy sector for disabled people and it is taken for granted that economic integration, even if not a sufficient condition of social integration, is certainly a necessary one.

This reflects accurately enough the values which permeate our society, and so can be welcomed as a sound position since it stresses that disabled people have the same basic needs and aspirations as others — and the same basic capacities. To this extent the Commission's choice of employment as the first theme for treatment at the policy level would appear to be justified and was in fact welcomed as a natural one.

Even however as we accept this high value set on employment, we must beware of a danger contained in it: since it is not by any means clear that paid employment, at least as that is generally understood, is actually or foreseeably a realistic option for all disabled people, no matter how severe their disability, we could fall into the trap of trying to centre our whole integration policy on an objective which is not, perhaps could not be, available to some of those for whom the policy is intended. By this means those with the greatest difficulties could be even more downgraded and marginalized by the very policies intended to advance their cause.

We can avoid this danger if we remember that the aim on which our initiatives are founded is not the development of any one activity or sector but something much more general and incontestably appropriate for everyone — the attainment of the best possible quality of life for each individual. On this basis we are free to recognize that for very many disabled people open employment, with its offer of rewarding occupation, social status, working relationships and financial independence, is the most precious of all the benefits which an effective equality of opportunity has to offer — so much so that success or failure in this could be regarded as the prime criterion of the validity of all equalization policies. In addition to that, we can and must assert that the proportion of disabled people for whom open employment is a real possibility is continually increasing, that no limit to that positive trend can be foreseen and that no one must presume to set such a limit. Although therefore we cannot yet quite say that the notion of 'unemployability' is altogether meaningless, we can be confident that it is useless in practice and should therefore be treated as obsolete.

Barriers to employment

In most member states of the Community a major effort has been made to establish legislation in order to promote the economic integration of people with disabilities, and to set up or encourage services which facilitate this. Yet it is certain that as a general rule the unemployment rate of disabled people is very much higher than that of the population at large,[1] and that the figures would be more negative still if there were not a considerable number of disabled people who have given up looking for jobs. There are likely to be numerous factors contributing to this, some at least of which can be identified with reasonable certainty.

For one thing, the positive effects of legislation, and in particular measures which impose quotas of disabled workers on employers, have been somewhat disappointing. Except in Germany, quota systems, introduced at a time of universal economic growth, have proved difficult to operate and have up till now failed as guarantees of equality of opportunity in times of relative restraint.

Nor is there a great deal we can say in favour of the other principal form of direct legislation for this purpose — the establishment by law of certain specific jobs (such as car-park attendants, lift operators or telephonists) as reserved occupations for disabled people. The trouble here is that this approach, welcome enough when it was first introduced, is now out of harmony with attitudes as they have developed among disabled people and their families, the professionals concerned with disability and even the general public. Any tendency to identify disabled people with a few limited occupations, above all ones which are somewhat lowly and undemanding of skill or training, is generally felt now to smack of discrimination in the bad sense and to be contrary to the dignity of the individual.

Another important set of difficulties derives from a mismatch between rehabilitation and employment policies on the one hand and benefit systems on the other. In a few economically well favoured countries, disability pensions have actually been generous enough to act as a disincentive to active vocational rehabilitation in response to disability incurred during working life, so that the oft-repeated slogan 'rehabilitation before pension' can hardly be seen to apply. Even where this is not the case problems can arise in the relationship between the way disability benefit systems work and certain kinds of employment patterns that can be of special interest to disabled people — part-time work above all, but also trial periods of work and the gradual taking up of work or return to it. There may be particularly powerful disincentives to otherwise useful trial schemes, since it may be difficult, if the trial period is not a success, to retrieve a benefit once lost, or at least there may be damaging delays. Lack of flexibility in the systems may moreover create special difficulties in relation to the patterns of mental illness.

I must mention here too the problems of environment which will be the main occupation of my next chapter. Progress in creating the physical conditions — in terms of usable transport, accessible built environment and adapted housing — needed to support a positive employment policy has been generally too slow and too sporadic. This can entail insuperable limitations to the employment opportunities really available, and virtually nullify the operation of a quota system in (for example) the public sector. It should be observed here that many of the most promising opportunities for physically disabled people at present are in the tertiary and specifically the office sector, and that this trend is likely to continue. Yet many modern office blocks have no offices on the ground floor, and there may well be serious problems not only in entering the building but also in being able to leave it quickly in emergency.

An important group of difficulties concern vocational training. In spite of the examples which exist of high quality training in well resourced establishments, whether specialized or not, the overall picture of the training of disabled people is one of basic inadequacy often combined with limited resources for adaptation, so that there is an increasing mismatch between the skills disabled people have to offer and the few vacancies available, and an over-provision of low-level training which does not equip disabled people for available jobs. Partly because of a lack of training opportunities, or because of difficulties in undertaking training which are directly related to a specific disability, a considerably greater than average percentage of disabled workers are unskilled with little or no prospect of on-the-job training; they are therefore exceptionally vulnerable to redundancy as a result of recession, restructuring or technological change.

Specific technological progress may indeed entail serious loss of classes of employment which have been particularly helpful to people with certain disabilities. Automation for production purposes has already reduced the occupations in secondary industry suitable for many disabled people including those with mental impairments. Another example is provided by telephone systems, until now an important area of employment for people with visual disabilities, but now put at risk by the fact that new exchanges are increasingly visual in their operation. Overall, the effect of new technology on employment opportunities for disabled people is ambiguous: advanced information technology has already proved its ability to offer new openings for people with physical or sensory disabilities, while the total effect on job chances for mentally handicapped persons is likely to be negative.

As for attitudes, evidently those of the employers themselves are the most crucial. Naturally the reality here is a diverse and complex one, yet there are some elements in it that stand out. In a world where many employers may feel that the only choice is that between stagnation and failure on the one hand, and aggressive competition on the other, it is perhaps understandable that at least some regard vocational rehabilitation as a luxury they cannot afford. With manning a major preoccupation, the employer may feel that for every disabled employee he will have to invest more in order to get less return.

The best-known study on this subject refutes this opinion: according to the Dupont Survey, undertaken in the United States in 1981, rehabilitation pays off. But the

American situation is different, since there the employer (at least through his insurer) may well be paying industrial pensions as well as wages. In Europe governments must count the social cost. In my experience, it is disputed or unclear among government experts in Community countries whether pensions cost more than rehabilitation; besides, if there is a suspicion that a thorough research of this point might produce the wrong answer officialdom may well be content to leave it unexplored.

There is ample evidence from professionals and from those employers who have engaged seriously in economic integration that disabled workers can offer exceptionally high motivation and reliability. Yet in its very nature this kind of experience is not easy to communicate. At all events, as long as it is believed by a significant number of employers that taking on disabled workers will reduce the company's competitivity, the problem of employers' attitudes cannot be seen as merely one of irrational prejudice, even if their opinion is wrong on this issue. Moreover wherever the motivation of employers even to resettle those of their own workers who incur disability is uncertain, it is obvious that disabled workers looking for a job from outside the company will have poor chances. These chances are even further reduced by the fact that those who are doing this are likely to belong to one of the three most vulnerable categories, young disabled workers looking for a first job, redundant disabled workers with low qualifications if any, or workers unemployed as a result of a new disability incurred when over 50 years of age.

Since negative attitudes towards questions of physical appearance and speech defects associated with certain disabilities are still widespread among the general public, it would be a miracle if no employers were inclined to caution; we have seen in Chapter 3 how this affected the employment in a bank of a young French woman with cerebral palsy. There is without doubt a major hidden barrier here to the recruitment of disabled people into jobs in the tertiary sector of the economy (commerce, tourism, general office work, personal services) for which they may otherwise be particularly well suited, and which probably constitute one of the most important domains of opportunity for the future.

A disappointing feature, of which there is evidence from more than one country, is the relatively poor take-up by employers of financial incentives offered by governments in order to encourage the taking on of disabled workers. Another problem is that in some countries there is little evidence of concerted effort to engage the interest and influence of the trade union movement in support of the employment of disabled people. Notably variable too among the different member states is the extent to which the representatives of disabled people are involved in the framing and implementation of measures to promote economic integration.

Principles of action

Before I proceed to give an account of some of the positive measures which have been adopted, and interesting projects undertaken, in Community countries, it could be useful to itemize here the chief *principles of action* which I believe should form the foundation of a policy for the economic integration of disabled people.

1.   It is essential to give more stress to the *positive capacities* of disabled people and

to underline that even the most severe impairments imply only a limited range of disabilities. Equally, the Community effort must avoid elitism or any tendency, in recognition of a highly competitive climate, to concentrate efforts only on the most talented among disabled workers.

2. The effectiveness of employment and vocational training measures depends on the support of actions to ensure an *environment* (in terms of transport, access and housing) which is favourable to independent living.

3. However successful efforts may be to integrate disabled people into the open employment market, there will always be a need for *alternative and supported forms* of employment. Flexibility and innovation in this domain are the only way to ensure that disabled people can have a reasonable number of realistic options to choose from. This issue is one where European co-operation and exchange of experience is particularly needed. It is also essential that those engaged in supported employment should have all the status and rights of workers, and that the development and control of such situations should be an integral part of employment policy.

4. National policies for *vocational rehabilitation* should ensure that recruitment to training is flexible, that new methods as well as contents are introduced to special as well as to integrated courses and that integrated vocational training is encouraged.

5. There should be a coherent set of employment measures comprising *a comprehensive policy* which combines legislative provision with other positive actions. Such measures should include initiatives in the fields of consultation, information and public awareness as well as technical and financial support to employers and services of training, guidance, placement and follow-up. There needs to be a continuing *dialogue and co-operation* involving employment services, the two sides of industry and disabled people and their representatives.

6. The notion that government must make a choice between *compelling employers and persuading them* is simplistic. The point sometimes made by employers' organizations that if they are effectively compelled by legislation to employ disabled people, their goodwill is going to be lost and they will no longer co-operate should be seen as a negotiating position. Nor is there any necessary incompatibility between good information, advice and financial incentives on the one hand and compelling legislation on the other.

NATIONAL MEASURES TO PROMOTE EMPLOYMENT AND VOCATIONAL TRAINING

Open employment measures

Quota legislation

Inevitably, much discussion of employment measures for disabled people focuses on the merits or demerits of *legislation which imposes quotas on employers*, requiring all those employing more than a given number of workers to include in their workforce a specified percentage of officially recognized disabled employees. To accept this stress is not to deny what has just been said about comprehensive measures or to imply that quota schemes are a panacea.

A chief reason for this interest is the relative success of the German 'equalization' quota scheme, and the consistency with which that success has been maintained. Moreover, it has been achieved within the most successful and powerful economy in the European Community; this simple fact satisfactorily demolishes the argument, much loved by British employers, that an effective quota system would impose an intolerable burden on employers and put them at an insuperable disadvantage in relation to their competitors.

The Germans define as handicapped someone whose integration into society (not merely the labour market) is affected by a temporary or permanent disability. A person is severely handicapped if, whatever the cause of the disability, his or her capacity is diminished by 50 per cent (or 30 per cent combined with the inability to find a job). All employers with a work-force of 15 or more are obliged to employ 6 per cent of severely disabled workers, on penalty of payment of DM 150 (about £50) per month for each quota place not fulfilled. The funds acquired by means of these fines are spent exclusively on practical action to promote and support the employment of disabled people. Hence the notion of 'equalization': contributions from the passive employers help to meet the costs of the active ones.

On the most recent figures available 5 per cent of the total work-force is severely disabled; this means that the scheme is, within its own terms, 83.3 per cent successful. In the private sector, 4.7 per cent of the workers are severely disabled, while the figure for the public sector is the very high one of 5.9 per cent. Of the 122,700 employers involved in the scheme, 21 per cent have fulfilled their quota or exceeded it, 39 per cent have partially satisfied it and 30 per cent are employing no disabled workers. The total number of places available for disabled people in the scheme is little short of one million.

At the time when the Commission was first preparing its proposal for the Recommendation on the Employment of Disabled People adopted by the Council in 1986, it was beginning to look as if the German experience was and would remain a unique one, quota systems in all the other countries, where they existed, having been proved a failure and now visibly drifting into oblivion. However, in no fewer than three countries, important changes were taking place at this very time which have put the approach by means of quota right back into the centre of the discussion.

In 1986 the Greek government introduced legislation which extended its quota system, previously applied only in the public sector, to make it operate in the private sector also. At the same time the details of how the scheme should operate and of its exemptions were brought up to date, and the role of representative organizations of disabled people in its implementation clearly established. Also in 1986, the Netherlands adopted an important new Disabled Workers Employment Act (the 'WAGW'). The most interesting aspect of this genuinely innovative act was the creative use of the dimension of time as a means for offering to employers a 'fair chance' to comply with the requirements of the law. The aim was to achieve a 5 per cent rate of employment of disabled people in both the public and private sectors, but employers were given three years in which to achieve this goal voluntarily, using various suggested means and drawing on the help of official services. Only after this period would employers who had failed to satisfy the criteria be subject to an imposed quota, set at between 3 per cent and 7 per cent. So as to avoid the disincentive of specific registration in order to benefit from the scheme, all disabled people who receive disability benefits or an invalidity pension are eligible as well as disabled employees for whom special provision in relation to their disability has already been made.

The third example of an initiative in the mid 1980s which restored the quota approach to the centre of the scene took place in France and also exploited the dimension of time in a pragmatic way. A 6 per cent quota is to be achieved over a designated development period, the target rising by 1 per cent per year from 3 per cent in 1988 to the intended 6 per cent by 1991. In other ways too the reform exhibits a conscious determination to replace a previous system, characterized by the fatal combination of unreasonable demands and ineffective sanctions, with its opposite — sensible requirements that are actually required. Before, the quota was set at 10 per cent but an employer was exempted if he had not found a disabled candidate for a post within a fortnight of having advertised it. Now, in addition to the lower percentage and the dispensation of time, the criteria of disability are not severe and there are various actions, other than the direct taking on of workers who are disabled, by means of which an employer may satisfy the law, for example by entering into a contract with a sheltered workshop. Moreover an employer who fails to meet his quota is given the opportunity to make a voluntary contribution at a determined minimum level; only if he fails to do that will a fine be imposed on him, at the rate of 25 per cent above the voluntary figure.

The funds which the French authorities acquire from employers by way of voluntary contributions or fines are attributed to the Association nationale de gestions des fonds pour l'insertion professionnelle des handicapés (National Association for the Management of the Fund for the Vocational Integration of Disabled People), in the operation of which representatives of the 'social partners' and of organizations of disabled people are involved. At heart, therefore, what the French have done is to adopt the equalization strategy of the Federal Republic. But they have also adapted it and refined it to suit their own needs and possibilities.

Meanwhile, it should be mentioned, the Germans themselves have also reasserted their faith in their own quota system by reviewing it and updating it. The approach of two Community countries is on the other hand in complete contrast to this and to the Greek, Dutch and French initiatives which I have just described. In Belgium, where there is a quota system applying in the private sector only,[2] official policy is not to enforce it on the grounds that it does not work. The same is true of the United Kingdom, where the quota also applies only in the private sector.[3] The British authorities argue that it does not work, that it militates against the cultivation of positive attitudes among employers, that sanctions cannot be applied when it comes to the point, and that (for all the protestations of the representative organizations) disabled people in practice show little enthusiasm for the scheme and a dislike of registration — there are in fact more theoretical places under the scheme than there are registered disabled people to fill them. The official conclusion is that, while it may not be possible for cosmetic reasons to abolish the scheme, there is every reason not to enforce it.

Of both countries it must in all fairness be said that a great deal is done to promote the open employment of disabled people by other means. Yet it is beyond reason to expect that, once the post-war boom was over, anything but failure could attend schemes which applied only to the private sector and where consequently no significant example of good practice is offered to private employers who have to compete in a market by public employers who, as a rule, do not. Besides, all the British arguments are unconvincing. The Germans and the French show how the problem of sanctions can be dealt with, the equalization principle deriving its political strength from a combination of practicality and solid morality. The Dutch experience proves that there is no need to make heavy weather of registration. If over any period there are more quota places than there are eligible disabled people presenting themselves, then one could simply lower the quota or the criteria of disability or both. And, as we have already seen, the crowning argument that a quota system is a threat to competitiveness is, given the whole German reality, untenable.

Lack of available figures makes it difficult to interpret the experience of the quota systems in operation in Spain and Italy;[4] the Italian picture is moreover obscured by the involvement in it of other categories of disadvantaged persons, such as widows and orphans. In Ireland the scheme applies only to the public sector and there are no sanctions; an enquiry carried out by the National Rehabilitation Board in 1985 produced a recommendation not to extend it to the private sector. This explains the fact that Ireland worked more vigorously than any other Community country (other than Denmark) to ensure that the reference to the quota approach in the European Commission's draft Recommendation was reduced to a harmless level.

There is no quota scheme in Portugal or in Denmark. The Danes explain that the idea of a compulsory quota conflicts with their culture and the values of their society. This position the Danish authorities can support by what looks at first sight the strongest of all arguments — that disabled people in Denmark do not want a quota system, which they would regard as discriminatory in the pejorative sense. There are problems both with the internal consistency of this position and with its relevance to the needs of the Community as a whole.

Officially, the Danish government recognizes no definition of 'disabled people' in the context of employment policy, all those who are in need of advice or practical help in developing their capacities, including those who are 'socially handicapped', being considered together. Yet, in spite of this, a regulation of the Ministry of Employment provides for priority access for disabled persons to certain posts in public or semi-governmental administrations, institutes and enterprises. How it can be that this provision is not undesirably discriminating is not clear. At least it would suggest that the Danish positions on the existence in law of disabled people as such and on the desirability of direct action to ensure jobs for them may not, after all, be unassailable.

The most recent developments show a mixed pattern. The 1990 White Paper of the British government shows no enthusiasm for the institution of a quota system which would work. The Dutch government, now that the three 'grace' years are up, does not appear to be in any hurry to take the further steps promised. In France, on the other hand, in April 1990 forty directors of the most important firms met at the Secretariat of State for the Handicapped to pledge their support for the integration of disabled workers and to elaborate a common charter. On this evidence a quota need not undermine the motivation of employers at all.

The subject of employment quotas is not only important in principle but very much alive in practice. If at one time it looked as if the Community might be well advised to ignore it and concentrate on other aspects of employment promotion, it is clear from the account I have just given that that cannot be the case now. By offering to employers the opportunity to make a voluntary financial contribution to the Fund as one of the legitimate options available to them, the French have disposed of the punitive aspect of quota enforcement and reduced the scope for gratuitous fuss about other people's consciences. Some such device as the availability in town halls of precise details of the performance of every local employer would ensure the inclusion in any scheme of the essential element of public awareness. I shall return to the implications of all this for Community policy in Part III.

Other positive measures

It is now time to reassert the importance of a policy made up of *a diverse but coherent set of measures*. There is no value in debating whether these are more or less important than an effective quota system; they can and should be complementary to each other, and any idea that they are exclusive alternatives is unfounded. By way of examples of positive action I propose to choose, from a great number of possibilities, some measures in the fields of financing and management, of incentives and advice to employers, of new technology and of voluntary initiatives, before taking rather longer looks at the two subjects of supported employment and vocational training.

Apart from the equalization funds acquired in Germany and now in France as a result of quota legislation, the most remarkable strategy for *financing positive action* in a Community country is that of the National Fund for the Social Resettlement of Disabled People (Fonds national de reclassement social des handicapés) in Belgium. The secret here is the simple device of accumulating very considerable funds by exacting, more or less painlessly and often unconsciously, small sums from a large number of people, notably by a modest premium on every single motor insurance. Since ownership of a car is proof of resources, social justice is respected. The management council of the Fund includes representatives of the 'social partners' and of organizations of disabled people in the usual mainland manner.

What impresses one most about the Fund is the width of its range of responsibilities. The key to this is the ability of the Fund to give direct support to individuals as well as to employers and institutions of rehabilitation and training. In 1988 over 2,000 training places were supported by the Fund, including a few in universities. The Fund is also responsible for careers guidance and for placement of disabled applicants in open or sheltered employment in the public or private sector. It is interesting that while in 1987 only 34 employers applied for grant aid from the Fund for the adaptation of working posts, in the same year no less than 1,859 benefited from incentive grants (available for one year only) which compensate the difference between the minimum wage and actual productivity of a disabled worker. The Fund can also give financial support to disabled individuals setting up their own business, but it seems that only a very few applications of this kind are received.

Sometimes to the outside observer it may seem that too much in Belgium is left to depend on this one institution,[5] and that there may in consequence be a disincentive for other statutory or voluntary bodies to take their share of the responsibility. Yet the efficiency of the Fund and the quickness of its responses cannot be doubted. Drawing on the British experience, the Commission included as one of the main items in its proposal for a Recommendation on Employment of Disabled People the idea of a national Code of Good Practice in each member state. The idea was immediately taken up and put into practice by Armand Maron,[6] then Director of the Belgian Fund.

Incentives and compensations for employers play an important part in the economic integration policies of a number of member states. *Subventions to employers* taking on disabled workers have been successful in Spain. An increase of two-thirds in the amount of the grant in 1984 led to steady increase in the number of beneficiaries over the next three years, and although that increase did not continue beyond 1986 it has settled at about 3,500, four times the 1983 figure. As in Belgium, the number of beneficiaries from a scheme to support the setting up by disabled people of their own business is rather disappointing (127 in 1987) and actually declining. A striking feature of the Spanish national approach to integration is the close co-operation between the National Employment Institute and the National Social Service Institute (INSERSO, Instituto nacional de servicios sociales), and the ability of the latter to promote, through its National Centre for Personal Autonomy and Technical Aids, the essential environmental supports to employment and training policy.

In France too considerable attention is given to *incentives for employers*. These comprise support for individual vocational rehabilitation contracts, for the costs of adapting work-places and of additional staff and for the cost of the training of disabled apprentices, as well as a scheme of recruitment grants over three years for employers who agree to take on disabled workers and to promote their rehabilitation and training. If the productivity of workers engaged in fulfilment of the quota is substantially below the norm, it is permitted for the employer to reduce the wages he pays, the sum being then made up for the disabled worker by the state. Disabled people setting up their own enterprise are eligible for an installation grant in addition to the grant available to all unemployed workers starting their own business.

In the United Kingdom also there is a well developed package of provision to promote employment and self-employment for disabled people, and to provide for employers both advice and practical support (short-term 'introduction' grants, 50 per cent contribution to adaptation costs, loans of special equipment). Of particular interest are the Code of Good Practice already mentioned, the establishment of a specialized Disablement Advisory Service and the provision that companies employing more than 250 workers are required to include an account of their policy for the employment of disabled people in the directors' annual report.

Though, as we shall see, the introduction of *new technology* into the vocational training available to disabled people is quite widespread in the Community, it is interesting that when in 1983 the quinquennial reform of the European Social Fund offered new opportunities for innovatory projects, it was the French and the British who were the first to respond with applications in favour of disabled trainees. In both countries attention has been given to the particular opportunities which computer-based work undertaken in the home ('telework') can offer to people with motor or visual disabilities. In the United Kingdom an ambitious scheme of promotion and support of individual disabled people in work of this kind has been energetically operated by the Department of Trade and Industry. In France the development was launched by a pilot scheme in 1984, involving the co-operation of two Ministries (Employment and Post and Telecommunications) and a consultancy firm (Etudes et Planification des Communications, EPC); the initiative was based on a 1981 study of the possibilities completed by EPC and GIRPEH (see below). In its second phase, started in 1988, telework posts for 60 disabled people are being created in six regions over three years.

In France and the United Kingdom too the complementary support given to statutory agencies by *voluntary and other independent bodies* is well developed. Equipes de préparation, placement et suivi (Preparation, Placement and Follow-Up Teams), some under public and others under voluntary auspices, operate in many departments in France, offering flexible, mobile and highly individualized services to workers with all sorts of disabilities. A valuable contribution is also made in France by the Groupements interprofessionnels régionaux de l'emploi des personnes handicapées (GIRPEH, Regional Interprofessional Societies for the Employment of Disabled People) established since 1977, which play a catalytic part in facilitating the resettlement of workers who become disabled and the placement of disabled applicants for a first employment, and maintain links between employers, statutory agencies and sheltered employment.

In the United Kingdom as elsewhere voluntary initiatives are specially prominent in promoting the integration of people with learning difficulties or mental handicaps into the open employment market; Pathway and the Shaw Trust are examples of this, and again the individual approach and attention to follow-up are salient features. Yet we must stress the aspect of complementarity and flexibility; as is proved by the Blakes Wharf Project of the Hammersmith social services department and many other examples, it is by no means the case that local statutory authorities invariably leave the problems of mental handicap for voluntary bodies to deal with on their own.

Finally there is great encouragement to be had from recent measures in Germany to *enable disabled people to undertake open employment without economic risk.* Detailed provision makes it possible for the disabled person to enter into work gradually with only a proportional loss of disability benefit, and to be guaranteed against financial loss if the attempt is unsuccessful. This is one of many practical examples of how elements which could make up a European Code of Good Practice are to be found already operating in member states.

Supported employment

Sheltered workshops

I have already said that, in addition to integration in the open labour market, there will in my opinion be a continuing need for *special and supported employment* for those disabled people for whom simple economic integration is not the best, or even perhaps a possible, choice. In all Community countries, apart from Greece, Italy and Portugal,[7] sheltered workshops are an established part of the economy of disability; in some there is also a distinct separate class of institution, such as the Adult Training

Centres in the United Kingdom and the Centres d'aide pour travail (CAT, Work Support Centres) in France, which offer structured but essentially non-productive occupations for those with more severe disabilities. While there is in general a great diversity of size, responsibility (both public and private) and — it must be said — quality, among the sheltered workshops throughout the Community, there are certain essential features which are common to all. The workshops though subsidized have to operate as enterprises and meet production targets; while their costs are subvented, their products, apart from privileged tendering or labelling in some instances, have to compete on the open market.

Distinct features of the European scene include the specially prominent role played in both the United Kingdom and Ireland by single organizations, Remploy and the Rehabilitation Institute respectively. Unique also are the Social Workshops in the Netherlands which are open to people with social handicaps as well as to those who would normally be classed as disabled, and in which an astonishingly large number of people are engaged — not much fewer than 80,000, almost the number of people to be found in sheltered workshops in the Federal Republic.

For many thousands of disabled people sheltered work has offered and continues to offer the principal effective contact with society and the only available means to a reasonable level of financial independence. Three problems however can be seen to beset sheltered work in its traditional form. The workshops have tended to concentrate on light manufacture or packaging without new technology, and the market for their goods therefore may be increasingly hazardous. Secondly they cost governments money, in a context in which pressures to reduce public expenditure are fairly constant. And thirdly there is a general feeling that what they have to offer in the way of integration is less than people are nowadays looking for.

In theory the last point can be met in so far as the workshops are able to develop, at least for some of their clients, a more typically transitional role — that of a flexibly organized staging post and training ground between special needs education or functional rehabilitation and the open labour market. In practice however it is not easy to reconcile the continuous and planned loss of the best workers with the workshop manager's production quota, and the endeavour to solve that problem by means of premiums may not be easy to finance.

Various initiatives are being undertaken in the attempt to meet these difficulties. Some of these take the form of measures to improve the effectiveness of sheltered workshops and the extent to which they meet the needs of their clients without changing their basic structure. Such measures include the introduction of new activities, as alternatives to the more traditional manufacturing or assembling processes; commercial services using computers are one promising area and intensive horticulture is another. In France since 1986 a considerable effort has been made to lessen the isolation of the workshops by encouraging commercial links between them and public or private enterprises operating in the open market.

Innovatory structures

Other measures consist of *innovations in the actual structure of the employment*, offering alternatives to the sheltered workshop which yet provide the level of support appropriate to the disability of the individual worker. The whole subject has been recently treated at length in a study carried out by the European Centre for the Development of Vocational Training (CEDEFOP, Centre européen pour le développement de la formation professionnelle) in Berlin.[8] Here I shall simply indicate some of the developments of greatest interest.

One method is the inclusion of small groups of disabled people (sometimes known as *enclaves*) working together within normal enterprises. Since there is a danger that this may lead to the perpetuation of ghettoes, the structure actually tending to increase the barriers between the disabled employees and their fellow workers, the tendency now is to prefer the integration of individual people ('sheltered' or 'supported' posts), who have a better chance of being fully accepted by their fellows because they work in the same conditions for the same reward. In Denmark this method of individual supported posts is well developed, the employer paying a minimum of 60 per cent of the wages and the remainder being made up by the district and commune.[9] A similar system of sheltered posts operates in the United Kingdom.

One of the most characteristic of all developments in the European Community has been the *co-operative movement* in Italy, which has in effect taken the place of the establishment of sheltered workshops and whose importance must be understood in the context of the closure of psychiatric hospitals on a national scale. Two features of outstanding interest are the participation of non-disabled and disabled workers together in 'mixed' co-operatives (the three co-operatives associated with the Capo d'Arco centre outside Rome, a member of the Community's network of rehabilitation centres, are good examples of this) and the fact that participation by the working members in the decision-making of the enterprise is provided for by law. Co-operatives, the majority of them not mixed, have also been developed in other countries, including the Federal Republic, the United Kingdom, the Netherlands and Ireland. Among the most important of these initiatives has been the 'Self Help' movement among users of mental health services in Germany. An example of a successful mixed enterprise outside Italy is the Goodwill project in Glasgow.

Finally, there have been successful projects to create employment in *specially designed enterprises* which operate on the open market, are supported by special services and respond flexibly in relation to individual needs but which are not either sheltered workshops or co-operatives. Typically these are run by voluntary organizations; vocational training often plays a large part in their activities. The enterprise operated by the Institut pour promotion sociale (IPS, Institute for Social Advancement) in Montpellier is an example of this; there is integration of disabled (about 60 per cent) and non-disabled workers, and the work consists of office cleaning and the maintenance of buildings, and the upkeep of parks, gardens and other open spaces. The large Promi Centre created by Dr Perez Marin at Cabra near Cordoba in Spain and the Rehabilitation Centre managed by Norbert Heintz at Capellen in Luxembourg include programmes for integrated housing in addition to vocational training and high quality production. An interesting feature of the Promi Centre is the employment of people with physical disabilities as instructors of the mentally handicapped trainees and workers who form the main clientele.

Before leaving this brief review of sheltered and semi-sheltered employment, I can suggest in summary five key issues which it could be useful to keep before one's mind in any reviews of Community or national policy concerning sheltered or alternative employment:[10]

- improving the quality of less successful workshops or centres so that they approximate to the best
- introducing new forms of activity and production (for example, in the computer sector) which are both more interesting and commercially more successful
- increasing the amount of genuine training available in workshops
- developing the transitional role of workshops, i.e. their function as assessment and personal development centres coming between basic education, rehabilitation or a period of unemployment and entry to the open labour market
- reducing segregation by developing operational links between sheltered workshops and open enterprises, by establishing sheltered posts or groups within normal companies, by creating co-operatives (particularly ones which integrate disabled and non-disabled workers) and by devising other forms of employment which offer individualized support to disabled workers without isolating them.

Vocational training

As we have just seen, *vocational training* often forms an important and integral part of the activities of centres which offer supported employment to people with disabilities, and it is important that its presence in traditional sheltered workshops should be enhanced. Yet many of the most important centres of either integrated or specialized training in which disabled people are enrolled do not also offer employment as such, and the topic needs therefore some treatment of its own.

Achievements of the Community's network of centres

Vocational training is the most important single activity of the Community's network of rehabilitation centres, already mentioned in Part I of this book. For a number of the centres the value and quality of the training has been enhanced by its setting in a wider context of operations. Centres such as the Stiftung Rehabilitation of Heidelberg, the Reine Fabiola Centre in Charleroi, Belgium, and the Lucas Stichting voor Revalidatie at Hoensbroek near Maastricht in the Netherlands are very large institutions with various functions including medical rehabilitation as well as vocational training. A number of centres cater for basic education as well as training: among these are the Theotokos Centre near Athens and the Oporto Centre (both for mentally handicapped children and young people), the Gulbenkian Centre in Lisbon for children with cerebral palsy and the Juan Amades Centre for the blind in Barcelona. Another instance is the centre run by what was then the Cork Polio and After Care Association which provides housing and other community services in addition to training and education.

Another source of strength for an establishment for training disabled people is membership of a *national network*. In Spain the government has established a network of Rehabilitation Centres for Physically Disabled People (Centros Recuperación

Minusválidos Físicos), fed by another network of assessment centres of which there is one in each of some 50 provinces. Of the main centres, one, in Cadiz, is a member of the Community network of centres, and another, in Salamanca, an integral part of one of the district projects set up in the first action programme.

Equally impressive, in a very different way, is the nationwide network of training centres managed in Italy by the National Organization ACLI for Vocational Integration (ENAIP, Ente nazionale ACLI per l'integrazione professionale). An independent body with its origins in the Christian trade union movement, ENAIP has played a major part both in contributing to the vocational training needs of mentally handicapped and psychologically disabled people in the framework of the 'democratic psychiatry' and in facilitating the contribution made by the European Social Fund in support of the national effort in this field.

Different again but also beneficial has been the effect of networking on the vocational training of disabled people in Germany. I have heard it said by the senior civil servant responsible in the Federal Ministry of Employment that it is the vocational rehabilitation programme, and not the famous quota system, which is the most important element in German measures to promote economic integration. Resettlement training for adults is available in some 20 further training centres (Berufsförderungswerke) and for young disabled people in 37 vocational training centres (Berufsbildungswerke). The centres are well equipped, the residential accommodation is excellent, the trainees are financially well looked after and the quality of training is high; much is being done to introduce the trainees to computer-aided design and production.

Integrated training

Integration is a trend perceptible almost everywhere in the Community in vocational training as in general education. It must however be remembered that it may be a far less important issue for someone who incurs a disability through accident or the onset of a disease in late adolescence or early adulthood, let alone for someone requiring rehabilitation much later in life, than it is for those whose disability has been with them from birth, infancy or early childhood. The former group are already socially integrated because of a more or less long personal history without disability; a limited period of intensive training or retraining in a separate, even residential, institution may offer no threat to that integration whatever. For the latter group, social integration may be a slow and continuing process which could be seriously set back by interruption.

Integration during training may be total, the disabled trainees spending all their learning time in a centre where the majority of the members are not disabled. This can mean simply participation in the mainstream training system, the instructor being supported in his role of integrator by special professional training or at least adapted teaching materials and advice on teaching methods; this kind of integration is, for example, increasingly practised in the United Kingdom and in Ireland. Alternatively particular centres may make it a chosen part of their mission to practise integration; this approach is exemplified in the Community's network by the Don Calabria Centre in Verona.

Integration may also on the other hand be organized by a division of the disabled trainee's learning time between a mainstream establishment and a special one. Training of the very highest quality, involving something of the 'best of both worlds', is provided by these means in the training centre for deaf students in Essen in North Rhine–Westphalia (not a member of the Community's network), and in the Copenhagen Handvaerkskolen, which is managed by Ib Nielsen[11] on behalf of the SAHVA organization and which offers training to students with various physical disabilities (including deafness) or with problems of mental health or social adjustment. There is an interesting contrast here between the ways in which the students' time is divided in the two institutions: in Copenhagen the practical work takes place in the specialized SAHVA centre, the students going out to mainstream provision for their theoretical lessons; for the deaf students in Essen the process is reversed.

Four examples of innovation

It would be appropriate to end this account of some of the interesting approaches and developments to promote vocational training for disabled people in the Community with a tribute to the spirit of *innovation and the aspiration for quality* which is such an encouraging feature of this domain. Here are four examples.

Under the inspiring leadership of Marguerite Mutterer the Centre for Rehabilitation in Mulhouse in France, enjoying as it does a world-wide reputation, has exerted a seminal influence in promoting improvements in the quality of vocational rehabilitation in the Community. The centre is above all famous for the development of the modular method for structuring training programmes, thus ensuring the maximum flexibility in meeting individual needs — including the freedom to enrol for immediate full-time provision at any moment in the year. Not quite as well known but equally important has been the pioneering work undertaken in Mulhouse to develop the role of the disabled students in determining the objectives and structure of their own training programmes.

My second example of an innovatory and creative approach is the National Training College founded in the early 1980s by the Irish Rehabilitation Institute at Roslyn Park, Sandymount, near Dublin. The college offers higher level training to about 150 young people with physical disabilities or histories of mental illness; some of the students have had problems of alcoholism or drug abuse. The aim is to ensure that all the training is relevant to actual employment opportunities in a contemporary economy; the focus of all the programmes is therefore on the acquisition of employable skills, but much attention is also given to general personal development. Courses include business and computer studies, graphic design, mechanical draughtsmanship and electronics, and there are supporting programmes of remedial education, communications and computer appreciation. A feature of special interest is the existence of an advisory group for each course with responsibility to monitor the continuing relevance of the course in a rapidly changing economy. The groups contain potential employers from the sector concerned as well as teachers, practitioners and other professionals.

My third example of innovation could equally well have been included just now under the heading of 'Integration': it is the Vocational College which the Royal

National Institute for the Blind (RNIB) has recently set up for students with visual impairments, in association with Loughborough College in Leicestershire. Rather according to the model of the Higher National Institute for the Deaf at Rochester in the State of New York, this new college is making a bold leap forward in combining the best of integration and special provision. All the necessary special training, in the use of braille and equipment exploiting new technology, together with the systems of education and support needed by visually disabled students, is available in RNIB's own newly built college. At the same time the visually disabled trainees will be able to take courses in the established mainstream college according to individual programmes, and free to share the social facilities there with the main student body. I should hope that the Loughborough project will prove a model for similar developments throughout the Community, above all for the benefit of students with impairments of sight or hearing.

For my last example of creativity and training, it is appropriate to go to one of the economically least well favoured regions of the Community, and to a centre which was both a member of the Community's network of rehabilitation centres and prominent in one of the first action programme's district projects. The ENAIP Vocational Training Centre at Melfi in the Mezzogiorno region of Basilicata is not large, but there is a co-operative associated with it, and there are many disabilities (physical, intellectual and psychological), some of them severe, among the student body. The key to the splendid creativity which is the hallmark of this centre is the strategy of promoting at one and the same time technical skills, basic education and social development by means of group projects devoted to the production of major works of craftsmanship. The re-creation in all its detail of a traditional agricultural wagon is one example of such a project; the highly original creation of wondrous figures for a children's playground in the town is another. Dramatic and festival projects are also an integral part of the programme, and individual work includes personally conceived ceramics, something very different from the somewhat uninspiring output that we too often see in a rehabilitation context. It is significant that the director of the Centre, Franca di Trana, is herself an educationist, one too who bases all her practice on theory, theory which is itself always subject to discussion and review. There is a lesson here to be learned by all those whose contempt for theory sets such narrow limits to their achievement.

THE INTERNATIONAL AND EUROPEAN CONTRIBUTION

The international organizations

A great merit of the work of the Council of Europe (Partial Agreement in the Social and Public Health Field) has been its capacity to consider the issues of vocational rehabilitation and economic integration in the wider context of all the essentials of independent living. This comprehensive view was finally and effectively brought home by the publication in 1984 of the document 'A Coherent Policy for the Rehabilitation of Disabled People'. Another important association, too often neglected, is that between employment and education. In extending its programme on the Education of the Handicapped Adolescent to investigate the transition from school to working life, the Centre for Educational Research and Innovation (CERI) of the OECD has therefore explored issues of priority concern to everyone working in the disability field. Of the high quality of the work undertaken in both these contexts there can be no doubt; how great its influence has been, whether on policy-makers or practitioners, is in the nature of the case difficult to assess.

I have already described the exciting progress that was made in the involvement of organizations of disabled people in the process of adoption of the 1983 Convention and Recommendation of the International Labour Organization on the Vocational Rehabilitation and Employment of Disabled Persons.[12] As to the content of these documents it may be said that they contain, and do not contain, all that one would expect. What has mattered of course has been the attitude of the various countries towards ratification, without which the constraining force of the Convention is void. So far, of the member states, only Greece, Spain, Italy and Portugal have ratified. It is a depressing subject, not to the credit of the Community.

The European Community

The European Social Fund

Returning now to the European Community, enough has already been said about the contribution which has been made to the dissemination of good practice throughout Europe by means of the Community's network of rehabilitation centres, and examples have been given of initiatives to promote economic integration within district projects under the first action programme. In Part I, too, I referred to the valuable support afforded by substantial grants of money from the European Social Fund in favour of the vocational training of disabled people and to the 1981 Mulhouse seminar at which some of the most striking results of this support were presented. Among these was the impulse which the Fund has given to the exploitation of new technology in the training and employment of people with disabilities; examples highlighted at Mulhouse included the Leersum project in the Netherlands to develop a light-spot typewriter for people with upper- or lower-limb disablement, and a Belgian project, developed by means of co-operation between the National Fund and IBM, for training visually disabled people as data processors and computer programmers. More recently, we have seen a highly individualized approach to the training of disabled people in the new technologies developed in the West Berkshire district project within the first action programe, also supported by the European Social Fund.

A second outstanding feature of Fund intervention has been the priority given to projects undertaken in the economically less favoured regions of the Community — the Mezzogiorno of Italy, notably, Ireland and Northern Ireland, and latterly Greece, Portugal and the poorer regions of Spain. Support for the vocational training of disabled people in Basilicata in the late 1970s, for example, extended to nine centres including the Melfi Centre I have just referred to in the previous section. The nature of Fund priorities, on the other hand, has not favoured a significant contribution towards meeting those problems of disability which are specific to inner city areas.

The Greek experience

The extent to which the European Community can make a decisive contribution towards the solving of problems of special difficulty where national and local resources are limited or wanting is surely one criterion of the value of Community investment of money and effort in the disability field. Before therefore completing this chapter with a look at the content and future prospects of the Community's one strictly political initiative on economic integration (the 1986 Recommendation on the Employment of Disabled People), I shall give some account of the special efforts that the European Commission has made to promote rehabilitation in Greece.

As one of the actions intended to facilitate the integration of Greece into the European Community, the Council of Ministers adopted a programme of 'Exceptional Financial Support for Greece in the Social Field'. The programme has two strands: support to a nation-wide radical reform of the system of psychiatric care, and support for development of the whole vocational training provision. The psychiatric programme was aimed at the progressive closure of all the large psychiatric hospitals and their replacement by emergency units, local mental health centres and programmes of active rehabilitation including training; in the general training programme was included all vocational rehabilitation for disabled people other than users of mental health services.

As far as concerned those of its parts which affected disability, the implementation of the programme was well prepared by the Commission. A study of the vocational rehabilitation needs and possibilities, based on visits and discussions in Greece, was prepared by a group of experts which included John Furey of the Irish National Rehabilitation Board and Francesco Calmerini of ENAIP, both of whom had considerable experience of European co-operation as well as holding key positions in their own countries. A report on the psychiatric reform, also derived from direct experience, was presented by another group led by the Irish psychiatrist Ivor Brown. That in spite of this foundation work the programmes ran into serious difficulties and soon fell behind time is not our main concern here. As far as the psychiatric reform is concerned, a fair assessment of results would have to include some criticism of the Greek authorities. Yet an incomplete picture has been presented by the concentration of public interest on the failures on the island of Leros and at Daphni, while the successes, for example in Thessaloniki and Tripolis, have been overlooked.

In order to give additional help for the implementation of that element of the Greek vocational training programme which concerned disabled people, the Commission decided to offer an activity of technical assistance to complement the Community's financial contribution. This was to involve a close collaboration between my Bureau, which controlled the Commission's technical networks in the disability field, and colleagues working in the European Social Fund responsible for administering and funding the Exceptional Action.

The network of rehabilitation centres had already mounted two major technical seminars in Greece in support of rehabilitation developments there, and backed this up by giving priority to Greece over a two-year period in its exchange programme. It was not therefore going to be difficult to mount a concerted programme of technical assistance which, while not interfering with the network's own activities or depending on the credits earmarked for these, would be able to draw on the abundant resources of knowledge and skill of which the network could dispose.

Nor was it difficult for me to choose the person who, if he could make himself available, would be the best leader of the technical assistance team. Ib Bjerring Nielsen, director of SAHVA's Handvaerkskolen in Copenhagen, was world chairman of the vocational training committee of Rehabilitation International, and in his own centre had long experience of the successful training of young people with a number of different disabilities. He already used four Community languages and was interested in adding Greek to these. He had the clarity of vision and determination needed, and was highly respected as a professional and as a person in the network and in the wider world of vocational rehabilitation. And, by good fortune, he was able to give some of his time over several years to the project.

Fortunately it was possible to extend the project, which did not start till late in the first action programme, over into the second one, Helios; progress was steady, but could not possibly be easy or quick. Hidden opposition had to be flushed out and overcome by a combination of obstinacy, reason and good humour; in particular the persistent hostility between the voluntary and state sectors in Greece had some-how to be coped with. Nielsen's approach was to concentrate on technical solutions and practicalities and so communicate the message that there were such things as possible solutions, something in which many of those concerned had ceased to believe. He won the confidence of the Ministry by delivering a hundred wheelchairs to Greece, together with a plan for ensuring that they would be used in the best way possible. A training workshop of disabled people would be set up in the State Vocational Rehabilitation Centre on the outskirts of Athens, and here the disabled trainees would learn to maintain and repair the wheelchairs. The chairs would then be lent out by the Ministry to disabled people living in the open community, made available and maintained, repaired or replaced free of charge. Meanwhile the training workshop would be developed as a production unit for the making of chairs as well as for their repair.

This notion of 'double benefit', involving the development of the service function of a training centre, has been used by Neilsen, for a number of different services and products, throughout the programme of setting up or reinvigorating Greek training centres which he has successfully carried out in both the voluntary and the public sectors. The 'open workshop' has become his hallmark. In fact, there are more than two benefits. Apart from the practical advantages, to the members of the public (whether disabled or not) who are consumers of the product or the service, and to the disabled trainees who are offered a meaningful and quality-oriented training, there are political and social gains. The Ministry gets the kudos for these practical successes; and the public's view of disabled people is improved, since the disabled people are visibly associated with activity and success.

I have dwelt on this activity because I believe it is important for its own sake but also contains an important lesson for all those interested in European co-operation in the disability field. Exchange of experience between countries is a valuable activity, but being reciprocal in a simple sense depends for its usefulness on the partners being at more or less the same level of development. Where this is not so, exchange activity will not be enough; there will be a need also for technical assistance pro-grammes, which are not simply reciprocal, and which involve the provision of a service of advice and support by experts representing more developed systems for the benefit of decision-makers and professionals working in a less developed country.

I believe we need to face up to the implications of this in our programme design, even though that may not be easy to do in a Community context. I think too that this applies, as far as disability is concerned, to the field of education (as I shall explain in Chapter 6) as much as it does to training, and that it is fundamental to the needs of Portugal as well as Greece in these areas. If I am right, what we shall need is the integration of technical assistance elements into future action programmes. There could be important implications here too for the way in which we open up our relations in the field of disability with countries in central and eastern Europe.

The Recommendation

In Part I we saw how the 1986 Council Recommendation on the Employment of Disabled People, although in some ways in its final form a disappointment to both Parliament and Commission, not to mention the organizations of disabled people, had at least for the first time put disability firmly on the Community's political agenda and established a policy foundation on which the Commission could build something more complete and more solid in the future. Before the first action programme finished at the end of 1987, we had taken the first steps in following up the Recommendation. A working party of representatives of national Ministries of Employment or of paragovernmental agencies had started work with me in designing the structure of the report on implementation of the Recommendation which the Parliament had successfully insisted on being presented in 1988. I was also lucky in being able to engage a former collaborator, Stefanos Grammenos, as the consultant to help the Commission with its part of the work.[13] How this has all progressed since 1988 within the Helios programme I shall explain in Chapter 7.

By way of summary and conclusion of this chapter I shall set out, in concise form, the main points contained in the 1986 Employment Recommendation and the Model Code of Positive Action annexed to it, as they were presented in the Commission's draft proposal.

The Draft Recommendation on the Employment of Disabled People in the European Community, January 1986

1. The principle of *fair opportunity* in employment and training, applied in relation to:

– Access to employment and training, including services of guidance, placement and follow-up
– Retention of employment and protection from unfair dismissal
– Opportunities for promotion

2. For this end, establishment of coherent, comprehensive and positive policies, taking account of developments elsewhere in the Community, in particular by means of:

(a) Elimination of negative discrimination

- Revision of laws etc. contrary to fair opportunity; protection from dismissal on grounds of disability
- Protection from refusal of access to specific training or employment on grounds of disability
- Access to courts etc. when fair opportunity has been breached
- Protection from disadvantage in taking tests of entry or validation in training

(b)   Positive action

- Establishment of target percentages of disabled employees for all enterprises of 20 or more workers; publication and enforcement of this
- Introduction of national Codes of Good Practice, based on the Recommendation and the annexed Model Code of Positive Action
- Obligation on employers to adopt a policy for employing disabled people and to report publicly on progress
- Obligation on employers to co-operate in resettlement of all their workers who incur a disability for whatever cause.

The *Model Code of Positive Action* which the Commission annexed to the draft Recommendation was set out under these headings:

- Job creation (including the new technology sector)
- Incentives to employers
- Placement and support in the work-place
- Sheltered employment, co-operatives, etc.
- Social security systems: their compatibility with positive employment policy
- Transition, vocational rehabilitation and vocational training
- Assessment and guidance
- The supporting environment (housing, transport, access)
- Consultation, co-ordination and participation
- Information and advice
- Research.

Of these, the supporting environment constitutes a sector in its own right and discussion of it will occupy the next chapter.

NOTES

1   That this is recognized by governments is made clear in the Council Conclusions of 1989; see References below.
2   There are some places reserved for disabled people in the Belgian public service, but this provision is distinct from the quota system.
3   In the UK the Ministry of Health and the National Health Service have voluntarily decided to apply the quota to themselves. Some local authorities, of which Lambeth is one of the most prominent examples, have done the same.
4   For the Commission's current statistical studies, which offer hope of real progress here, see Chapter 7, p. 153.
5   Recently the fund has been divided in accordance with political devolution in Belgium.
6   Maron is now director of the Helios experts team; see Chapter 7.
7   There are sheltered workshops in Portugal, but on the most recent figures available only some 300 persons are employed in them.

8   The study was co-ordinated by the CEDEFOP expert Tina Bertzeletou, a former trainee in the Commission's bureau. For authorship etc., see References below.
9   This method of support must be distinguished from induction allowances which are only temporary.
10 These points are taken from the guideline framework for positive action annexed to the 1986 Recommendation; see References below.
11 For Nielsen's leadership in launching technical assistance in Greece, see p. 78 above.
12 See Chapter 3, p. 55.
13 For Grammenos, see Chapter 2, n. 7.

REFERENCES

Community policy documents

Memorandum of the Commission to the Council concerning the employment of disabled people in the European Community (COM (86) 9 of 24 Jan. 1986).
Resolution of the European Parliament on the above of 15 May 1986 (O.J. No. C 148/95 of 16 June 1986).
Opinion of the Economic and Social Committee on the draft Council Recommendation on the employment of disabled people in the European Community of 23 Apr. 1986 (O.J. No. C 189/90 of 28 July 1986).
Council Recommendation of 24 July 1986 on the employment of disabled people in the Community (O.J. No. L 225/43 of 12 Aug. 1986).
Report from the Commission on the application of the Council Recommendation of 26 July 1986 on the employment of disabled people in the Community (COM (88) 746 of 15 Dec. 1988).
Conclusions of the Council of 12 June 1989 on the employment of disabled people in the Community (O.J. No. C 173/1 of 8 July 1989).

International Labour Organization policy documents

Recommendation No. 99 on the vocational adaptation and rehabilitation of the handicapped, 1955.
Recommendation No. 168 on the vocational rehabilitation and employment of disabled persons, 1983.
Convention No. 159 on the vocational rehabilitation and employment of disabled people, 1983.

Commission studies and conference reports

Georges Rouault, *The Handicapped and their Employment — a statistical study*, Luxembourg 1978. (DE, EN, FR)
Guy Mangin, *The Handicapped and their Employment — a statistical study*, Luxembourg 1983. (DE, EN, FR, IT)
Robert Feeney, *A Functional Assessment of Disabled Workers in the Light of the Task Demands of New Micro-electronic Devices*, Loughborough (Institute of Consumer Ergonomics) 1983. (EN, summary in FR)
Mary Croxen John, *Overview: disability and employment*, Brussels 1984. (DE, EN, FR)
Eliane Vogel-Polsky, *The Economic Integration of the Disabled: an analysis of measures and trends in member states*, Brussels (Centre de sociologie du droit social) 1984. (EN, FR)

Commission report of a workshop on the employment of disabled people held in Brussels, 21–23 Mar. 1984, Brussels 1984. (DA, DE, GR, EN, FR, IT, NL)

Wil Albeda, *Disabled People and their Employment*, Maastricht (European Centre for Work and Society) 1985. (DE, EN, FR)

Pierre Olivier, *Analysis of Current Needs and Initiatives in the Field of the Adaptation of Vocational Training for Young Handicapped People to the New Employment Realities*, Nanteau 1986. (DE, EN, FR)

Other Community study

Erwin Seyfried and Thibault Lambert, *New Semi-sheltered Forms of Employment for Disabled Persons — an analysis of landmark measures in the member states of the European Communities*, Berlin (Centre européen pour le développement de la formation professionnelle, CEDEFOP) 1988. (DE, EN, FR)

Chapter 5

The Environment for Independent Living

INTRODUCTION

We have seen how, for very many disabled people, employment is both a vital means to independent living and an important part of it. To stress this is not in any way to downgrade the other aspects of daily life — life in the home, family life, social life, cultural life and so on. The distinction between work and leisure is a somewhat artificial one which we have to make in order to plan and organize; in reality they interact and form part of one whole.

That is true for everyone; yet it holds good above all for people with disabilities, for the reason that the relationship between employment or training and the other aspects of life can go wrong for them in a way and to an extent that simply is not true of other people, even other disadvantaged people. Since for disabled people choices are limited in all aspects of life, it is obvious that uniquely for them the combination of choices that work for all these aspects is both essential and difficult to find. The chances of finding an accessible living environment within manageable distance of an appropriate job opportunity are made all the weaker from the circumstances that there is normally no means for co-ordinating improvements in accessibility over the three essential sectors, employment, transport and housing.

In this chapter therefore we look at what is being done to create or adapt the physical environment in all its aspects so as to make it fully accessible and usable. It is convenient to explore this domain under three heads:

- transport and other aspects of mobility
- access to and within public buildings and facilities
- housing and services delivered to the home.

Of course these three elements overlap: effective transport systems must comprise accessible stations and termini as well as vehicles and other carriers, and the objectives and standards for these will often be the same as for other public buildings and for adapted housing. Yet the whole field is so vast that some breakdown is needed and the one suggested (which is also the one adopted by the European Commission in the structuring of its policy proposals) has the advantage that it corresponds to the distribution of administrative responsibilities in our various countries.

I have explained earlier in this book how in its strategy for the bringing forward of formal policy proposals to cover all the environmental needs of independent living, the European Commission has decided to treat the theme of transport and mobility first. It follows that policy development work on this topic is more advanced than it is for the others. In this chapter therefore I shall not only treat it first but also deal with it at greater length.

MOBILITY INCLUDING TRANSPORT

Scope and national response

If we are to promote the personal mobility, in town and country and across frontiers, of all disabled people, there are four main fields of operation which will have to be covered:

1. Public transport of all kinds (rail, including underground; buses, trams and coaches; airways; travel on water; public taxis), ensuring accessibility of stations and termini as well as of vehicles and craft.
2. The availability and expansion of special transport services, designed specifically for people with disabilities, especially severe ones.
3. The encouragement and support for as many disabled people as possible to own and, whenever they can, drive their own car.
4. Freedom to move about the street and in other pedestrian areas, particularly for those using wheelchairs or with visual disabilities.

In addition there will have to be other supporting measures which relate to all four of these areas — education of the general public, for example; training of transport staff; information, training and advice for disabled people; research.

One of the most encouraging aspects of the national initiatives which are being taken to meet these needs is the setting up in Ministries in a number of Community countries of units with a general responsibility to co-ordinate the promotion of mobility in all these areas. In France and the United Kingdom, for example, these units are located in the Ministry of Transport; in Spain this activity is part of the work of the National Centre for Personal Autonomy and Technical Aids in the Ministry of Social Affairs.

Units such as these can perform a number of useful functions. They can advise Ministers and participate in the drafting of legislation, on the basis of consultation processes which they have themselves organized. They may be able to support research and training; they will certainly be able to carry out, or enable others to carry out, a wide range of information measures, including the dissemination of examples of good practice, the production of guides and brochures and the clarification of rights established in law. The existence of such units is a guarantee that mobility needs will not be entirely neglected, that there is a prominent and permanent point of reference and source of initiative, that standards are being monitored and that co-ordination of services among the various public and private operators is encouraged.

The contribution of these units is almost as great at the international as at the national level. All three of those I have mentioned are represented on the Ad Hoc Working Group on Transport for Disabled People of the European Conference of Ministers of Transport, the importance of whose work is explained below. Ann Frye, head of the Disability Unit in the British Ministry of Transport, is convenor of that Working Group and was responsible for the organization of the important conference 'Transport without Handicap: a Priority for Europe' held in London in 1986. The COLITRAH (Comité de liaison pour le transport des personnes handicapées) in Paris, under the leadership of Catherine Bachelier, publishes and updates each year an international compendium of measures to make public transport accessible, to develop special services and to facilitate the ownership of private vehicles; this publication is all the more valuable for including as well as data on the member states, information about countries in western Europe not at present members of the Community as well as about North America and developed countries in the Pacific region (Australia, New Zealand and Japan).

Public transport

Air transport

When we review the level of specific services and facilities in the different member states we must admit that we find great variations among them. Convergence is, not surprisingly, most evident in air transport, since here the standards provided on airports and in aircraft have been favourably influenced by relatively powerful international agreements and pressure groups. None the less even here serious problems remain. These include the deplorable development (which has spread now to Brussels of all places) which requires passengers to pay for the use of trolleys on airports, and the increasing number of delays during peak periods which cause particular hardship to disabled passengers as well as to some other categories. On the aircraft themselves there can be difficulties about special apparatus and a lack of information about these — wet batteries are the most often quoted example.

There are however three problems which are of wider application. Facilities which are available on larger aircraft and on main routes are often not provided in smaller aircraft which yet may be the only means of public transport for certain journeys; since the point here is not the level of comfort but the ability to travel at all, more needs to be done to upgrade all provision to the level of the best. Secondly, requirements for medical certificates can be troublesome and, at least according to some passengers, more rigorous than necessary. And there are still differences of practice and controversy on the question of 'escorts' accompanying disabled passengers. Not everyone could accept that the most favourable solution is a reasonable expectation: this would imply that in all cases the disabled person could choose freely whether to be accompanied or not, and that whenever he did so choose the escort would travel without charge. On the other hand there is at present too much variation in the strictness of requirements for disabled passengers to have a companion who must pay the full fare — Lufthansa is notably less severe on this than Alitalia, for example. A good compromise might be to allow certain categories of disabled passengers (those with severe or total visual impairments, for example) to travel with or without an escort as they pleased and to offer reduced fares for escorts on certain lines; for other categories of disability (chiefly, those requiring continuous or specialized attention) an escort would always be required but a reduction in the fare of the escort always offered. A harmonization of European regulations on these lines would be a big step forward.

Travel by rail

In spite of these problems the relative satisfaction of disabled people with the general level of provision for travellers by air needs to be stressed. The same cannot be said of travel by rail, where the difference between the best and the worst is enormous. It may be thought that the best example here is that which has been set by the German state railways (Bundesbahn). What distinguishes this effort has been the capacity to look at all stages and aspects of the passenger's journey and to plan ahead by setting targets which will be achieved over time. In this way the German authorities both establish a clear direction of policy and make it possible to reduce costs (which none the less remain an important factor) by taking the opportunities offered when new models are required or general restructuring taking place. Among the many improvements which have been introduced and are being multiplied are fully accessible stations (ramps, lifts, etc.), reduction of gaps between platforms and carriage entrances, widening of these entrances, and fully adapted seating and toilets in the carriages themselves. By the end of 1987, 118 such fully adapted carriages were in service on the German inter-city network. Equally encouraging is the recognition in Germany that suburban services are at least as important as longer distance ones if disabled people are to play a full part in economic life.

While some national main-line systems have made little progress towards accessibility, others have made headway comparable to the German achievement. On the underground networks however the situation is generally very much worse, at least as far as wheelchairs are concerned. In London, wheelchairs are not permitted on most of the network at any time, for reasons of security; on those sections where this does not apply, access is only permitted outside rush hours, if there is an escort and (as if that were not enough) after written permission has been obtained in advance. In Brussels, one of the cities where the most important underground constructions are under way, a decision has been made not to include accessibility to wheelchairs among the facilities planned. It is not possible to reconcile this with a declared national policy to promote the economic integration of disabled people.

Yet there are examples to prove that even underground systems can be made fully accessible if the will to do this exists. Lille in the north of France is probably the most famous example and pioneer; the same success has been achieved in Amsterdam and Rotterdam in the Netherlands and in Newcastle upon Tyne in the United Kingdom. The metros of Marseilles and Lyons are partially accessible to wheelchairs; that of Paris is not. Good progress has been made in Germany with access from the platform to the train itself. In Milan lifts and ramps are planned for all new stations but the vertical distance between platforms and carriages remains a problem. The conclusion is clear enough: total accessibility of underground systems even to wheel-chairs is a practical proposition and therefore should be a declared target; the speed with which it can be achieved is a factor of financial strategies as much as of priorities.

Buses and trams

For many people buses and trams play an even more important part in daily life than trains — or would do if they were accessible. The frequency with which they stop and start means that particular attention has to be given to safety in the design of seats, corridors, platforms and handrails. It also implies that there has to be a large number of stopping places and that the cost of making these suitable for disabled and elderly people may be considerable. It must be remembered too that if people with disabilities are to be able to have a full choice of holiday packages and cheaper long-distance travel, then both coaches and the facilities of coach stations must be fully accessible as well as local service vehicles and open bus stops. It is essential too to consider both the needs of users of wheelchairs — who, unless significant adap-tations are made, simply cannot use buses at all — and the greater number with less severe impairments who none the less find that the combination of discomfort, exhaustion and insecurity makes the stress of trying to use the system more than they can manage and so have to accept a serious limitation to their freedom of movement.

One of the most useful approaches to the making of real headway without exorbi-tant and ineffective cost is the selection, at least for the first stage of planned improvement, of a limited number of key urban routes, the choice being based on a carefully conducted survey of consumer needs. An excellent example is the service which has been operated in Annecy in France since 1984. Six minibuses, adapted for severely disabled passengers including users of wheelchairs, run four times every day (five times on Sundays and holidays) on special routes which are diametrical to those used by the regular services. Deviations to pick up individual passengers may be arranged with prior notice. Fares are at the normal rate and the buses are filled, on average, to about half their capacity; the system is however subsidized as an inno-vation of exceptional interest.

A different innovation has been introduced in Leicester in the United Kingdom. Here since 1982 three buses equipped with lifts run a shuttle service on each of eleven carefully chosen routes leading to the centre of the city and back; detours for individual passengers are made. That the service is of real benefit to people with severe disabilities is proved by the figures: of the average of 360 passengers who use it every week, 180 use the lift, and of these 72 are in wheelchairs. It is also instructive that in Coventry, where a less ambitious service is operated (one adapted bus running on two routes to the centre without individual detours), this is said to be more popular with disabled people than special call-up services, because although there is no individual pick-up there is always a place, the journey is more comfortable and the stigma of social assistance is avoided.

To improve the accessibility of vehicles and stops on regular lines, on the other hand, no country of the Community has done more than the Netherlands. The provision of raised platforms at tram stops in The Hague (a method also in use at bus stops in Oslo) appears to have been a success. New models of buses include better designed steps, the provision of an adapted seat and extra handrails which are brightly coloured to help passengers with visual impairments. Incorporation of modifications such as these when new models are brought out goes a long way towards solving the problems for those with moderately severe disabilities; more severe handicaps raise other problems, including the intractable difficulty of accommodating wheelchairs. Here the Dutch experience does not yet encourage the view that the physical modification of buses built to operate on regular routes can meet the needs. A proposal to develop and introduce kneeling buses, supported by the Netherlands Council for the Disabled (Gehandicaptenraad), was not upheld by the responsible Ministry; the objection was not only the capital cost but also the need for extra buses to maintain a given level of service owing to increased delays at stops and the extra space needed to accommodate wheelchairs inside the vehicles. A reasonable conclusion might be that, whereas adaptation to regular stops and vehicles is of the greatest importance to those with light or moderate handicaps (including a very large number of elderly people), ingenuity in devising complementary services, such as those pioneered in Annecy and Leicester, may be the best way ahead for those whose disabilities are more severe. Even this, as we shall see, will not foreseeably dispense with the need for special services which are totally distinct from normal provision.

Before leaving the question of transport by bus we should notice that it is a sector where all improvements are particularly vulnerable to the effects not only of drives to reduce public expenditure but also of privatization. The operation of this effect in rural areas has been observed widely and long since, with consequent severe isolation and immobilization of many disabled and elderly people living in the country. More recently, similar trends affecting a larger number of people can be observed in some towns. Where a number of private urban companies are running minibus services in close competition the likelihood that space or time will be afforded to passengers with moderate impairments becomes increasingly remote, while the chance of any provision whatever for the more severely handicapped is virtually non-existent. Nor, as the processes of privatization become more sophisticated, is it likely that public authorities, interested in selling their asset at a good price, will be over-zealous in prescribing the obligations concerning access established by law.

Transport by water

Of all forms of public movement, transport on water has, as far as concerns the needs of disabled and elderly people, attracted the least attention and been the object of the least serious study. Yet the question is an important one, both for holiday-makers and for the day-to-day employment and other needs of those who live by water, whether on the coast or inland. Generally, it would appear that, while quite a lot is done in the way of concessionary fares, no great effort has yet been made to make ferries, water-buses, hovercraft, hydrofoils, etc. physically accessible, except in Sweden and perhaps other Scandinavian countries. French ferries operated by SNCF (Societé nationale des chemins de fer, the French national railway) or other companies between France and England or Ireland are however designed for the circulation as well as the access of wheelchairs, and this is also true of the majority of cross-Channel ferries run by British companies.

Public taxis

It would be a great mistake, also, to underestimate the importance of public taxis, which may provide not only the quickest, most comfortable and safest means but the only possible means of starting or finishing a journey or of making the vital link between two different modes of transport in mid-journey. To understand the problem we must imagine the situation of a disabled man or woman of business arriving in a foreign city at night, or of a family with a disabled parent travelling on holiday, who find that there is no taxi-driver at the airport or station of arrival able or willing to take them to their hotel or other centre.

In many countries examples can be found of commercial taxi companies who on their own initiative make available an adapted taxi which can be ordered by telephone. Such a service is evidently useful, above all wherever special provision of the kind I shall describe in the next section is not available. Of more general importance, however, for the reasons given above, is the extent to which the vehicles on taxi ranks are accessible. Again the picture is a mixed one: there are plenty of examples of good practice, but it is not generalized and cannot be relied on. In Paris drivers are specifically forbidden to refuse disabled passengers or guide-dogs, and the government has encouraged the production of accessible vehicles by means of a competition. In Germany adapted taxis, some with pivoting front passenger seats, are available in many cities, but provision typically depends on the offer of grant aid from the local authority. Taxis in Madrid will now accept wheelchairs and guide-dogs without extra charge, while in London and other British cities the introduction of the new CR 6 model of taxi, which can accommodate any kind of standard wheelchair, has been a significant success. Current resistance on the part of taxi-drivers to the efforts of the local authority in Newcastle upon Tyne to introduce fully accessible vehicles is an indication of the difficulties in this area. It will be a long time before disabled people will be able to rely on finding a service which meets their needs beyond the capital cities of certain countries.

Principles of accessibility

If the endeavour to make public transport accessible to all disabled people throughout the Community is to be well directed it will have to be founded on clearly identified and articulated principles of action. It might therefore be useful to set out here the twelve 'general policy approaches' which I proposed as applicable to public transport in the 1989 ERICA report which I shall refer to later. No doubt this formulation could be considerably improved; certainly it has no claim to be definitive. It is however the outcome of considerable study and consultation, and at the very least may help to clarify what is meant by the term 'principles of action' and what ground such principles might cover. The twelve listed in the report are these:

1. Recognition that the access of all citizens to public transport is a civic right; development aimed at implementation of the principle that public transport is accessible to all who *wish* or *need* to use it, not only to those who *can* use it under obtaining conditions; acceptance that this is a fundamental responsibility of transport providers, not a merely marginal welfare issue.
2. Recognition that the installation or adaptation of accessible public transport is always a normal solution, and that the existence of special services and the development of car ownership are not excuses for avoiding this responsibility.
3. Adoption of comprehensive legislation to establish standards and protect rights, of measures to ensure legislation is implemented and of means to monitor this.
4. Abrogation of laws or regulations which provide that on principle certain categories of disabled people are forbidden to use certain forms of public transport.
5. Recognition of the cross-sector benefit of accessible public transport and encouragement of accessibility by contributions to its cost by health and social services.
6. Adoption and enforcement of laws and regulations to ensure that all new provision is accessible from the start, and that existing inaccessible provision is adapted as soon as possible (e.g. when repairing, restructuring, etc.).
7. Commitment to the guarantee of accessibility of all public transport to all ambulant disabled people very soon or immediately, and also to all users of wheelchairs for all long journeys; extension of this to users of wheelchairs for short journeys whenever and as soon as possible.
8. Development of positive measures, including financial concessions, based on the consequences (not the cause) of disability, but without prejudice to already existing measures.
9. Implementation of measures according to priorities, e.g. adaptation first of key routes and establishment of minimum networks.
10. Improvement of the co-ordination and articulation of services at international, national, regional and municipal levels; planning for all elements of a journey especially between major centres, between centres and stations/terminals and from door to door.
11. Co-ordination between the initiatives of voluntary bodies, associations of travel agents, tourist boards, service providers, etc.
12. Consultation of disabled people and their representatives in the planning of measures, and arrangements for their partnership in implementing them.

Concessions

It will be observed that this list refers to concessions as well as to the physical aspects of access. I do not however propose to deal fully with the whole question of fare concessions in favour of disabled travellers here — not because it is not important but rather because it is too complex to cover satisfactorily in a general survey such as this. National practice in member states has often been based on a policy of reward and compensation to those disabled when serving their country in time of war. More recently concessionary arrangements have been introduced on a far wider basis than this, yet on a firm foundation in so far as they express, in part or entirely, commercial principles. To a considerable extent it is evident that fare concessions will encourage many disabled people to travel who would otherwise not have travelled at all, or at least less frequently or by another mode; such incentives are all the more effective in view of the high proportion of disabled people who are on low incomes.

The commercial value of concessionary schemes for the operators is obviously considerably heightened if it is linked to off-peak travel, as is often the case with arrangements in favour of senior citizens — an increasingly important group which of course includes a very large number of people with disabilities. It should also be remembered that off-peak travel can be an attractive proposition to younger disabled people too, provided they are not engaged in full-time employment, since it may offer more comfort and security — though there could be the danger of unwelcome discrimination and isolation if this were carried too far.

There are a number of useful concessions in operation which are specific to certain situations or transport modes. On British and Irish ferries, for example, and on some French ones, the car of a recognized disabled driver is carried free of charge. The facility to travel first class with a second-class ticket, as on the Paris Metro, is also an appropriate concession, particularly at rush hours or when suitable seating is not otherwise available.

Special priority, in my view, should be given to schemes which allow the escorts of disabled people to travel free of charge, and all those with the interest of disabled people at heart owe a debt of gratitude to the International Railways Union for having achieved the breakthrough by means of their agreement that the escorts of blind passengers may travel free of charge on railways throughout Europe. Bearing in mind that this concession is afforded already on the railways in the Netherlands to the escorts of all disabled people who cannot travel unaccompanied, there is no reason why we should not aim to extend this facility throughout the European Community for all disabilities and all modes of transport, including even airways (see p. 85 above). I shall return to this point in Chapter 7 in my discussion of the idea of a European Travel Card, which should facilitate a European agreement to ensure free carriage both for guide-dogs (already more often than not conceded) and (what may be more difficult to achieve) for essential apparatus.

Before leaving concessions, I must mention an arrangement which is unique to the United Kingdom: the mobility allowance, a global regular grant which is afforded to all those in the United Kingdom who are assessed as having a significant mobility handicap, to be spent in whatever way the beneficiary chooses — on public transport fares for example or on the costs of running a private car. The scheme has the great advantages of allowing disabled people themselves a good range of personal choice and of eliminating the need for complicated detailed concessionary schemes covering various disabilities and transport modes. It does not however seem likely that a European agreement could ever be reached to generalize this approach. If this is right, it confirms the view that European efforts at harmonization should concentrate on concessions for escorts rather than on those for the disabled people themselves which are likely to remain divergent on national lines.

Finally, it could be useful to record here the basic principles which I suggested in the 1989 ERICA Report should underlie our approach to concessionary provision:

1. The principle should be established that concessions are based on the effect of disability, but without prejudice to already existing measures.
2. Concessionary schemes should not be allowed to develop haphazardly, but should be co-ordinated nationally so as to constitute a coherent and fair set of measures; they should not be based merely or fundamentally on market principles but on the right to equalizing compensation for disability; their financial advantages should however be stressed, both from a merely transport point of view (attraction of customers who would not otherwise travel) and a more general one (promotion of independence).
3. The existence or development of concessionary schemes must not be seen as an alternative to making public transport accessible.
4. Either mobility allowances for disabled people or a system for the reduction of fares covering all modes of transport should be developed.
5. Where fare reductions are offered, they should apply to season and other special tickets; travellers should be able to acquire them in the country visited, not only before departure from their own; there should be special reductions for the family of a disabled person travelling together.
6. Disabled people should never be required to sign declarations discharging responsibility.
7. National mobility cards should specify clearly all services or benefits to which disabled people are entitled.[1]

Special services

Leaving now the whole area of public transport we come next to consider that of what are commonly called 'special services'. By these I mean systems which normally offer a door-to-door service, which may be run by a public local authority or by a voluntary organization and which only authorized disabled people and their escorts may use. It is above all this last point which distinguishes such provision from supplementary services (of the kind described on p. 87 above) which, though designed with the needs of disabled passengers chiefly in mind, are provided by the normal local bus transport operator (whether this is a private commercial company or a local public authority) and may be used also by non-disabled passengers.

It must be observed at once that the expression 'special services' to describe the systems we are now discussing is not always recognized as appropriate. It has, for example, been put forcibly to me by representatives of disabled people in Spain that such provision should in all circumstances be recognized as a 'normal' extension of mainstream services, and that therefore the term 'special' must be avoided when referring to it, since it militates against the acceptance by public authority that it has a statutory responsibility to ensure that this service is available. I believe that we should respect this point of view and look for a terminology which would satisfy it; meanwhile, I shall continue to use the term 'special services' for want of any other.

Special services raise difficult issues of policy and, even more perhaps, of the way policy is presented and so generally understood. Ideally, it might be supposed, all such provision should be superseded as the accessibility of normal public transport progresses; it should therefore be the declared aim of any national policy to eliminate the need for special services within a reasonable time. It would follow that, assuming that 'a reasonable time' means 'the foreseeable future' it would be a mistake now to do anything which would encourage the expansion or multiplication of special services, since that would merely be to invest in planned obsolescence.

Yet I believe that such a view would be both unrealistic and damaging — damaging above all to the interests of those with the most severe disabilities, including multiple handicaps. While it would be wrong in principle to say that no public transport system could ever be adapted to meet the needs of this important group, we must recognize that we cannot imagine how this could be done; it would therefore make no sense even to discuss a possible time-scale for achieving it and it follows that even to conceive its achievement as an ideal to be borne in mind is likely to be an unhelpful diversion.

Since from numerous examples in different cultures special services are known to be operated efficiently and to offer a provision which is both essential to the aim of independent living and unattainable by any other means, and since there are many cities and districts in all Community countries where no such provision exists, then it is evident that it should be a part of declared Community policy and of the national policy of every member state to promote and enable the extension and generalization of these services by every possible means.

Yet there is an obvious danger in this. As soon as it is known that it is a part of policy to extend and generalize special services, there will be a tendency for transport operators, the world at large and even disabled people themselves to suppose that this is the whole of the policy, or at least its main thrust. It is a short step from there to the belief that special services are *the* provision for disabled people; from this it would follow that disabled people were not to be expected as passengers on public vehicles, that any claims they were to make on them would be wrongly directed and that public transport operators had no obligation to make their services accessible. It is evident that this negative effect can only be forestalled if transport policy for disabled people is planned and presented as a whole made up of a number of interlocking parts, of which accessible public transport and the development of special services are two important and complementary elements. And this global approach to action and publicity must be assured at all levels — the European Community, the nation, the region and the municipality or local district. At the local level, in particular, it is vital that everything which is done by public authority, by commercial operators and by voluntary organizations is co-ordinated and manifested as a totality which both covers the ground of need and offers as many options to as many disabled people as possible.

It is no matter therefore of mere chance that the European Commission chose the subject of door-to-door services for its first study activity in the whole domain of the mobility of disabled people. What came to light then (in 1982) is confirmed in more recent accounts: though provision is scattered and its existence cannot be relied upon, examples of well-established good practice are numerous and widespread.

In Denmark the only initiatives recorded have been in the public sector, the voluntary organizations not apparently seeing this as their province; the most developed service is that in Copenhagen, run by the city's transport company on behalf of the Department of Health and Social Welfare. In the Netherlands, by contrast, there are many diverse services throughout the country, some (as in Rotter-dam) operated by the municipal authority, others by voluntary bodies, others yet again by commercial companies. An initiative of particular interest has been the research and development pilot programme launched by the central government in the province of Groningen, aimed at extending a special service for handicapped children so as to include all disabled people in all municipalities. In Belgium, like Denmark, the most noteworthy development has been in the capital city and under public auspices; the special minibus service is operated by the Brussels transport company on behalf of the city's central administration ('agglomeration'). Its efficacy has been evaluated by a commission on which disabled people are represented; it has been shown that its popularity justifies it as an effective means of promoting independent living, but its cost may well prevent its extension beyond Brussels to other communes.

In the German Federal Republic, as in the Netherlands, services are numerous — they existed in 60 towns and cities when information was last available — and are operated by various voluntary bodies (such as the Red Cross) as well as by munici-palities. Provision exists in many of the major cities (such as Bonn, Hamburg, Frankfurt-on-Main, etc.) and in many cases is offered without charge to the disabled clients. At the last count I have seen, nearly 150,000 journeys a year were undertaken. Of even greater repute than this widely dispersed provision is the celebrated 'Telebus' service of (West) Berlin, originally launched with substantial federal support and now under the responsibility of the social service department of the Berlin Senate. The service, possibly the most highly developed in Europe or indeed the world, operates for 24 hours a day every day of the year; the research on the basis of which it has been established offers valuable evidence about the needs and wishes of people with various disabilities.

In the United Kingdom, as in Denmark, the initiative has lain in the public rather than voluntary sector. In Coventry the scheme, which is supported by the social service department of the local authority after initial financial aid from central govern-ment, has been evaluated and proved its worth. Yet, though there are well established schemes in other provincial cities (such as the 'Ring and Ride' service in Birmingham) special services are not perhaps as widely or as evenly spread in Britain as one might have expected. One of the most impressive provisions is to be found in London, where 'Dial-a-Ride' schemes operate in all the 29 boroughs of the city.

In France special services are numerous and widespread; the latest COLITRAH report lists over 60 towns and cities where such provision exists under various aus-pices, in addition to over 30 places where services are run by or associated with one voluntary organization, the Group for the Integration of Physically Disabled People, the GIHP.[2] Either local public authorities or voluntary associations may be involved, and co-operation between them is common. The national network created by GIHP is of outstanding interest and indeed one of the most fruitful autonomous develop-ments in the disability field in the whole of Europe. Its network structure has enabled GIHP to improve standards of performance in the light of varied experience. Moreover, in addition to its special transport service, each GIHP branch offers a number of other services of advice and support to physically disabled people in its locality. And — what is perhaps the most remarkable feature — GIHP was created and is administered by disabled people themselves.

Special services have proved their worth — their utility from the consumers' point of view, and their flexibility in being equally amenable to public and voluntary management. 'Consumer friendliness' however appears to vary considerably: requirements to make arrangements 24 hours or more in advance and restrictions as to the geographical limit, frequency or purpose of personal journeys are quite often encountered and naturally unpopular; not all services operate at weekends or on public holidays, or during unsocial hours; restriction of use to local members is also common and, though quite understandable, evidently not compatible with the longer-term mobility aspirations of disabled people. Standards of management, in terms of cost-effectiveness and security, are also somewhat variable. It follows that well organized exchange of experience, leading gradually to the production of European guidelines, would be of exceptional value in this area. Meanwhile, here are the 12 principles for the operation of special services which I set out in the ERICA report and which might form the basis for discussing future developments at Community level:

1. It should be publicly established that door-to-door and similar services are only 'special' in that they cater for clients with special needs; they are not apart from public transport provision but an extension of it; their existence or development must never be conceived as an alternative to the adaptation of public services, still less as an excuse for delaying or avoiding this.

2. Equally it must be realized that special services will continue to be needed in the long term, especially for those with severe disabilities; and that since special services are by no means evenly or adequately distributed over the countries and regions of the Community, they will need to be extended, not merely maintained.

3. While it is recognized that, when demand exceeds supply, priority may be given to local residents, all special services should be open also to disabled visitors from other regions and other Community countries; they should not be limited to those who, as well as being eligible on other grounds, are members of a family owning no car.

4. Responsibility for the cost of special services should be borne by those responsible for public transport provision and not by public welfare authorities; responsibility for planning and running them should be shared among these together with voluntary organizations and with disabled people and their associations.

5. The cost of subsidizing special services should be considered as balanced by the financial benefits of deinstitutionalization on the one hand, and on the other, against the cost of individual allowances which offer no benefits of scale such as shared journeys.

6. The cost-effectiveness of special services should be promoted as far as possible, for example by organizing transport for several passengers to one or more destinations ('many to one', 'many to many') as well as priority journeys for single persons ('one to one'); the cost-effectiveness of locally restricted services should also be considered.

7. Consumers should normally contribute to the cost of the system by paying the cost of public transport over the same distance; the same principle or that of free travel should apply to escorts; there should be no extra charge for the guide-dogs of blind or deaf people or for apparatus including wheelchairs.

8. Whoever operates the special service, the purchase of adapted cars or minibuses should be grant-aided if possible and certainly exempt from VAT; a European market for specialized vehicles should be developed.
9. In large cities, municipal authorities could run a regular service of wheelchair-carrying vehicles to reduce the need for on-demand special services.
10. It should be recognized that it is not always possible to establish special services in rural areas, where some alternatives (such as a taxi-card system or accessible post-buses) may be needed.
11. Regulations for the granting of licences to drive minibuses should not be so strict as to make it impossible for voluntary bodies to maintain their transport services for disabled people.
12. Regular adapted services to schools, training establishments, hospitals, rehabilitation centres or employment should be separately provided and responsibility for their provision should rest with the appropriate authority (education, health, etc.).

Privately owned vehicles

We come now to look at the contribution which is made to mobility by privately owned vehicles. By this of course is meant vehicles owned by disabled people themselves; we should however bear in mind that while very often the disabled owner of such a vehicle will be the normal driver of it, this is by no means always the case: it may also be useful for someone, the nature of whose disability makes driving impossible, to own his or her own vehicle and to be able to travel as a passenger in it, driven by his or her partner or a friend. It is important too to recognize that we are not entering now on a topic which is less essential, more marginal, than those of public transport or special services. Although a number of disabilities obviously preclude driving, ownership of a car offers to very many disabled people by far the best solution to their mobility problems, and may even offer them more in terms of equal opportunity and social integration than any other element of their lives. There is perhaps nothing quite like the possession of a car for enabling a disabled person to feel that he or she shares freedom of movement with those who are not disabled. Above all for those who spend a large part of their lives in wheelchairs, the ability to own, and in many cases to drive, a car offers relatively more than to any other member of society — given that even in the best circumstances of adaptation the use of public transport will be for the disabled person always difficult and quite often impossible.

To this we can add a number of other factors. Not only are people throughout the Community living longer: an increasing proportion of elderly people are continuing to drive their own cars, including many who are incurring various levels of disability with old age. Technical advances also are continually making driving a possibility for people of all ages the severity of whose disability made this impossible in the past, and this process of extending opportunity will continue. Finally we must take into account the extent to which the motivation, even the necessity, to drive is being everywhere increased as urban planning, including the location of shops and other facilities, is more and more dominated by the demands of the motor car. For all these reasons it is clear that the encouragement and support afforded to a growing number of disabled people to own a vehicle is as important a component of a positive mobility policy as any other.

Support may take the form of help towards the cost of buying a vehicle or of adapting it or of running it. Important aspects of encouragement include the reduction to a minimum of the difficulties involved in receiving driving lessons, taking a driving test and obtaining a licence — a licence too that is not hedged about with limitations.[3] Special parking rights are a major feature of positive policy in all member states, and increasing attention is now being given to the accessibility of facilities essential to drivers, such as petrol stations generally and the whole range of services on motorways. The easy availability of advisory services covering all the numerous and complicated problems facing the would-be disabled car-owner is also essential if the full potential of this form of mobility is to be realized.

As we have already found with other components of mobility, there is considerable variation in the quality and range of provision to help disabled car-owners in the different member states. In general (except sometimes in the matter of parking facilities and rights) local variations are not significant and everything depends on national regulations and national procedures for affording grants. In some countries, such as Belgium, Germany, Ireland and Italy, financial help is virtually restricted to those who need a vehicle for the purposes of work or training; in Denmark and Luxembourg on the other hand this limitation does not apply. Both in Denmark and the Netherlands provision of grant aid is decentralized, to local authorities and workers' welfare organizations respectively. Decentralization also applies in Italy, where it is said that help is hard to obtain and procedures lengthy. For those who are eligible under vocational criteria financial support in Belgium appears to be good, no doubt because it has been administered by the National Fund for the Social Resettlement of Disabled People, the effectiveness of which we have already observed in the discussion of employment; disabled passengers as well as drivers may benefit — blind people, for example, are eligible. In the United Kingdom the existence of the mobility allowance, mentioned in the section on 'Concessions' above, puts disabled people who receive it in an exceptional position of choice. In the United Kingdom too the part in assessment and advice played by the voluntary body Motability is also of particular interest; a similar function is performed in Belgium by a private commercial organization, CARA.

The official issue of cards or badges which afford special parking rights to disabled drivers is an important measure in all Community countries; in some it is available to disabled passengers as well. Not surprisingly, there are considerable differences between the various schemes both in the criteria of eligibility and in the range of facilities and privileges which card-holders may enjoy; the extent to which local variations of practice are significant is another variable — it would seem to be relatively high in Spain, Ireland and Italy. Generally cards are thought to be relatively easy to obtain in Italy, particularly difficult in Luxembourg; recent concern in the United Kingdom about possible abuses of the system and doubts about the wisdom of awarding cards to those who have difficulty in carrying (i.e. impairments of the upper and not of the lower limbs) are evidence of the genuine difficulties experienced by those trying to draw the lines of eligibility fairly and consistently.[4]

Cards and badges normally permit their holders to park without charge where meters or similar systems apply, to disregard time limits, to pick up and put down where this is not normally allowed and to use special parking places officially reserved for them. Provision of such reserved places and the strength of measures making such provision obligatory are exceptionally well developed in France. In France also much has been done to make motorway facilities accessible and to publicize these facilities by means of an excellent brochure; by 1983, 70 per cent of motorway service stations and shops were accessible.

International agreements and harmonies are intrinsically valuable to disabled car-owners for obvious reasons. Where more favourable conditions can be found over the border, disabled drivers may already take matters into their own hands: regulations surrounding the award of a driving licence to a disabled person in Italy are so severe that disabled Italians go to Germany for their licences — an excellent recourse, since not only are attitudes generally much more positive there but also licences (except in the case of certain deteriorating conditions) are granted for life.

In spite of the many differences of detail, there is more than enough evidence of convergence of approach and policy aims throughout the Community to justify the hope that harmonization, so appropriate if not essential in this field, could be achieved in the foreseeable future. This prospect will be further explored in Part III.

Opinion presented to me when I was preparing the ERICA Report led me to identify eight general principles to underpin the promotion of car ownership by disabled people:

1. It should be recognized that ownership of a vehicle, a car or van, offers the highest degree of freedom of movement for both disabled passengers or non-drivers and disabled drivers. It should also be recognized that for those who are severely motor disabled, whether passengers or drivers, ownership of a car or van often offers the only means of journeying away from home. The principle that all disabled people should be encouraged and assisted to obtain and maintain a suitable vehicle, and that those who can do so should be encouraged and assisted to obtain a driving licence, should therefore be universally acknowledged and put into practice.
2. Laws or regulations which forbid any category of disabled person from holding a licence should be abolished. The criterion for obtaining a licence should be the individual's ability to drive, not the category of his or her impairment.[3]
3. Special measures should be introduced to ensure that all disabled people have an equal opportunity to obtain a licence; the needs of those with specific disabilities (e.g. small people, drivers without hands) must be considered; general licences, rather than licences to drive only a specific vehicle, should be afforded where possible.
4. Disabled candidates should have the right to a driving test at the same standard as other citizens.
5. Disabled drivers and passengers should, where this is necessary, be exempted from the requirement to wear seat belts.
6. Financial as well as technical assistance should be afforded to assessments to match passengers or drivers to suitable vehicles, purchase (including adaptation for passenger or driver), replacement and running costs of the vehicle and assessments of driving ability and driving lessons. The assistance should include:

help with purchase costs; interest-free loans; exemption from VAT; exemption from tax on imported cars or vans; contributions to hire-purchase charges; exemption from road or registration tax; help with the cost of maintenance, repairs, spare parts and accessories (exemption from VAT or reduction of it, percentage contribution to bills); exemption from petrol duty; contribution towards higher insurance premiums resulting from the higher value of an adapted car, and protection from arbitrary premium surcharges; and, for disabled drivers, grant aid to driving instruction fees (especially where the cost of additional lessons is necessarily incurred) and exemption from test fees.

7. Financial help should be afforded to those authorized to act for and looking after people with mental disabilities and, where appropriate, to an institution or association purchasing and maintaining a vehicle for the use of disabled residents.

8. No element of financial help should be restricted to disabled drivers or passengers who are employed.

Movement in the street

The last of the four components of mobility identified by the European Commission comprises movement in and about the street. The problems here concern mostly people with visual disabilities, those who have difficulty in walking, carrying or standing and those who use wheelchairs. Such movement brings disabled people sooner or later to the entrance of wherever it is they want to go; this topic therefore shares a frontier with the subject of access to public buildings and facilities which is treated later in the next section of this chapter. Street movement however involves problems which are mostly quite different from those which are encountered when entering or using a building, and is better grouped with the other aspects of mobility even though it does not involve the disabled person in the use of a vehicle or a transport system. In this connection it is worth remarking that it is important that as a general rule wheelchairs should not be classified as vehicles and that users of them should have the same rights of movement on pavements and other pedestrian areas as those moving on foot.

Among the chief elements to be considered when planning an accessible pedestrian environment are the pavement, the kerb, the crossing, movement between levels and rest places. Pavements should be level, slip-resistant and free of obstacles; temporary obstacles or dangers (such as manholes) must have secure barriers and be well lit at night. Kerbs should be low and ramped at crossing points to facilitate the passage of wheelchairs; their approach should be signalled to pedestrians with visual disabilities by means of surface variation. Crossing signals should be audible as well as visible and should allow a reasonable time for those with difficulties of movement to cross in safety; pedestrian refuges should have space for wheelchairs. In principle, shopping precincts ought to offer a much improved environment for disabled shoppers; yet if, as is often the case with newly built precincts, they extend over more than one level there may be less accessibility than in a traditional street. Ramps as a supplement to steps are certainly better than nothing but are likely to require a number of disabled people still to be dependent on an escort. The frequency and siting of rest places need careful planning.

This is of course by no means a complete list of what is needed to ensure a safe and accessible pedestrian environment for all those disabled people who need to use it. It is enough however to remind us of what we all know — how far we are in Europe from achieving anything like a reasonable standard, let alone a reliable level of general provision, in this field. On the whole, much more has been done in the United States, and we must be grateful for this example. Efforts to follow it have of course been made in a number of European cities, including some capitals; the best-known and most comprehensive in its conception is probably the demonstration project carried out in the town of Gouda in the Netherlands.

The argument that the creation of an accessible street environment is unattainably costly cannot of course be simply ignored; it would however be more convincing if good opportunities offered by new developments and by necessary repair work were not so frequently missed. The reality is that an enormous amount needs to be done, involving a significant change in public attitudes. No doubt there is a vicious circle at work here: disabled people are generally not visible because the street environment rejects them, while the general public is unaware of the potential, needs and even existence of disabled people because they are not visible.

Nothing less than a concerted European effort is likely to be able to have sufficient impact to bring about significant change in the mid term. I shall return to this prospect later; meanwhile here are the six general principles for the promotion of an accessible street environment which I set out in the ERICA report:

1. It should be recognized that walking is still by far the most important form of movement for the majority of disabled people, and that the use of wheelchairs and other mobile aids in the street by disabled and elderly people is constantly increasing.
2. There is a general need for more co-ordinated planning, based on published guidelines which are derived from well-tested solutions, in order to ensure an integrated approach at local level to the lay-out of public spaces and the establishment of priority key routes which are barrier-free and well equipped.
3. It is essential to involve disabled people and their representatives as well as town planners, architects, engineers and builders in the preparation both of guidelines and of local development and adaptation projects.
4. In assessing the cost-effectiveness of proposals, it must be stressed that all citizens (above all the elderly) benefit from an urban environment accessible to disabled people.
5. The principles of safety (including road safety), good lighting, clear signs and regular maintenance should form the basis of all planning.
6. It should be recognized that non-motorized wheelchairs are not vehicles; they should have complete freedom to use pavements and pedestrian crossings; this principle should be extended to motorized wheelchairs as appropriate.

European initiatives

The European Conference of Ministers of Transport (ECMT)

Any account of European initiatives to promote the mobility of disabled people should start with a tribute to the ongoing work of the European Conference of Ministers of Transport (ECMT), whose Working Group on Transport for Disabled People was set up in 1985 and is presided over by the head of the Disability Unit in the United Kingdom Ministry of Transport. All member states of the Community are members of the Conference and all except Greece and Portugal participate in the Working Group. Continuity of key membership, an effective secretariat (located in the building of the OECD in Paris) and a clear vision of its mandate are some of the factors contributing to the high quality of the work undertaken by the Group, which stands out as a model of fruitful international co-operation. Already in 1977 the Conference had produced a Resolution on Reciprocal Parking Arrangements which pioneered freedom of movement for disabled drivers across frontiers in Europe.

Since being set up in its present form, the Working Group has worked systematically both at the level of policy foundations and at that of technical detail. Three of its most important reports are 'Meeting the Needs of Disabled People' (1985), 'Comparisons of Practice and Policy with Recommendations for Change' (1986) and 'International Co-ordination and Standardization of Measures and Policies to Promote Mobility' (1987). Two of the most significant conclusions to have emerged from the activity of the Working Group are the need to stress the importance of cross-sector benefit when assessing the financial implications of mobility measures, and the need to distinguish between those measures which can and should be prescribed in terms of precise standards and those where the clear but non-numerical statement of an objective is more appropriate.

The European Commission has regarded it as essential to establish and maintain close co-operative relations with the European Conference and its Working Group. This co-operation was publicly demonstrated when Mr Clinton Davis, then European Commissioner responsible for transport, gave one of the keynote speeches at the December 1986 London Conference on 'Transport without Handicap'. The contribution made by members of the ECMT Working Group to the 1989 ERICA report has also been of great value.

In December 1989 the French government co-operated with the ECMT in the organization in Dunkirk of a European conference on the theme of transport for disabled people. At the main conference the results were presented of an open ECMT seminar on bus transport. From the side of the French government, the conference was addressed by President Mitterrand as well as by the Ministers for Transport and Disabled People. The conference also provided me with the opportunity for the first public presentation of the 1989 ERICA study. Soon after this, in 1990, the ECMT produced yet another valuable report comprising a 'Review of Provisions and Standards for Journey Planning and Pedestrian Access'. Of special value here is the up-to-date detail on precise access standards, another big step forward in the direction of technical harmonization as an essential element in a European policy aiming at a guarantee of accessibility everywhere. Since then the

ECMT has been co-operating with the Commission's Directorate-General for Transport in the preparation of studies on funding and administrative arrangements.

The Council of Europe

The Council of Europe has also concerned itself with the mobility needs of disabled people, in the framework of the Partial Agreement in the Social and Public Health Field, the nature of which has been described in Part I. In 1975 the Committee of Ministers adopted a Resolution on Ways of Facilitating Access to and Use of Public Transport by Disabled People. A section on mobility is included in the Council of Europe's compendium of legislation on the rehabilitation of disabled people and also in their publication of a coherent policy in this field.[5] The European Commission and the Council of Europe keep in regular contact with each other's work although more active co-operation is somewhat inhibited by the difference between countries' participation in the Partial Agreement and membership of the European Community.

The European Community

As for the European Commission itself, its interest precedes the adoption of the 1981 action programme. In its response to the Commission's report on the 1974–81 action programme on vocational rehabilitation the Council stressed among other things the importance of measures undertaken at local level. Taking up this point, my predecessor, Dr Umberto Vidali, as a first initiative, decided to commission a first-ever European study on door-to-door transport schemes in the European Community, thus setting the pattern of policy-oriented surveys which I followed and which has formed the basis of all the Commission's policy work on the employment and environment of disabled people during the last nine years. This first study was entrusted to a British independent research institute, ERICA (European Research in Consumer Affairs), whose president, Mrs Eirlys Roberts, has been an active champion of consumer interests as a member of the Community's Economic and Social Committee. The study was prepared by Claudine Van Lierde, the Flemish consumer economist who played such a large part in the co-ordination of the district projects in the first action programme (1982–7) and who is now doing the same for the local model activities in the Helios programme.

The study proved that in the special transport field there existed in the Community local developments of exceptional interest and effectiveness, which however were not generalized in practice or even widely known. There was a clear implication as to the need for dissemination of information and exchange of experience, and as to the responsibilities of the Commission in that regard. Equally important was the policy implication: the study demonstrated that special transport provision was a topic concerning which a policy initiative on the part of the Commission was both desirable and possible.

We have seen in Chapter 1 how the United Nations International Year of Disabled People (1981) proved to be a turning point in the approach of the European Community to the needs and potential of people with disabilities. The objective, instead of being merely 'vocational rehabilitation' (limited by the more traditional and restrictive view of the competence of the European Community, as something confined to the economic sector), was now 'social and economic integration'. Though the Community was only beginning to comprehend what the expression 'social integration' might imply and comprise, it was already in 1981 at least partly understood that mobility and transport were elements that could not be ignored. The European Parliament, which it will be remembered was the first of the Community institutions to respond to the challenge of the International Year, refers to transport in three articles of its 1981 Resolution on Economic, Social and Vocational Integration; it called for, among other things, Community recognition of national passes and parking rights and for the dedication of Social Fund support to mobility schemes, as well as taking up the Council's point about the importance of local initiatives. Four months later (July 1981) the Social and Economic Committee included a section on 'Access and transport' in its Opinion on The Situation and Problems of the Handicapped; of particular interest is the Committee's view that Community action in this regard should be founded on the articles of the Treaty which deal with free movement and the common policy for transport.

The European Commission's own 1981 initiative, the proposal for the first social integration action programme, was far more concerned with the general character of that concept from a policy point of view than with its specific contents, its other preoccupation being the prescription of new programme targets and modalities; about transport the only specific statement concerns the need to co-ordinate Commission activity in this and other fields. The Council in its Resolution of December 1981 adopting the action programme does indeed stress the need to 'develop and implement measures on the housing and mobility of handicapped people and improved access to public buildings, transport and other public facilities', but these words come in the section of the Resolution addressed to member states and there is no explicit invitation to the Commission to work in the transport field.

However the open nature of the action programme itself, above all the reciprocal exchange of visits and opinions between the staff of the Commission and its experts in the Interact team on the one hand and the district projects and leading non-governmental organizations on the other, soon ensured that the essential importance of mobility and transport to social integration became something taken for granted in the programme. At the same time it was brought upon us that we needed to accelerate and promote in importance, as an integral element of the programme, formal proposals directly aimed at the establishment of Community policy and the development of policies in the member states. As was explained in Chapter 2, I decided that the first of these initiatives was to be concerned with employment, and that this would be followed by a series of proposals on environmental topics, starting with mobility and transport. This required following up the first ERICA study on door-to-door transport systems by other studies which would aim to survey the whole range of issues and measures on this topic at European level.

The first of these was again entrusted to ERICA, and carried out on their behalf by David Yelding of the British Consumers' Association. Published in 1985 under the title 'Everyday Mobility for Disabled People', the report covers three main areas, the pedestrian environment, private cars and adaptations to existing public transport vehicles. For the last two there is a precise statement of the situation in each of the then ten member states, while the pedestrian environment is treated by means of a more extended analysis of problems, measures and standards. A valuable summary of conclusions covers all three areas and there are recommendations for possible Community action. As well as reinforcing both the possibility and the necessity for Community action in the field, the study provided much of the technical basis on which such an action could be founded.

To complete the main components of its technical base the Commission then invited the Netherlands Consumentenbond to prepare an equivalent report on longer-distance travel. The authors, J.R. Vorderegger and C.J. Verplanke, produced a report in two parts, of which the second consists of a detailed analysis of the needs, approaches and facilities in eight of the member states as well as Canada, Spain (not then yet a member), Sweden and the United States. The first part, also published in 1985, compresses this mass of material, the core of which is presented in the form of a survey of findings and conclusions followed by proposals and recommendations. The work covers accommodation for travellers as well as travel by rail, air, bus and coach, sea and car, and for each of these reviews the state of legislation and guidelines, financial arrangements, the provision of information and examples of practical facilities. There is also a look at the probable direction of future trends in the member states. In its entirety this was a monumental work, and again the Commission was fortunate in finding experts able to extract from an intractable mass of material generalizations and conclusions amenable to policy application.

Following the operational principle that the various elements of the action programme should complement each other, the Commission made sure that the Handynet information project and both the network of district projects and the scheme of co-operation with the leading non-governmental organizations of and for disabled people contributed to the political effort. For Handynet the Gruppe Hardtberg in Bonn produced a report on the information needs concerning access to transport. The plenary seminar of the districts held in Piacenza in 1986 was devoted to the practical problems of independent living, including mobility and the provision of accessible transport. The national secretaries of Rehabilitation International in the Community countries, by providing up-to-date information on the state of measures in their own member states, made a useful contribution to the work of bringing together all information relevant to the possibility of developing an international or European mobility card for disabled people, a task undertaken by Bernard Vanderhaeghen within the Commission's Bureau itself. Mobility was also one of the principal themes of the RI expert seminar held in Athens in 1988.

Valuable contributions were also made by the autonomous action of non-governmental organizations, notably the seminar on mobility organized by the European Blind Union at Tarquinia in 1986, and the report on 'Access, Mobility, Housing and Leisure' published by the European Community Secretariat of the World Federation of the Deaf. Also in 1986, but outside the framework of the action programme itself, a group of French organizations concerned with mental handicap, including the Union national des associations des parents d'enfants inadaptés (UNAPEI, National Union of Associations of Parents of Children with Mental Handicaps), produced a report entitled 'Mentally Disabled People and Public Transport'. By these means the Commission was able to get information, not easy to obtain, about the transport needs of those with other than motor disabilities.

Following the successful method used in the development of the Recommendation on employment, we were by the end of 1986 ready to hold a consultation workshop in Brussels which would give us the concentrated results of intensive discussion about already well prepared questions on the part of representatives of national Ministries and international transport organizations, of independent experts and of members of the Commission's own networks (the district projects, the non-governmental organizations, Rehabilitation International and the rehabilitation centres). Organized for us by Monique Stilmant's European Co-ordination and Information Bureau for Disabled People (BECIPH, Bureau européen de coordination et d'information pour les personnes handicapées), the workshop included the largest number of disabled people who had ever been brought together in the programme, and therefore no doubt for any Community purpose. At this workshop too the co-operation of the Commission with the Working Group of the European Conference of Ministers of Transport was reinforced, the keynote address being delivered by the convenor of the Working Group, Ann Frye. An interesting factor of the workshop was the emergence of a convincing majority opinion in favour of the idea of a European Travel Card.

It was possible to arrange the workshop to coincide with a hearing organized, also in Brussels, by the Transport Committee of the European Parliament, in the context of the report on the transport of handicapped and elderly persons being brought forward by the Spanish Socialist MEP, J. Ramirez Heredia. The hearing, itself an important step forward in the development of effective democratic action in this domain, certainly contributed to the strength and direction of the own-initiative Resolution of the Parliament adopted in July of that year. The Resolution incorporates a considerable number of detailed recommendations for the provision of accessible routes in towns and cities, and for the improvement of the accessibility of public transport vehicles and infrastructures. It firmly states the right of disabled and elderly people to mobility and the responsibility of public authorities to meet this. It also reinforces the Commission's view that, for social and economic integration, mobility is a central issue, not a marginal one: 'Access to transport and greater mobility constitute a vital means for giving the handicapped person an active rather than a dependent role . . . mobility is essential to some disabled people in finding and retaining a job.'

Preoccupied as it was with achieving the adoption of the second action programme (Helios), the Commission did not possess in 1987 the resources to follow up immediately the strong position it had established on mobility and transport. Careful technical preparation, consultation with the representatives of the clients and co-operation with ECMT had required a considerable expenditure of resources, and given the Commission's exiguous personnel this meant that reliable progress could not be made quickly. This problem of pace was a perpetual worry for us in the Commission's service and I believe often a source of disappointment to our supporters outside. But at least a solid platform for effective final action had been built.

It was also clear what needed to be done next: a first draft of a European Code of Good Practice could be prepared, a practical scheme for the institution of a European Mobility Card for disabled people devised and a political strategy for the Commission to follow worked out. How these tasks have been addressed in the Helios programme will be revealed in Chapter 7.

ACCESS TO PUBLIC BUILDINGS AND FACILITIES

International initiatives

In deciding that transport and mobility should be the first of the three environmental themes for treatment at policy level the Commission was not implying any hierarchy of importance; access to public buildings and facilities is no less essential to independent living, and housing may be thought to be the most basic provision of all. The importance of access has been widely recognized by the International Organizations. As early as 1972 the Council of Europe adopted two Resolutions, one on the planning and equipment of buildings to make them more accessible and the other officially adopting the International Access Symbol devised by Rehabilitation International. The United Nations (Centre for Social and Humanitarian Affairs) co-operated with RI in the publication in 1974 of a report on 'Barrier-Free Design', and followed this up, in the context of the 1981 International Year, with an excellent illustrated guide to the adaptation of the built environment for disabled persons, under the title 'Designing with Care'. Design guidelines on 'the functional needs of handicapped persons' were produced in 1979 by the International Standardization Organization as part of its ongoing work in this field.

The European Community

The work of the European Community on access and buildings during the 1970s has already been described in Part I. Yet in spite of this background, when we came, at about midway through the first action programme, to tackle the topic of accessibility we had no doubt that it needed as careful preparation as had been given to transport. First, we entrusted to the Dutch Council for the Disabled (Gehandicaptenraad) the preparation of a European policy study which would analyse the key issues of accessibility, and summarize the principal statutory and practical measures which member states had undertaken in the field. Under the title 'Accessibility of Public Buildings for the Disabled' the report of this study was submitted by its author, Johan Galjaard, in 1986. As well as covering the ground of the subject, Galjaard stressed the importance of the International Access Symbol introduced by RI and of control of its use, gave details of a number of successful projects to make museums accessible and insisted on the need to plan not just single buildings but whole environments which are accessible.

   The report was presented as the main working document of a consultation workshop on 'Access to Public Buildings and Facilities' which we organized with the co-operation of the Dutch Council for the Disabled in Utrecht in 1987. In addition to general conclusions, this workshop produced sets of recommendations from six working groups made up of representative disabled people, professionals and experts from all member states. Meanwhile, our understanding of the subject at European level was further augmented by the report of the Danish expert Klaus Blach entitled 'The Need for Information on Access for Disabled People', prepared on behalf of the Commission in the context of the development of the Handynet information project. Knowledge of the problems and of useful solutions was further advanced by two seminars organized by RI under Commission sponsorship, the first on 'Environment and Housing' at Bois-Larris, Chantilly, in 1984 and the second the 1987 Athens seminar already mentioned (p. 104).

As a result of this work we were able to clarify what the term 'accessibility' should comprise, and to appreciate the importance of including in the concept both 'reachability' and 'usability'. More precisely, full access consists of the freedom to perform these actions:

- getting to the entrance
- getting into the building, through the entrance, lobby and reception facilities
- finding one's way round the building, including the ability to read and interpret signs and directions
- getting around the building, including managing doors and the use of lifts
- using all the facilities of the building which are relevant to the nature of the visit (for example, sanitary facilities, switches, control buttons, taps, communication apparatus)
- getting out of the building rapidly and safely in emergency.

Secondly, we were able to clarify the point that by 'public buildings and facilities' we meant those that were offered for public use (whether they were under public or private ownership or management), but also 'mainstream' establishments open to special populations, such as schools and work-places. If we distinguish these two main classes as 'general public buildings' and 'special public buildings' respectively, we find that under the 'general' head we must include:

Administrative etc.: advice centres, municipal offices, social welfare and security offices, tax offices, post offices, registry offices
Judicial: police stations, courts
Health: health centres, hospitals, clinics, sickness insurance offices, rehabilitation centres
Commercial: banks, insurance offices, travel agencies, estate agencies, shops
Utilities: sanitary and communication installations in public places
Cultural: theatres, concert halls, cinemas, art galleries, libraries, museums
Religious: churches, chapels, parish halls
Recreational: restaurants, buffets, cafes, bars, pubs
Touristic: holiday centres, youth hostels, camp sites
Sporting: gymnasiums, stadiums, swimming pools, sports centres
Other outdoor: parks, public gardens, nature trails, safari parks, zoological gardens

As for the 'special public' buildings, there seem to be three main classes of these — work-places, educational and training establishments, and hotels. Of these the first two come within two of our main policy sectors, and are treated in the chapters which deal with these (4 and 6 respectively). As to hotels, it is important that they are not thought of merely in a touristic way. Already many disabled people need accessible hotel accommodation when they travel for public or private business purposes (as they do, for example, in their participation in the work of the United Nations or the European Community); as the promotion of independent living takes effect in the Community there will be an increasing demand for these facilities. The point is all the more important because abuse of the International Access Symbol is widespread; the availability of accessible hotel accommodation in major European cities is generally poor and quite often non-existent.

The number of those closely concerned in problems of access is much greater than one might at first sight suppose. They include:

- disabled people, their associations and (where appropriate) their families
- politicians and officials, at European, national, regional and local level, responsible for policies and programmes to construct or adapt buildings and facilities, and for urban planning
- architects, town planners and engineers; also students of these professions and their teachers
- workers in the health sector, the social services and voluntary organizations, concerned with promoting the independent living of disabled people in the open community
- producers of building materials and products and of technical appliances relevant to access problems.

It has also been possible to establish two basic operational principles, on which all national policies should be founded:

1. All new public buildings, facilities and environments should be designed so as to be accessible to all, including all disabled persons (the 'macro' approach); this should be ensured by means of national standards which respect European guidelines, and which have to be precisely followed if building licences are to be awarded.
2. Already existing public buildings and facilities which are not fully accessible will be adapted or replaced over time as resources permit; to promote this, national governments should lay down priorities and require the responsible regional or local authorities to present and make public their annual and mid-term plans in this regard.

The pace at which the Commission's policy initiative on access can be brought forward, and the strategy which will be used to achieve this, will evidently depend on the experience which the Commission has on the theme of transport and mobility. More recent progress will be described in the account of the Helios programme in Chapter 7.

HOUSING AND CARE IN THE HOME

The operation over a decade of the scheme of grants to support housing projects for disabled people has meant that the Commission has acquired a unique amount of evidence of good practice on this subject from all the countries of the Community. In order to bring together and make available the results of this experience, the Commission offered to a research centre in Bonn, the ABT Forschung, a subvention in support of a study which would survey the legislation and provision in the member states and prepare profiles of a considerable number of outstanding projects. At one time it was also hoped that this co-operation would produce a data base of contacts which might become a module of the Handynet information project, but this did not materialize.

Many of the most useful projects have concerned the provision of urban apartments fully adapted for people with severe physical disabilities. One of the first of these to be supported by the Commission was the project to establish 15 new and 57 adapted dwellings in the new town of Evry on the outskirts of Paris. Of the Belgian projects profiled in the ABT report, the most celebrated is perhaps the Cité de l'Amitié, where some 15 per cent of apartments in a large development were designed for physically disabled people. The Association nationale pour le logement des handicapés (ANLH, National Association for the Housing of Disabled People) responsible for the project was one of the pioneers too of the principle of 'care without institutionalization', by providing for assistance services.

The problem of the link between the provision of the assistance needed on the one hand and the possibility to live independently in adapted housing on the other was studied in 1988 by a member of the Helios experts team, Mary Kyriasopoulou, who had also been a member of the Interact team in the first action programme. Kyriasopoulou undertook an analysis of three approaches in different member states. The first was Crossroads Care, a British voluntary organization which employs 1,300 staff bringing supplementary care to some 11,000 people each year in 132 projects; the scheme is also being taken up in the Netherlands. One of the Crossroads' main merits is the flexibility with which it meets the needs of disabled people and their carers for regular, occasional or emergency supplementary care provision. Supported financially by the local statutory authority, it offers a typical example of 'indirect action'.

The other systems studied were the Fokus in the Netherlands (originating from Sweden) and the individual assistance method widespread in Denmark, including the locality of the Danish district project in the first action programme, the city of Aarhus. The disadvantage for Fokus clients is that they have to be grouped together in designated accommodation, whereas those benefiting from the Danish scheme can live in any accessible accommodation they choose. Indeed the so-called '48.3' scheme in Denmark, initiated in Aarhus, offers an exceptionally well funded and flexible system which enables disabled people committed to an active and independent life to employ their own assistants for as many hours as has been agreed with the local authority. Yet this is balanced by a very considerable difference of cost. Though Kyriasopoulou noted the difficulties in making direct comparisons, her figures of 72.21 ECUs per resident-day for Fokus and 175 ECUs for the Danish method cannot be disregarded.[6]

One of the most important projects more recently supported within the Commission's housing scheme is also in the Netherlands. Under the responsibility of the National Housing Council (NRW, Nationale Woningraad), it aims to generalize the 'macro' approach, by multiplying throughout the country the practice of renovating and building dwellings in such a way as to make them easily adaptable in case of disability at any time in the future, whether through a change of occupant or change in the occupant's personal condition. Also to an institute in the Netherlands, the Housing Research Institute, we entrusted the task of preparing the key policy study as a basis for the political initiative which it was planned should succeed that on access. Published in October 1987 under the title 'Towards Autonomy in Housing for the Handicapped', the report distinguishes between the existence of information (on adaptability, accessibility and aids) of which there is a great deal, and the dissemination and availability of this information which is quite inadequate. Moreover, the authors (A. de Jonge, J.H. Kroes and P.P.J. Houben) note that 'Architects and policy makers don't use the available knowledge; they don't seem to be aware of the fact that disabled people exist in society and need housing; therefore this subject should be part of their training and education'.

The report identifies seven key themes relevant to autonomy in housing for disabled people:

1. More awareness and attention in European policies concerning disability.
2. Better data to make the housing situation of disabled people more visible.
3. A clear definition of the entitlement of disabled people to housing and care.
4. National building codes ensuring the adaptability and accessibility of all new and renovated housing (the 'macro' approach), as more desirable than special housing for disabled people.
5. The improvement of the socio-economic position of disabled people, as more important than good housing and services.
6. A further stimulation of the process of deinstitutionalization by improving and extending care and services in the local community.
7. Especially at European level, the stimulation of new developments in housing . . . implying a more innovative development programme and better education of European architects and policy-makers.[7]

A great strength of the report is that it gives as much attention to the needs of people with mental handicaps and to users of mental health services as it does to those with physical disabilities. Not surprisingly, the Commission has encountered these needs within its scheme of housing grants, above all in the context of the operation of the philosophy of 'democratic psychiatry' in Italy, where in centres such as Trieste and Rieti important advances have been made in facing all the consequences of deinstitutionalization. In Ireland, too, important use has been made of the scheme in providing small-scale supported housing for mentally handicapped people, and a scheme of adapted housing linked to new communal facilities was launched in the framework of the Irish Midland Counties district project.

Among other notable housing developments within the district project network I can mention integrated housing for mentally handicapped people in Dordrecht and new housing for people entering the local community on the closure of wards in the main psychiatric hospital in Montpellier. Outside the district projects, another creative approach to the problems of mental illness has been adopted, for example, in the Bürgerinitiative für Soziale Rehabilitation in Marburg by means of the provision of short-stay homes with a carefully worked out programme of rehabilitation and prevention. Yet another innovation has been the training of ward-based staff to provide ongoing care to elderly psychiatric patients resettled in the community from the Springfield Hospital in south London.

The Commission's consultation workshop was not held until the second action programme (Helios), but in other respects the theme was as well prepared as the other two (transport and access) identified as essential to the promotion of independent living. As with them, we shall see in Chapter 7 how the Commission has been able to move its initiative forward within the Helios programme.

OTHER ASPECTS OF INDEPENDENT LIVING

Incomes and benefits

Any reader, and above all any disabled person, may well be tempted at this point to reflect that the Commission's programme of policy development to promote independent living is vitiated by a glaring omission: there has been no mention of the whole issue, complex yet fundamental, of incomes and benefits.

It is not that the Commission has never been engaged at all with these questions. In 1981 Brian Abel-Smith of the London School of Economics prepared on behalf of the Commission a report on the social security provision for longer-term disabled people in eight member states.[8] Moreover, in the context of the guaranteed rights of Community citizens moving from one country to another, the Commission is dealing with the social security claims of individuals, including disabled people, on a day-to-day basis.

There have been other initiatives which have contributed to an understanding of the topic at a European level. As early as 1978 the Disablement Income Group in the United Kingdom prepared a comparative report on 'Social Security and Disability'. In 1987 three experts produced a report for the World Rehabilitation Fund entitled 'Social Security Disability Programs: an International Perspective'.[9] It covers three member states of the Community (Netherlands, United Kingdom and the Federal Republic of Germany) together with Austria, Canada, Finland, Israel and Sweden. More recently still, the European Community secretariats of RI devoted one of their annual seminars supported by the European Commission to the theme 'Income, Benefits and Services: Public Social Protection for Handicapped Persons in the European Community Countries'. The seminar took place in Madrid in November 1988 and the results have been brought together in a report.

Some basis of knowledge of incomes and benefits on which a Commission policy proposal could be founded does therefore already exist. However, given the differences between the social security and other benefit schemes among the member states, and the frequency of substantial modifications of these, the topic remains a uniquely complicated and intractable one to tackle on a European scale. For this reason the Commission has decided, rightly or wrongly, to treat the themes of employment, environment and education first and to tackle at a later stage any remaining anomalies or injustices in the systems of supports and benefits, whether in cash or in kind.

The Commission made its view clear in its July 1987 proposal for the Helios programme: 'The Commission has also previously signalled its intention to choose the theme of Incomes and Benefits for the third in its series of policy initiatives. The Commission has started preparatory work in this field, not with the intention of establishing proposals which would cover all aspects of this enormous domain (an inappropriate and probably impracticable aim), but rather in order to identify those priority issues in respect of which Community action would be most justifiable and effective.' It is evident that, unless the Commission were to change its view as to the number of core staff needed to operate the programme, the chances that policy proposals in this area could be ready before the end of the century are not bright.

Sport

There are two quite different aspects of a full and independent life for disabled people which engaged the attention of the Commission quite early on and should therefore be mentioned here. The first of these is sport. Very soon in the first action programme the Commission found itself being asked to give moral and financial support for Olympics-style games for physically and for mentally disabled people. It was not long before we found that we had entered into a domain where it was certainly good for the Commission to be active but where it was impossible for us to establish priorities or distinguish the merits of the various organizations engaged. This difficulty was happily resolved when, as a result of negotiations undertaken by Louis Van Amelsvoort, we were able to establish a regular co-operation with the World Fund Sports for Disabled in Amsterdam. We could then award a yearly grant to the World Fund who in turn could distribute it among the various European events taking place each year, with all the essential advantages of an understanding of the scene and a representative democracy on which to base its decisions.

The arts

The other is the practice by disabled people of the arts, which has come to be known as 'creativity'. One of our first approaches on this was from Luc Boulangé, of the voluntary body Creativity and Mental Handicap (CREAHM, Créativité et handicap mental) in Liège. A special interest in the topic was shown by a member of the Interact experts team, Lieven Joniaux, and we decided to organize a seminar in Liège on the subject, to which district project teams were invited together with others known to be both active in the field and interested in European co-operation. One of Rehabilitation International's annual European Community seminars, organized with Commission financing by the Royal Association for Disability and Rehabilitation (RADAR) at Madingley Hall near Cambridge in 1985, also discussed this theme, together with that of sport for disabled people.

From these beginnings a proposal inevitably gathered force for the establishment of some European forum or association on creativity and disability, so that the quality and continuity of co-operation and of the exchange of experience could be assured. From my point of view there were good reasons for setting this up without delay. The American organization Very Special Arts International was beginning to become active in Europe, and, though I was quite happy for a co-operation with the Americans, I was determined that on our territory it should be on our terms, and that there was to be no question of American leadership if I could help it. By the end of the first action programme the first steps in setting up a European Association on Creativity for Disabled People had been taken. Important advances have been made in this field, and also in that of sport, within the Helios programme.

NOTES

1 For the idea of a European travel card for disabled people, see Chapter 7, pp. 155f.
2 For this Association, see Chapter 1, p. 8.
3 Considerable concern is being shown by the deaf community throughout Europe in the face of current proposals for harmonized regulations for the granting of driving licences in the Community, since these threaten to be discriminatory against deaf drivers.
4 A lack of solidarity between people with different disabilities is also perceptible on this subject.
5 For these Council of Europe documents, see References to Chapter 1.
6 Figures for the Crossroads scheme are not comparable as the services offered are dissimilar.
7 For the education of architects see the report of the 1987 Milan seminar (in References below).
8 Except France 'which was not able to participate in the study'.
9 The experts were Monroe Berkowitz and David Dean from the USA and Peter Mitchell from the UK.

REFERENCES

Note For European Commission documents on access and housing produced before 1981 see References to Chapter 1.

Community policy document

Parliament Resolution of 16 Sept. 1987 on the transport of elderly and handicapped persons (O.J. No. C 281/87 of 19 Oct. 1987).

Commission studies and conference reports

Claudine Van Lierde, *Transport for the Disabled: door-to-door transport systems*, ERICA, London and Brussels 1982. (DE, EN, ES, FR, IT, NL)
David Yelding, *Everyday Mobility for Disabled People*, ERICA, London 1985. (DE, EN, ES, FR, IT, NL)
J.R. Vorderegger and C.J. Verplanke, *Travel and the Disabled*, Consumentenbond, The Hague, 1985. (DA, DE, GR, EN, ES, FR, IT, NL, PT)
Bernard Vanderhaeghen, *A Mobility Card for Disabled People*, Commission staff paper, Brussels 1985. (EN, FR)
Claudine Van Lierde and Mary Kyriasopoulou, *Independent Living*, report of a district projects seminar held in Piacenza, Oct. 1986, Interact, Brussels 1987. (EN, FR)
Johan Galjaard, *Accessibility of Public Buildings for the Disabled*, Gehandicaptenraad, Utrecht 1986. (DE, EN, FR, NL)
Monique Stilmant (BECIPH), *Mobility and Handicap*, papers of a Commission workshop held in Brussels, Jan. 1987, Brussels 1987. (DE, EN, FR)
Wolfgang Steinle, *Housing Schemes and Related Services for Disabled People*, ABT Forschung, Bonn 1983–7. (EN)
Y. Koster-Dresse *et al.* (Gehandicaptenraad), *Access to Public Buildings and Facilities*, papers of a Commission workshop held in Utrecht, Sept.–Oct. 1987, Utrecht 1988. (EN, NL)
A. de Jonge, J.H. Kroes and P.P.J. Houben, *Towards Autonomy in Housing for the Handicapped*, Housing Research Institute (RIW) Delft 1987. (EN, NL)
E.A.H. Nolte (Nationale Woningraad, National Housing Council), *Building Adaptable Housing*, Almere 1988. (EN, NL).

E.A.H. Nolte, *Building Adaptable Housing*, report of a consultation workshop held at Nunspeet, May 1989, Almere 1990. (EN, NL)
Roy van Hek, *European Manual for an Accessible Built Environment*, Central Co-ordinating Committee for the Promotion of Accessibility, Utrecht 1990. (EN, NL)
Patrick Daunt, *Moving to Independence*, ERICA, London and Cambridge 1989. (EN, FR)

Documents of international organizations (selection)

United Nations

Barrier-free Design, Centre for Social and Humanitarian Affairs in co-operation with Rehabilitation International, Vienna 1974.
Designing with Care: adaptation of the built environment, United Nations, Habitat (Centre for Human Settlements) with Swedish International Development Authority, 1981.
Report of the Secretary-General (A/AC 197/14 of 13 May 1982) on an international card for disabled people; adopted by the Advisory Committee of the International Year on 12 July 1982.
Road Traffic, Consolidated Resolution, UN Economic and Social Council, Inland Transport Committee of the Economic Committee for Europe, Geneva 1985.

International Organization of Standardization

Needs of Disabled People in Buildings — design guidelines, Geneva 1982.

European Conference of Ministers of Transport (ECMT)

Resolution on reciprocal parking arrangements, Paris 1977.
First report of the Working Group on transport for disabled people, Paris 1985.
Developing Accessible Transport: the role of demand responsive services, Paris 1986.
Comparisons of Practice and Policy with Recommendations for Change, Paris 1986.
International Co-ordination and Standardization of Measures and Policies to Promote Mobility, Paris 1987.
Accessibility to Public Transport by Bus for Persons with Reduced Mobility, report of an international seminar, held at Dunkirk, 29 Nov. 1989, Paris 1990.
Review of Provisions and Standards for Journey Planning and Pedestrian Access, Paris 1990.
Transport for Disabled People — funding and administrative arrangements, Paris 1989–91.
Transport for people with mobility handicaps, draft Resolution on buses, trains and coaches, Paris 1990.

Council of Europe (Partial Agreement in the Social and Public Health Field)

Resolution on the use of an international symbol indicating special facilities for the disabled, Strasbourg 1972.
Design and Planning of Buildings to Provide Easier Access for Physically Disabled Persons, Strasbourg 1972.
Resolution on the provision of facilities for substantially handicapped people, Strasbourg 1975.
Ways of Facilitating Access to and Use of Means of Public Transport by Disabled People, Strasbourg 1975.

Resolution instituting a European Card for substantially handicapped persons, 1977.
Adaptation of Housing and Surrounding Areas to the Needs of Disabled People, Strasbourg 1977.

National reports with European/international content

Transport without Handicap: a priority for Europe, papers of a European seminar, Department of Transport, London 1986.
Mesures en faveur des personnes handicapées dans les différents moyens de transport et les différents pays [Measures in favour of disabled people in different forms of transport and different countries], 18th edn, Conseil national des transports (COLITRAH), Paris 1990 (updated yearly).

Reports of non-governmental organizations, etc.

Resolution of the General Assembly of Rehabilitation International on the use of the International Access Symbol (ISA), New York 1974.
International Commission on Technical Aids (ICTA) of Rehabilitation International, report of seminar on 'Access to the skies' held at Mulhouse, Mar. 1980, Bromma, Sweden 1980.
ICTA, report of seminar on 'Public surface transportation for disabled people' held at Mulhouse, Apr. 1982, Bromma, Sweden 1982.
Mary Winner, *Concessions for Older People in the European Community*, Age Concern, London 1985. (EN, summary in FR)
Access, Mobility, Housing and Leisure, European Community Regional Secretariat of the World Federation of the Deaf, Carlisle 1986. (EN, FR)
Monroe Berkowitz, David Dean and Peter Mitchell, *Social Security Disability Programs: An International Perspective*, Rehabilitation International and World Rehabilitation Fund, New York 1987.
Seminario europeo di architetti ed esperti nel settore delle barriere architettoniche [European seminar for architects and experts concerned with architectural barriers], report of a seminar held in Milan, Sept. 1987, Associazione italiana assistenza spastici (Italian Association for Assistance to People with Cerebral Palsy), Milan 1987.
Ingresos y Prestaciones: la protección social pública de las personas minusválidas en los paises de la Comunidad Europea [Incomes and Benefits: Public Social Protection for Handicapped Persons in European Community Countries], report (in English) of a seminar held in Madrid, 17–18 Nov. 1988, Madrid 1989.

Chapter 6

Education — Integration and Special Needs

THE EUROPEAN AND INTERNATIONAL BACKGROUND

Laying the foundations of Community policy

When we move from employment and the physical environment to education we are moving between worlds which are vastly different in one important respect. If I go to Heffers Bookshop in Cambridge and enquire about books on special education, the staff at the general information desk will know exactly where to direct me and I shall find a number of shelves devoted to that subject; if I were to ask for books about employing disabled people or establishing an environment accessible to them, it would be difficult to find anyone who could tell me whether there were in stock any books on those topics or if so where to find them. There are such things as academic chairs and departments of Special Education, but not, I think, of Special Employment or Special Environments.[1] This means that, since I am ultimately concerned in this book with policy, some thought will have to be given to the extent to which policy is or should be based on the mass of knowledge actually available.

Robust as this subject evidently is in academe, it has proved a frail one in the corridors of Brussels. At one time the use of such an expression as 'Community policy' was controlled there by the legalistic approach which held sway until the late 1980s. While it was correct therefore to speak of an 'agricultural policy', the idea of a Community 'policy' on any aspect of education, let alone education for special needs, was both undesirable and anyway impracticable. Looking back, it is easy to see how the public was losing patience with a political institution so inclined to insist on the policies it did not have and did not want to have. Nowadays, it is permissible to agree that policies may exist at different juridical levels and express themselves by means of different common activities. This seems to me obviously a very good thing both for the European Community and for 'delicate' sectors such as education — including the education of children with special needs.

In Chapter 1 I described how the Commission had tried unsuccessfully in the late 1970s to persuade the Council and Education Ministers to adopt a programme of co-operation on special-needs education, and how it was not until 1984 that the political barriers to this development came down. Even then it was on the initiative of the French delegation to the Community's Education Committee, and not that of the Commission, that it was agreed that something could be done. The 'something' certainly was extremely tentative, less a programme than the cautious exploration of the possibility of one. On the other hand, the content of the work was overtly political: the theme was to be, not special-needs education as such, but the integration of children with special needs into mainstream education.

The Commission's formal proposal was not presented to the Council until March 1987. It was based on two years of work with a Working Group on Educational Integration, made up of small delegations of one or two representatives for each member state, officials from Ministries of Education or professionals (who might be inspectors or academics) nominated by them. The Working Group gave birth in 1986 to a report on 'Progress (in the Member States) with regard to the Implementation of the Policy of Integrating Handicapped Children into Ordinary Schools'. Discussions in the Working Group also made it possible for the Commission to present its 1987 proposal with confidence that the member states would, on the whole, welcome it.

These discussions were friendly and positive but by no means easy. My own position as chairman was made difficult by the fact that I believed I knew and understood something of the subject, an impediment to good chairmanship from which I did not suffer when other aspects of disability were at issue. A working paper which I presented to the Group with not a little pride was treated with more politeness I dare say than foxhounds treat their quarry but much the same result. I was fed up at the time with reading, in OECD reports and elsewhere, generalities about disabled or handicapped children, without ever a word to differentiate one disability from another. It seemed to me that we needed to analyse some of the differences of need and attitude towards mental, sensory and other physical disabilities and spell out the implications. The members of the Group were horrified: this would be to fall into the sin of categorization, which would be discriminatory and contrary to the spirit of the times. My attempt to analyse the differences between the educational environments of primary and secondary schools, highlighting the difficulties I felt to exist for integration of children over the age of 13 or thereabouts, was also received with dismay and disavowal. Perhaps it was inevitable that technical considerations should give way to political ones.

The consequence of all this was that the ponderous analysis which I should have liked to accompany the Commission's proposal simply was not there. The programme document itself was merely introduced by a brief statement of the general conclusions of the Group's work, comprising the discovery of two policy factors common to all member states.

The first of these 'highlights the theme of the educational integration of children with disabilities as a policy issue of exceptional interest and importance in all member states, because it is situated at the intersection of two developing lines of policy, one directed at the social integration of disabled people, the other aiming to improve equality of opportunity in the (whole) educational systems'. I went on to elaborate this:

The clear trends in social policy are towards stressing the capacity rather than the incapacity of disabled people . . . and towards recognizing the reciprocity of integration, and therefore the responsibility of society and its institutions to adapt in order to eliminate handicapping effects once thought of as inevitable but now perceived as the consequence of institutional and environmental inflexibilities. The similarity of these concepts with those which are generally prominent when the need for educational change is discussed are evident enough.

I was confident that here at least was a point which really emerged from the Group's discussions and which therefore the Commission could honestly present as an outcome of its work.

The same is true of the second policy factor identified by the Commission in its proposal. If the educational integration of children with special needs is not only compatible with the whole contemporary process of educational reform but an integral element of it, then it must share with the larger endeavour its evolutionary character. 'Integration', I wrote, 'must not be forced through . . . it should be encouraged and fostered.' From its evolutionary nature it also followed that, although no theoretical limits should be set to progress in integration, it should be thought of as a process in an agreed direction, not as a goal to be achieved by a given date. A second consequence was that integrated and specialized systems must not be allowed to drift into mere opposition: 'It is hard to see how professional demoralisation and family confusion are to be avoided if the coexistence is not translated into active co-operation.'

The stress on an evolutionary approach, apart from any other merits it might have, was politically essential, given the massive divergence of general educational tradition and of practice in regard to integration among the member states, comprehending the extremes of both radical and conservative policy. The notion of the importance, in an integrating situation, of co-operation between the integrated and specialized systems was also something worth underlining at the start, and has proved fruitful. But I should want to be somewhat more cautious and pessimistic now — only some four years later — in what I should want to say about the general direction of educational reform, at least as far as the United Kingdom is concerned. The distinction between integration seen as a process or as a goal also needs reviewing in the light of further discussion at the European level. I shall return to these points towards the end of this chapter (p. 139).

Later in its 1987 proposal, in the section headed 'Implications for a Community Programme of Action', the Commission identified five key issues to be addressed; these appeared in the Council Conclusions of May the same year, which gave a rather cool blessing to the action programme proposal, as four 'research themes'.[2] Since these represent very clearly the Commission's view of the conceptual framework of the topic of educational integration at the point when the Community was about to address it for the first time, and since they will bring us closer to practical issues, it should be useful to list these four themes at this point. They are:

1. Special systems and integrated situations

- analysis of systems for co-ordinating decisions and developments within integrating policies
- analysis of available data on cost-effectiveness in connection with different forms of provision

- case studies illustrating positive modifications of the role of specialized teachers/establishments in integrating situations
- practical models of positive collaboration between educational and other local services (health, social services, etc.) in support of integration.

2. Teachers and parents

- comparison of working models, and of evaluation data where available concerning:

    insertion of a component in initial training courses aimed to prepare general teachers for integrated situations
    in-service training of general teachers for basic roles in integrated situations
    in-service training of general or special teachers for leading roles in integrated situations

- case studies of positive experience aimed at involving parents of handicapped and non-handicapped children (and other family members) positively in the integration process, whether by means of information, training, discussion with professionals or participation in decision-making.

3. The classroom

- case studies of effective curriculum development, with a particular reference to the needs of children with different disabilities, involving any or all of:

    modifications of syllabus objectives and content
    modifications of teaching methods and organization, notably those aimed to encourage individualization
    contributions of new technologies as aids to communication and learning.

4. A full school life

- physical aspects:

    case studies, including financial data, of successful construction or adaptation and equipment of school buildings to enable full access to school facilities for physically or sensorily disabled children
    the same, for establishments of higher education
    similar studies concerning adapted transport between home and school, covering all levels of education and different environments (urban and rural)

- social aspects:

    analysis of studies (and preparation of new studies if necessary) of the social experience of disabled children in mainstream situations, based to a significant extent on the testimony of such children themselves and of their peers.

It is worth observing that the heading of the fourth of these themes, 'A full school life', was in the first instance translated into French by the Commission's official translation service as if it meant 'full-time attendance at school'. Fortunately this curiosity was spotted in the Education Committee before the document came before the Ministers.

Some highlights of CERI's work

It is somewhat ironical that in 1987 I found myself writing a programme of Community co-operation on the integration of children with disabilities in ordinary schools, since when I was first working on special-needs education, in the late 1970s and early 1980s, I was opposed to this approach to the problem. In particular, I believed that CERI (the Centre for Educational Research and Innovation of the OECD in Paris) had made a mistake in choosing 'Integration in the School' as the first theme of its programme, then already under way, on 'The Education of the Handicapped Adolescent'. This was not because I was against integration in principle — far from it; I simply felt that one ought not to beg the question as to how far integration was the most important issue in the whole domain of special education, and also the most suitable one to explore in an international context.[3]

Certainly the early work of the OECD appeared to have a somewhat missionary flavour, and the influence of radical Italian integrationist philosophy looked to be paramount. In her 1979 report on 'Integration of Handicapped Children and Adolescents in Italy', Dr Yvonne Posternak describes how, in a locality in the province of Lecce, 'all the handicapped children of compulsory school age were brought to school in *pompa magna* with flags and music. It was a hard won victory.' With a triumphant conclusion, evidently.

Yet of course the OECD was right: the choice of a theme rather than merely a domain both raises the political temperature of the activity and gives the experts a direction which will take them quickly to the heart of the matter, the relation between theory and practice in real situations. The approach soon paid off in terms of insights: as early as 1981 the CERI secretariat was able to report the simple but vital discovery that 'the contributions to date have highlighted the differences between ordinary schools which are good situations for young people who have handicaps and those which are not'.

I shall not attempt here any overview of CERI's substantial and still continuing work in this field; it would not be practicable, and besides CERI produces its own syntheses and conclusions. But, before summarizing the lessons from the CERI programme as they presented themselves to us when we were preparing our 1987 proposal, I want to draw attention, as an example of the quality of the CERI work, to the 1981 paper of the French inspector Aimé Labregère on 'Changes in the Educational Systems Favouring Integration'. There are a number of insights in Labregère's paper that make it in my judgement of outstanding interest. I am impressed by the way in which the attitudinal changes which empower the integration 'movement' are set by Labregère in a socio-economic context:

> Once a society becomes 'post-industrial' and begins to question the idea of unlimited growth of production, yield and profitability, it rediscovers a number of human values, represented fairly well in the concepts of quality of life, coexistence, right to differ, respect for the environment and life style . . . The focus . . . is on the quality of the relationships between people.

In an important section headed 'Changes that would be required in the school system in order to integrate the handicapped', Labregère tackles directly the problems both of functional and pedagogic integration and of social integration in respect to different kinds and degrees of disability, an approach not often enough taken in international work, according to my view. After this and other practical considerations, Labregère returns to conclusions which I believe are central to all our problems in this domain and not often enough faced up to, at least in international activities:

> Community demand is essentially a vehicle for the social aspirations of the individual members of the group. So emulation, competition, forcing the pace and exclusion become practically inevitable . . . like it or not, the integration of the handicapped into the normal environment, if it is not limited to the intelligent physically handicapped, poses problems whose solution will not be found only in modifications to school architecture or traditional pedagogy. It would be a pity to let too simplistic a view of the problem block the avenues that might be opened up by current thinking on this question.

In spite of these reflections, an overall impression was given by the promotional literature of the time that school integration should and could be carried through with relative speed at least in the developed countries of the West, and some of the voices heard took on a certain doctrinaire if not triumphalist character. Not surprisingly, and perhaps as an inevitable reaction, defenders of well-resourced systems and establishments, where these existed, could be perceived to be entrenching themselves against this assault.

But by 1986, opinions appeared to be less polarized. At the ministerial conference marking the end of a phase of their project which CERI organized in Paris in December 1986 enlightened pragmatism was more the keynote. Integration could be expected to go ahead everywhere, but not necessarily with great rapidity; the mistakes made by some of the pioneers should not be repeated; the cost of simply running integrated and segregated systems in parallel needed to be watched. Simplistic views were further discouraged by the powerful Swedish delegation which, after taking the lead in reasserting the rightness of radical mainstreaming, in proclaiming the importance of individualization and in rejecting categorization, startled the Conference with the news that in Sweden it was policy that profoundly deaf children should be educated in special schools, not in the mainstream.

The climate implied in Paris at that time was a good one in which to launch a European Community initiative, since it promised that, rather than the exchange of slogans fired from behind prepared positions, there could be a genuine exchange of experience, with the possibility of applying to new developments the lessons learnt elsewhere in the recent past. I shall now give some examples of that experience as it has begun to emerge in the early days of the Commission's work in this field.

APPROACHES IN AND OF MEMBER STATES

It is not my intention here to give a systematic account of developments in the integration of children with special needs in the mainstream of the school systems of all the European Community countries, with comparable sections devoted to each. As far as the official view is concerned, this exists already in the Commission's 1986 Progress Report. For an independent treatment worth reading a whole book would be needed to cover the ground in anything like a systematic way. All I aim to do here is to illustrate the ways in which integration is being tackled in the European Community in such a way as to highlight both the issues which are of common concern and the differences among the approaches which are being adopted. I have called this section 'Approaches *in* and *of* member states' because for some countries (the United Kingdom and Germany), where the educational structure is broadly speaking decentralized, it is more revealing to emphasize particular projects and initiatives ('approaches *in* the country'), whereas for others it is more appropriate to stress rather the total intention and effect of national policy ('approaches *of* the country').

Nor shall I refer at any length to all the countries of the Community; so 'approaches of member states', not 'of *the* member states'. It does not appear that integration is yet far enough advanced in Luxembourg, Greece or Portugal for significant illustrations of the process to be drawn from those countries, though of Greece and Portugal I shall have before the end of this chapter something specific to say that I believe is important. I also find it difficult to exemplify developments in Belgium or Ireland in a way that would help to illuminate the theme. I ask myself whether confessional conservatism has not acted as a brake on governmental initiatives in these countries; certainly the complexity of the educational structure in Belgium does not facilitate concerted reform even when that is official policy. In case these omissions from my account are taken to be judgemental, let me add that a more purposeful approach to integration is now perceptible in Ireland, and pay tribute to the outstanding contribution to the Commission's Working Group on Educational Integration made by the inspector representing the Flemish community in Belgium, Auguste Dens, and to the innovative work of Jean-Jacques Detraux.

I shall group these notices of national approaches under four heads:

- radical integration: Italy, Denmark
- the gradualist approach: France, United Kingdom
- the conservative tradition: Germany, Netherlands
- new departures: Spain.

Radical integration

Italy

For the development of a concerted and radical policy of school integration, Italy has enjoyed a number of advantages. For one thing, separate special education was not well developed: the effort to establish special provision only predates the initiation of integration by less than a decade. This has meant that in practice not a great deal has had to be done in the way of rapid or gradual running down of a system to be superseded, with all the complexities of changing roles and relationships, and of resource transfer, which that entails; it also means that there is not a substantial, well-organized core of sponsors, administrators, professionals and parents with a vested interest in preserving the status quo.

Secondly, the Italian system is, relatively speaking, not only centralized, but also uniform; virtually all the establishments of basic education are run by the state, so that the influence of local authority, and of confessional or other private ideology, is less prominent than in many other cultures. Thirdly, there was already a movement with a coherent philosophy to which educational mainstreaming could adhere, the attack on the psychiatric hospitals and other residential institutions mounted by Basaglia in the 1960s. This enabled the Italians to seize and maintain a simple but powerful basic position: the need for radical social integration is accepted, and this implies radical educational integration, since integration in society and segregation in school are mutually contradictory.

The Italian law of 1971 established school integration as a right for all children with disabilities, a right based on the guarantee of equal *status* to all citizens under the constitution. In 1975 it was clarified that severity of disability could not in itself justify exclusion. The reports of CERI have made it clear how much of the implementation of the law depended on the initiatives of local multidisciplinary groups of professionals offering the guarantee of their technical and moral support to the developments which they encouraged. Yet it may be that standards were not always well guarded in these early days, later to be known as the period of 'integrazione selvaggia' (wild integration). In particular the provision of supporting personnel was irregular.

It was further legislation in 1977 which addressed these problems and established the pattern that has since characterized the Italian approach to integration. An integrated class should not number more than 20 pupils or include more than two children with special needs, and a support teacher must be allocated to it. I shall return to examine this class-by-class strategy for solving the problem of progressive implementation of a total policy later in this chapter.

Moreover at the same time the system of 'giudizi' (precise marks, requiring an overall annual 60 per cent if the child is to be promoted to the next year group) was to be superseded by profiles — probably the most dramatic single example on record of the adaptation of an established mainstream system in favour of those whom it disadvantaged.

Since then further progress has been made. Partly at least as a direct result of the process of mainstreaming, all primary classes are said now to number no more than 20 children — an effect no doubt made possible by the combination of falling rolls and the protected employment of teachers deriving from their status as civil servants. At a time when 28,000 support teachers were in post, there was calculated to be an average of one for every four integrated children; there are now 35,000. It is claimed too that much headway has been made in overcoming what was one of the identified weaknesses of the process, the preparation of the support teachers — a fundamental problem, given that there was virtually no body of teachers trained for special needs on which to draw. All support teachers operating at primary level have now received some training, and this provision is being extended to the 'scuola media'.

Another development with positive implications for integration was the setting up of Local Health Units (USLs, Unità sanitarie locali) throughout the country in 1978. Co-operation between these relatively small but by no means powerless bodies, the local authorities (with responsibilities for transport and school buildings) and the schools themselves ensures the participation of the local democracy in what could otherwise be an over-centralized system. In particular, the USLs (in Modena for instance) have been able to ensure the provision of sophisticated technological support for severely motor disabled children working in ordinary schools, another area of previous weakness about which there seems to be little that the education service itself can do.

It would be wrong to suggest that there have not been serious problems in Italian integration, or to deny that these have occurred in the generalization period which has succeeded the measures of 1977 as well as in the 'wild' period which came before it. Yet my impression is that the reform is emerging from this second phase of backlash. At the CERI conference of December 1986 the Italians did not seem to have as much to say as one would have expected; now there is I believe some revival of confidence. There is no going back on the original conception that integration means 100 per cent; no alternative aim has effectively presented itself. The emphasis now is on quality, not whether to integrate but how. The willingness, or perhaps one should say the necessity, in Italy to ensure that the children benefit from demographic decline in terms of better staffing levels is a considerable resource in support of this endeavour. But there will be a need for other innovations too, I suspect, and the future of such ideas as district support centres for children with severe disabilities may be crucial.[4]

Denmark

At first sight it might seem paradoxical that Denmark and Italy are the two member states which have gone furthest in the direction of mainstreaming, seeing that these two countries are, one might say, at the extremes of the cultural traditions represented in the Community. Yet they have one thing at least in common, enough in my view to explain their similar levels of achievement in mainstreaming: both Italy and Denmark operate what are substantially monolithic secular systems of basic education. And there is another common factor in support of this: they are the two countries which have extended universal comprehensive education beyond the age of 11, Italy in the 'scuola media' up to 13 and Denmark in the folkschool until 16.

Naturally there are differences too. The Danes have been able to bring to integration certain advantages denied the Italians. For one thing, Italy has brought forward its integrating initiative more or less in isolation within the Mediterranean region; the Danish reform has fitted comfortably into the much wider context of social and educational progress throughout the Scandinavian and indeed Nordic countries. Danish folkschools too have always enjoyed relatively favourable staffing levels, and the Danes have had far greater possibilities to provide advanced technical aids in support of children coping in mainstream classes with disabilities of sight, hearing, speech, or movement and control. New information technology as a support for the education of children with learning difficulties is also well developed in Denmark, as reported for example from Odense in Jørgen Hansen's study for the European Commission. The positive effects of that extension of education to 16 in the strongly class-based folkschool also comes in here.

On the other hand the Danes, unlike the Italians, have had to grapple with the problem of running down, as a consequence of integration, a developed system of special schools. Nor have they been able to dispose of the same abundance of relatively inexpensive personnel in order to support the mainstream teacher in the classroom as have the Italians. It may be doubted also whether the integration of children with mental handicaps is not more difficult from a cultural point of view in Denmark than in Italy. As to the rigidities resulting from central control of curriculum and textbooks it is not possible to make any accurate comparison; all that can be said is that in both countries there is awareness of this as an impediment to successful integration.

A few years ago there was the impression that mainstreaming in Denmark had about run its course. Achievement by 1984 was already impressive. Of all children in the folkschool 14 per cent were receiving an education adapted to their special needs. Of these, 88 per cent (12.5 per cent of the whole folkschool population) were fully integrated into the ordinary school; 6.2 per cent were in special classes within or attached to ordinary schools; only 5.7 per cent were in separate provision, representing less than 0.8 per cent of the whole folkschool population. More recently however the official representatives of the Danish Ministry are talking of a new initiative, aimed at the total elimination of segregated education by the end of the century.

I believe that we should regard the Danish achievement in school integration as a precious contribution to the improvement of the quality of life for disabled people throughout the Community. We could summarize its sources of strength as these:

- The nature of the folkschool: its ethos for one thing, but also the continuity of its class- (or form-)based structure; since the form teacher typically stays with his or her group of children throughout their school career, there are opportunities here for the development of an understanding of the children and contact with families which cannot fail to be a vital support to successful integration.
- The quality and availability of higher professional support, above all that of the school psychological service, but also therapy including speech therapy.
- The involvement of parents, and children themselves, in deciding the right special programme for each child, combined with the flexibility to include in this temporary or part-time separate provision where this is needed.
- Good staffing levels and relatively ample provision of technical aids.

The determination of the Danish authorities to press on with integration so as to embrace the last few per cent still in separate provision within the next decade means that the Danish experience in the next few years will be of exceptional importance to all the other member states. In particular, it will be interesting to see how the Danes adapt their school life in order to receive those children whose severe disabilities are aggravated by other social, cultural or ethnic difficulties; already in their 1986 contribution to the Commission's Progress Report, the authorities in Copenhagen were admitting to concern about the relation between radical integration and the prescribed curriculum. Another uncertainty is how in the end the total aim is reconciled with the principle of parental choice so fundamental to Danish educational philosophy, since that principle must presumably include the freedom to insist on separate schooling for one's child. I imagine that there is at work here a robust Scandinavian faith in the power of reason: virtually no parents will want separate provision because virtually all parents will see that integration works and is better. It will none the less be interesting to see what actually happens.

The Community is indeed fortunate in having two exemplary countries in respect of integration which are so different from each other in other ways. It is an enormous advantage to be able to start with a living refutation of any suggestion that main-streaming can only work given one particular cultural framework — or given one high level of material resources available to the schools. It is evident that Denmark and Italy respectively are excellent potential models for the development of main-streaming in countries whose educational systems are relatively well and relatively poorly provided for in material terms.

The examples are all the more valuable both because in both countries the success-ful integration of children with severe disabilities is well attested and because both countries are determined to carry integration through to completion. Yet we must remember that this aspiration applies only to the primary and junior secondary levels. Quite as important in the future will be successful extension of integration into the upper secondary level, about which up till now one hears much less said.

The gradual approach

France

In France, although the principle of 'minimum exclusion' from normal education was pronounced as early as 1975, the effects of this were largely of an experimental kind, and limited to children with motor or sensory disabilities. Nor was France a prominent participant in the first phases of the CERI programme. A most significant step was the publication of an interim plan in 1981, and of circulars in the two succeeding years which laid down the principles of integration and established practical guidelines for their implementation. It is in this context that we can understand the French 1984 initiative in the Education Committee in Brussels which led to the first agreement that the Commission should address the topic of the educational integration of children with special needs.

From early on the French approach to integration has exhibited some special characteristics. The first and most important of these has been the insistence that mainstreaming should not be seen as merely compatible with the general trend of educational reform but as an integral part of it. The initiatives in the early 1980s were aimed not only at the need to desegregate children with long-term specific disabilities but also to reduce the failures among a much larger number of children, who for a wide variety of reasons were experiencing difficulty at school. There are important similarities here, as we shall see, with the British approach, notably as this is formulated in the Warnock Report. The concept is therefore of a single comprehensive objective of personal achievement and a single fight for equality, of which the promotion of mainstreaming is one element.

Secondly, the French approach though positive and active — as came out clearly enough in the CERI conference of 1987 — is relativist and gradualist. All changes of the child's situation which are from a relatively segregated personal programme to a comparatively normal one are counted as acts of integration; so much for relativism, a logically impeccable position but one which just might be misused as an excuse for unduly slow progress. Integration, again, is described as one of a number of means towards the full development of the child, and not therefore an end in itself; this idea too sounds incontrovertible at first hearing, but may need more careful exploration, since a thing may be both a means and an end at the same time. Moreover, a distinction is made between the 'expressed aim' of integrating all children, regardless of the nature or severity of their disability, and the individual attention which must be given to the educational need of each single disabled child. For the latter purpose there must be flexibility of provision, including the possibility of separate education for a greater or lesser period of time; and that in turn implies that the special and integrated systems must be seen as complementary to each other for the foreseeable future.

The drawing of this somewhat cautious conclusion from the principle of individualization may well be the result of the third French characteristic, which is the continuing influence of the health sector as a powerful factor in determining both the programmes of individual children and the general trend of policy. There are those who would question how far integration will be able to proceed as long as that influence is maintained.

The United Kingdom

The education of children with special needs is an area in which it could be said that the United Kingdom has established a framework of policy, not a thing for which the British educational system is well known. The official Warnock Report of 1978 on Special Educational Needs has been influential in and beyond the United Kingdom in a number of ways. It has done much to popularize the use of the expressions 'children with special needs' and 'education for special needs' in preference to 'handicapped children' and 'special education'. It has done a great deal to eliminate the evil effects of categorizing individual children — even though to my mind this has led to some confused opinion about the use of categories in general. Levels of need, the Report insists, should be seen as a continuum. Moreover action in response to special needs should take into account all the 20 per cent of children who have significant difficulties at some time in their school career, not merely the 2 per cent traditionally identified as in need of 'special education'; we have seen how closely this corresponds to the French view.

Perhaps the most important of all the insights in the Report is the recognition that school failure may be caused as much by faults in the curriculum or the ways in which it is delivered as by the limitations resulting from the child's own disability. There is no need to emphasize the importance of this explicit application to the education of children of the principle so fundamental to progress in response to adult disability, that handicap is not a necessary consequence of the disability itself but results from the interaction of the disability and an insensitive environment. For schools the perception that difficulty in learning is not simply 'the child's fault' is not short of revolutionary, with positive implications for all children, but especially for the 20 per cent for whom difficulty is, at one time or another, a serious problem, and above all for those whose special need, albeit specific, is of long duration. Again we see here a close affinity with the French approach.

The Warnock Report is cautious however on the subject of integration: the committee responsible for the Report was 'entirely convinced' of the continuing need for special provision, for the benefit of those with severe disabilities of whatever kind.

Yet even in the mid 1970s it should have been clear that severe visual disability (total blindness, in other words) is certainly not in itself incompatible with integration; since then it has been shown that the same can be said of disabilities of movement or control. With severe or profound mental handicap, severe behaviour problems and (for quite different sorts of reasons, of course) prelingual deafness the case is not nearly so clear; but these vital distinctions get lost from the debate if hostility to the use of categories becomes too rigid. At all events, although the Report avows its belief in integration 'in principle', this does not amount to much in the light of the conviction just referred to. Such support for coexistence would suit very well the British authorities, who are traditionally drawn to decentralization of responsibility to local authorities and so would be more than content to accept that nothing which a local authority did not do in respect to integration could be proved to be wrong.

The British government did however follow up the Warnock Report with legislation, and did this relatively quickly. The 1981 Act is a milestone in that it lays an obligation on all schools to identify all those of their children who have special needs and to provide for those needs; it also establishes the rights of parents to be involved in assessment, to be informed of decisions and to appeal against them. This has certainly had beneficial effects for the 20 per cent, and at least laid the foundations on which the integration of the 2 per cent could be built. But whereas required procedures for assessment and follow-up exist, for integration there are only principles which should be respected in deciding whether a child should be integrated or not. Nor are there to be any earmarked national resources or national guidelines, let alone regulations, concerning resources. This, from an integrationist point of view, is evidently highly unsatisfactory; there are very often going to be some arguments at least against integrating a particular child — indeed in certain settings against integrating any children at all. Unless there is a national strategy for promoting mainstreaming, incorporating not merely principles but also common recommended procedures, and backed up by guidelines (at least) on the resources needed, integration is unlikely ever to be more than a piecemeal affair. Resources can after all be *required* to go to a school or to a class which is launching itself on an integration programme, or as in the United States they can accompany the child moving from special to mainstream provision. If none of these things is laid down there cannot be said to be a national plan at all.

This need surprise no one, since the idea of a national plan has been contrary to the British tradition, let alone one that includes resource implications. Nor is it surprising that since 1981 government has shown little interest in the encouragement of mainstreaming or in monitoring its progress. In consequence it is only to be expected that progress in integration in the United Kingdom has been disappointingly slow, especially as far as concerns children with moderate or severe learning difficulties or behaviour problems.

More recently the prospects for mainstreaming in the United Kingdom have got worse. The 1988 Education Act represents a break with tradition since by means of it central government has acted to take away much of the autonomy of Local Education Authorities, allocating more power to the individual school communities but also imposing more demands on the system from the centre. It is the nature of these demands which — though it is too early to be sure of their total effect — looks at first sight to constitute a threat to the progress of integration. In my view the imposition of a common core curriculum should be entirely beneficial to all children including those at the extremes of intellectual capacity, even though there will inevitably be much room for disagreement about its design; it is after all what many of us working in the comprehensive movement were campaigning for twenty years ago. The combination of this with nationally determined attainment targets and periodical external testing is on the other hand a very different matter. Either the national curriculum is to be 'disapplied' to children with serious learning difficulties (from whatever cause) working in ordinary schools, which would not only be highly discriminatory in principle but would remove in practice one of the main reasons for wanting to move a child from a special school to the mainstream in the first place, or the published performance of those schools will be affected by the difficulty such children will experience in reaching attainment targets which have not been defined with their special needs in mind.[5] Had one set out to devise disincentives to integration it would have been hard to do better than that.

There are two consequences of this to be mentioned here. The first is that, while I have twice had occasion to refer to similarities between the United Kingdom and France, we have here come across a major divergence. The notion that the integration of children with disabilities into the mainstream is not only compatible with the general trend of educational reform for all children but actually an integral part of that reform can no longer be said to apply to the United Kingdom. Secondly, it is as certain as can be that for positive evidence of British integration in the foreseeable future we shall have to look for isolated instances of innovation or at best the achievement of particular Local Education Authorities who have made an early commitment to integration and have established a strategy for implementing it. Since this brings us back to what has for long been one of the most precious strengths of the British educational system, the capacity for local, even school-based and indeed teacher-based innovation, let us cheer ourselves up with a mention of one or two examples out of the many which could qualify.

My first two examples concern the problematic area of the education of deaf children. At Angmering in West Sussex the method of incorporating a specialized unit for deaf and physically disabled children within a mainstream primary school is well established, and it can fairly be said that the children have all the benefits of special and mainstream provision. While in the unit the deaf children, for example, have the services they need of specialized teaching and specialized facilities, yet individual timetabling, which can be frequently reviewed, allows them to benefit from the maximum of functional integration appropriate to their individual development. Of great interest here is the social model, including the opportunity offered for every deaf child to associate and communicate with other children who are deaf. This model of a 'community within a community' can be seen to offer a wholly appropriate preparation for adult life as a deaf person integrated in the open society but yet retaining a special place in the community of deaf people.

My second example is the programme, covering a wider range of both disability and age than at Angmering, for the education of partially hearing and deaf children in the city of Leeds. The service provides flexible and supported integrated education for the pupils concerned, and does so systematically throughout the city. This is done by establishing a network of 'resourced' schools at all three educational levels in all four zones of the city. Flexibility is ensured by the possibility to vary the extent to which the children with special needs spend time within mainstream classes, or within special groups within the resourced school where the service of specialist staff is more intensive and the hearing-impaired children can support each other. The operational philosophy, without which the development could not have taken place, is the promotion of total communication. The objective is to provide a service which is 'needs-based' and comprehensive; in other words the administrators responsible are operating a demanding consumer model rather than a convenient bureaucratic one. Other features of particular interest include the emergence of educational interpreters and prelingually deaf instructors as important team members; the emphasis on the consultation of parents and the deaf community and on the in-service training of staff; and the setting of the whole endeavour within a total 'equal-value' policy adopted by the education authority, embracing also multicultural education.

My last example is the global policy for the integration of children with special needs into ordinary schools which is operated by the county of Oxfordshire, and which has been well reported by Mike Burnham, the Senior Adviser for Special Needs Education, and his colleagues. Here the key strategy is the development of links between special and ordinary (secondary as well as primary) schools, links that are genuinely operational and committed to the progressive development of integration. This is backed up by the provision of an Education Centre (Bishopswood) which can accommodate 60 children between the ages of two and 16 for a period of their school lives, with a view to integration in the child's local primary or secondary school or in the Centre's own classes in neighbouring schools at both levels. Integration throughout the county respects the individual needs and possibilities of children and the wishes of parents and is flexibly implemented so as to allow individual programmes of total or partial mainstreaming. In this way careful headway has been made with the integration of children with severe learning difficulties, and with autistic and maladjusted children. On the side of physical disability, the Ormerod School had integrated 100 children in eight years by 1988, including 30 children in six years into the local secondary comprehensive school — one it should be noted where radical mixed-ability teaching was in force.

These most encouraging examples make it all the more disappointing that there is no purposeful support for integration at the national level, and that recent manifestations of national purpose in regard to education are more likely to impede integration than promote it. And this is in spite of the results, very positive to integration, of the research conducted by Seamus Hegarty and his colleagues in the National Foundation for Educational Research.

The conservative tradition

Germany

Although the thrust of this book, in line with developing Community policy, is unequivocally in favour of mainstreaming, I do not mean to imply that 'conservative' is used here in a merely pejorative sense. Allegiance to special schools in Germany reflects above all a recognition of the generous and purposeful investment, personal as well as material, that has been afforded to separate provision there and of the high standards which have often been achieved by those means. Naturally enough, therefore, the German contribution to the Commission's 1986 Progress Report on integration, while not negative in what it has to say about mainstreaming, is extremely cautious; indeed at secondary level it is implied that the integration of children with disabilities other than physical or sensory ones is not contemplated. As well as warning against change that does not guarantee improvement, the report quite correctly points out that the mainstream system was simply not designed with integration in view:

> It is impossible to make comprehensive changes in the existing separate types of schools while leaving the structural parameters for the education system as a whole unchanged. Rather, it is necessary to rethink the overall concept and framework of existing educational provision and initiate changes from that angle.

A clear implication of this is also spelled out in the report: there is an organic link between integration and the replacement of the traditional mainstream secondary structure of Hauptschule, Realschule and Gymnasium by the comprehensive school (Gesamtschule). The point is forcibly put: 'Consideration should be given to whether the setting up of individual types of special school had not been rendered invalid by the setting up of the comprehensive school.' But there is a further implication here, the likelihood that integration will become politicized along the same lines as comprehensivization has been, and that we shall have to look for significant mainstreaming developments, if anywhere, in those less politically conservative Länder where comprehensive secondary education has taken root — the three city states (Berlin, Hamburg and Bremen) together with North Rhine–Westphalia and Hesse.

It would of course be unreasonable to expect in Germany, where the fundamental responsibility rests with the Federal States, the same kind of nationally concerted approach to as difficult a subject as integration as we find in Italy or Denmark. As in the United Kingdom therefore, it is particular projects in particular places which are of chief interest when we are looking for examples of good practice.

Rudolf Schindele reported a valuable development in the field of visual disability in the first number of Seamus Hegarty's *European Journal of Special Needs Education*. He demonstrated clearly how a certain complexity of framework can make it possible to design models in which flexibility of school programmes in response to individual need is inherent. Having argued in favour of retaining separate provision for the most difficult cases (where there are severe retardation, multiple handicaps or acute behaviour problems; where previous educational experience or family background is exceptionally poor) Schindele identified the consultancy, itinerant and resource providing roles which specialized centres can provide in support of integrating programmes. To exemplify this model in operation he described the work of the School for Partially Seeing and Severely Visually Handicapped Pupils of the Land of Schleswig-Holstein, whose services include advice to children and parents, collaborative pre-school provision, educational and vocational guidance, specialized support to visually disabled children in regular or other specialized schools, discussion and training sessions for parents and in-service courses for regular teachers. Schindele also stressed the double benefit which comes from putting reflection, resources and drive behind the relationship between special and integrated provision: as well as offering the possibility of supported mainstreaming to those previously in special schools or otherwise destined for them, the expanding dynamic role of the specialists ensures much-needed support to many children in regular schools who before had none at all.

My second example is of the planned approach to radical integration of children with special needs into regular primary schools in the city state of Hamburg. The project is called an experiment, but has all the appearance of a phased yet ongoing development, school integration being seen as a goal rather than as a limited process. There can be little doubt that the favourable context supplied by an all-through comprehensive system following the primary school has been and will remain a supporting force here.

The initial strategy in Hamburg has been, in effect, to follow the Italian model. 'Integrated classes', of which as I write there are so far 47 in 15 primary schools, are identified and launched under strict rules as to class size, number of special-needs children in the class and the amount of additional staff support which is mandatory. There is also considerable stress given to achieving a consensus of parents concerned before an integrated class is opened. Already those responsible for the project corroborate the Italian experience that severity of disability is not in itself the chief cause of difficulties where these occur. A big difference between the two countries, for obvious reasons, is that in Germany the support teachers are fully qualified professionals from the special sector. The need therefore is for adaptation and retraining rather than for the initial training of a new class of professional as in Italy.

As the project proceeds, a more sophisticated notion is developing of the needs of a designated integrated class than can be met simply by additional personnel in the normal classroom. Increasingly there will be the provision of an 'integration kit', offering staff resources which can be exploited in a variety of ways (for example in the running of special learning groups in the class), as well as additional resources of aids and equipment. Here we can see a development strategy whose potential is only limited by the availability of resources.

The third example shows a German initiative in launching international co-operation between professionals in the Community. The author of this co-operation was W. Schumann of the Protestant College for Social Studies in Reutlingen, who set up links with the health, education and social services in Arezzo in Tuscany. Although there was at the time no officially adopted Community programme on special needs education, I was able to offer some financial support to the project in view of the particular significance of collaboration in this field between Italy and Germany. By 1986 a full exchange programme was launched, involving also now the Royal College for Teacher Training in Copenhagen and the London University Institute of Education. The exchange activities included public symposia, and the project became a strong source of support for local integration policy development especially in Reutlingen. Since 1989 the project has laid more stress on research, focusing on the quality of life of the children at risk.

The Netherlands

These examples are enough to demonstrate that, for all the official hesitations, Germany can already offer experiences of great interest to professionals and parents in other Community countries.[6] It is not yet possible to say that of the Netherlands, where a special school system has been developed which is, if anything, even more elaborate than that of the Federal Republic. There are fourteen different kinds of Dutch special school. Over 32,000 mentally handicapped children are taught in 332 schools specializing in their needs (MLK). There are also 322 schools for children with learning and behavioural difficulties serving over 40,000 pupils — more than half of whom, it must however be added, do not spend the whole of their school career in special provision. Nearly 75 per cent of the special schools are privately run, and of these the great majority are confessional. Since moreover these all enjoy the security of 100 per cent state funding, it would be a reasonable hypothesis that there is here a massive and powerful conservative force.

Current national policy for the education of children with special needs is incorporated in the 1985 Special Education Interim Act which encourages schools to adopt a developmental approach towards the education of children with special needs. The Act also encourages integration, and the Primary School Act of the same year promotes the ability of ordinary schools at that level to cater for a wide range of educational needs. The experience gained as a result of the Interim Act will form the basis of a new Act to be introduced in 1995. Evidently the Dutch are approaching reform as Hannibal's elephants crossed the river Rhône — *pedetemptim*, feeling their way with their feet.

It is on the other hand agreed that a will to make integrating progress exists, and that there is dissatisfaction among parents with the traditional structures. In this context the Dutch response to the setting up of a European Community programme specifically concerned with integration has been less reluctant than might have been expected, and there is official support for research in the University of Groningen which is looking at integration experience in other countries. It cannot be said however that evidence of much progress as yet is easy to find. In the city of Rotterdam, for example, although 12 per cent of children assessed as 'handicapped' are said to be integrated, there are 51 special schools as against 200 regular ones; this is said moreover to represent a lower proportion of special provision than in the country as a whole. Moreover, even in this 'City of Education' it was difficult to find examples of co-operation between special and regular schools. In principle, this should be one of the kinds of development most of all to be looked for under the Interim Act, yet the barriers seem to be not only practical but actually legal as well.

Yet I can end on a much more positive note. This is the setting up in six districts (two in east Gelderland, one each in Flevoland, North Holland, Friesland and Zeeland) of a network, known as the ZON project, whose aim is actively to promote mainstreaming and which it is intended to extend throughout the country. Certainly the aims are limited — the objective is merely to reduce the number of children in special schools with nothing like the Italian or Danish vision; but that is only to be expected. The project has two real sources of strength. One is what the French would call a philosophy, the promotion at the educational grass roots of affective as well as cognitive objectives, based on the work of L.M. Stevens of the University of Utrecht. The other is the existence in the project of a development strategy, in this case the creation of co-operative local clusters of special and regular schools.

It is appropriate to end this section in an encouraging way, as it will undo any impression that I may have given that our response to the situation in the Netherlands should be dismissive. There are sound and entirely respectable reasons for the fact that integration is not yet well developed there. Besides, for the sake of the solidarity within the Community's co-operative programme, it is excellent to have as one member a country which is economically favoured and generally progressive but not in the forefront of the development in question, since this works against the stereotyping of the haves and the have-nots.

A new departure — Spain

I am calling the developments in Spain 'a new departure' because the introduction of the key legislation which underlies them is relatively recent yet they exhibit a powerful sense of national purpose. Giving effect to the educational aspects of the Law of 1982 on the Social Integration of Disabled People led to the adoption in 1985 of a Royal Decree on the organization of the education of children with special needs. The result bears testimony to the advantages which sometimes accrue to the relative latecomer on the developmental scene: what the Spanish have created is a rational framework for that rarest of all political phenomena, the pursuit of radical aims by gradualist means.

In essence the plan has similarities to the Italian approach with important differences. Development will be by the method of designating integrated units, but in Spain the unit to be so designated is not a class but a school — the schools eligible being primary schools with at least eight classes together with an attached pre-primary school. The 'rules' which must be satisfied are a maximum of 25 children per class in the first year of the school, with the classes above being reduced to that level year by year after that, and the provision, also year by year, of two support teachers in the school.

But the planned aspect of the development is even more remarkable than that. There is a defined eight-year development plan, and one school is to become an integrated one for every 100,000 to 150,000 inhabitants per year. By this means 50 per cent of all schools providing basic education will be integrated schools by the end of the eight-year period. Moreover the choice of schools to become integrated will be arranged so that there will be at least one for each geographical section of the population every year. Given the current prominence of decentralization to the autonomous communities in Spain, this is a breathtakingly bold approach to the problems of the sporadic and uneven implementation of national policies which, as we have seen, bedevil other countries with decentralized structures.

The agreement of teachers and parents to the decision that their school will become an integrated one is also on the other hand an essential prerequisite. The Minister each year publishes an invitation for schools to join the integration programme, and all adhesions to it are therefore to be voluntary.

There are a number of other remarkable features to the Spanish integration plan:

– from the beginning the plan is a global one; there is provision for early intervention, initial and in-service teacher training, the operation of multidisciplinary teams, the adaptation of the curriculum and textbook reform, information initiatives for parents and teachers, and research

– there is close co-operation between the Education Ministry and the National Social Services Institute (INSERSO, Instituto nacional de servicios sociales) notably in the fields of assessment and technical aids
– the development plan has allowed for a gradual build-up, with no more than one or two integrated schools designated in each area during the first year (1985–6), and an increasing rate of development during the succeeding seven years of the plan according to needs and resources
– as in the United Kingdom and France, the development is specifically aimed at meeting the needs of the 20 per cent who experience school failure as well as the 2 per cent with specific disabilities.

It need hardly be said that the contribution of Spain to the Community's action to promote the integration of children with special needs in mainstream schools cannot fail to be a rich one.

POINTS FOR RESEARCH AND DEVELOPMENT

Out of all this experience it is obvious that there is a great deal of useful mutual learning to be gained from a Community programme of exchange and co-operation; the two fundamental criteria for the success of such a programme are clearly satisfied — there is enough unity of purpose to make exchange possible and enough diversity of approach and strategy to make it profitable. The field is so extensive and many aspects of development still so untested that there are inevitably a very considerable number of issues to address. Here I shall simply draw attention to eleven of these, without in any way implying that there may not be others which many people would regard as more important.

Development strategy

The lesson of the experience which I have so briefly illustrated in the previous section is surely clear, that the way to pursue significant let alone radical goals by gradual means is through a development strategy which is universally known and applied, and which enables those responsible not only to set the initial pace of change but subsequently to slow it down or accelerate it as circumstances require.

We have seen how in Italy and Hamburg the basic development strategy is that of designating a class to become an *integrated class*, provided there is consent and certain resource criteria are satisfied; in Spain we have the variation of a designated *integrated school*. A different approach, but equally authentic as a strategy, is the method of *school links* developed in the county of Oxfordshire; similar to this is the idea of *clusters* envisaged in the ZON project in the Netherlands. Such arrangements as the incorporation of a special unit within a regular school do not in my view constitute a strategy, since they do not in themselves imply any developmental dynamic, but they might well constitute a very important element in a strategy. It would not even be too pretentious to propose the usefulness of drawing up a European taxonomy of development strategies which would establish a conceptual framework to facilitate comparative study and evaluation.

Simply as an example of what a development strategy can offer, here are some of the advantages that the class-by-class method possesses:

- It is possible to select for development those situations which are ready for it. Above all that means classes where the teacher is both competent and well motivated towards integration, in schools which are not weighed down with other problems, and where the principal is behind the idea. Wherever 'parent democracy' is part of the system, the support of the parent class council can also be fostered and secured before anything is done. Once the reform is well rooted it can be extended to less favoured situations.
- Resources of staff and materials can be precisely targeted to the place of actual need at the time when they are needed. Cost-effective use of resources is a vital issue everywhere now; haphazard development is likely to be wasteful and the evidence of this may well be enough to endanger the whole reform.
- 'Rules', that is conditions which must be fulfilled if a class is to be declared an integrated one, can be relatively simple, designed to match realities in terms of resources and culture, openly publicized and therefore well known to professionals and clients, and strictly adhered to. In this way the reform can win a reputation for fairness and reliability in the professions and with the public. The maintenance of standards can also be reinforced — a key issue in mainstreaming.
- The pace of change can be regulated precisely, using the brake or the accelerator as policy, resources or professional and public attitudes require.
- Researchers will be able to offer a well-targeted service of evaluation, since the distinction between the development and control settings will be quite clear and all developments will have taken place at a known time under certain common conditions.

Of course this method will operate most effectively at primary level and in those lower secondary systems where the constant class or form remains an important element in the child's school life. Where the organization of the lower secondary curriculum is relatively complex, and at the upper secondary level, a link or cluster method might work better, though these depend of course on the existence of a well-developed special system. It might even be possible to combine class-by-class and link methods, provided the notion of an intelligible development strategy did not get lost in a mass of complexities and alternatives.

Categories

It could be useful to invite the professional philosophers to help us clarify our thinking about categories of disability. The greatest danger, and one that not only has been often and disastrously realized in the past but is still and probably always will be a serious menace, is that once having categorized a child (as moderately mentally handicapped, or whatever) we use our a priori knowledge of that category, rather than what we learn empirically from the child, to determine our total image of the child and all our predictions of his or her potential.

None the less, I think we should avoid falling into a paranoia of categories, which are useful, indeed essential if we are to construct training modules or organize the supply of technical aids, to mention only two of the many middle-level planning activities which actually could not take place at all without categorization.[7] That thinking about levels of activity may be helpful here has been demonstrated in an article in the *Harvard Educational Review*, by Judith Singer and John Butler, concerning the Education of All Handicapped Children Act in the United States.[8] In the process of implementing national legislation covering *all disabilities*, they report, 'special education directors at local level have continued to decide the range of placement and service options for *categories* of handicapped children, but have willingly delegated decisions about appropriate mixes of instruction and related services for *individual children*'. This pattern of three levels of responsibility implying three vocabularies could have a universal application. Yet here too there are hidden dangers. If what special education directors do is work out the kinds of special services or materials which categories of children are likely to need, well and good; but it would be quite unacceptable if they were to exclude certain categories from certain possibilities on the ground of kind or severity of disability. We have already seen, for example, how the European experience shows that severity of disability alone is not a criterion of failure in full-time functional and social integration.

It may be noticed before leaving this topic that categorization is not the only process which leads to predetermination of a child's development and potential in despite of real evidence — unless carefully used, an individual learning programme can have the same effect.

The ordinary school

The need for the ordinary school to be or to become functionally and socially accessible to children with special needs if integration is to be successful is self-evident. What is coming clearer is that we should not think of the regular school as 'having to adapt' — willy nilly as it were, and regardless of the interests of the majority of the children — in order to accommodate a minority of some 2 per cent of the population who want, or are thought to want, to get into it. If it is true that integration is not compatible with much that is traditional in our schools including the values which underlie what is done, then it is not enough to say that integration depends on that compatibility coming about by some mysterious means. Rather integrating must be seen as not merely compatible with the direction of general educational reform, but actually part and parcel of it. Implied here is the belief that the changes in the school's style and values which favour integration do not only benefit the 2 per cent or even only the 20 per cent but all the children. Both the mainstreaming of children with special needs therefore and the reform of the mainstream itself are all one process in so far as both are founded on the equal-value principle set out at the start and end of this book.

The snag is of course that in the United Kingdom at least this unity no longer exists. This means that in that country, and in any other which chooses to follow it in promoting competitive over co-operative values in their schools, it may be necessary to go back to the beginning and ask, and keep asking, whether the regular school is a fit setting into which to invite children with special needs to spend their educational lives. It also means that if, as I suggest at the end of this chapter, the

Commission proceeds over reasonable time to the formulation of a Community policy for the education of children with special needs, and if as one must suppose integration figures largely in that policy, then there is stormy weather ahead.

Upper secondary schooling

Far too little is being proclaimed or reported about the progress of children with special needs, whether in integrated or special settings, into either technical or general upper secondary education. The study completed for the Commission by the then National Bureau for Handicapped Students in London highlighted the end of the compulsory phase of education as a danger point for young people with disabilities and made it clear that far fewer of these pupils are passing on to upper secondary level full-time education than should be the case. It is to be hoped that the Community's action programme gives a priority to this problem in its next phase of work.

New technology

Co-operation at Community level should be able to make an especially valuable contribution to development of apparatus and software in support of the education and the school integration of children with special needs of whatever kind. This was already clear from preparatory co-operative work initiated during the first action programme by Jørgen Hansen in the Danish Ministry of Education, with the effective support of the European Association of Special Education (EASE) under its president, Philippe Lamoral of the Ghent special psychosocial centre, and by the working party, chaired by Lamoral, which reported on Community-level information services about special educational softwares as part of the Handynet project. There is good reason to hope that the programme as a whole, and the Handynet project in particular, will contribute to the strengthening of the European market in advanced educational technology, to the benefit of all concerned, above all those children living in less favoured areas who have been denied these advantages owing to the inaccessible costs and lack of information and maintenance services which a feeble market implies. New technology is an unpopular topic with some of those educationists who insist that all our efforts should be expended at the socio-political level. I suppose they are fearful of the exploitation of children as consumers of commercial hardware and software, as guinea-pigs even. But if we distinguish use from abuse and apply a bit of common sense, we can safely ignore these apprehensions and get on with it.

Teachers and parents

It is obvious that there is a vast area of our subject which I have hardly touched on here. It includes not only the initial and in-service training of teachers and their co-operation with parents, but the provision of information and training for parents and other family members themselves, as well as their participation in the preparation, making and implementation of decisions. These are issues which the Commission will address during the second half of the Helios programme. It is to be hoped that the Commission will be able to involve in this activity two voluntary associations, the Association for Teacher Education in Europe (ATEE),[9] and the European Association of Parents, both of which have shown a concern for the education of children with special needs. Another important partner would be the International League of Societies for Persons with a Mental Handicap (ILSMH), in which the interests of both parents and professionals are strongly represented and whose education committee presented a working paper unequivocally in favour of integration to the League's 1990 world congress in Paris. It is to be hoped too that such collaboration might lead to increased Commission support to the work of such organizations in the future.[10]

The universal benefit

We have seen under the third point above that the changes in the regular school which favour integration are believed by supporters of mainstreaming to benefit all the children. More than that, integrationists believe that the presence of disabled children in the school will in itself benefit all the children. The arguments in support of this are too complex for all of them to be treated now; I shall return to the point at the proper place in the last chapter. For now we need only note the central argument which is that disability is part of the human condition which in itself has more positive than negative characteristics, and that to be educated without any contact with this reality is a deprivation. Whatever is thought of that point of view, it is evident that this is a topic which calls for research undertaken over time in a number of different cultural settings.

Integration — how far?

It is quite often debated whether integration is a process or a goal, a means or an end. I believe it can properly be all of these things, although the two pairs of terms are not the same. Evidently integration is a process; for a radical integrationist it is also a goal (that is to say, the declared aim is to integrate all children), but not for someone who believes there is an immovable point beyond which integration cannot go. Of the seven countries from which I drew illustrations in the previous section, we might conclude that integration is a goal as well as a process in Italy, Denmark, some German Länder such as Hamburg, some British local authorities, and Spain, but that it is a process not conceived as a goal in France, the Netherlands, other states of Germany, and in many areas as well as at the national level in the United Kingdom.

At first sight, it might appear that integration is a means not an end, the end being social integration. Strictly speaking, social integration is not the ultimate end or aim, any more than (for example) is independent living. The end is a good quality of life, one component of which is that degree of social integration which is attainable by the individual and which the individual desires. Moreover, school integration is not merely a means to that element of the good life which we call social integration, any more than a child's life in school is merely a preparation for later life as an adult. Children should, in my view, have the same right as anyone else to live above all in the present; the preparatory aspect of their lives is important too but secondary to that. It follows that functional and social integration during school life is part of the end of enjoying a good life during childhood, as well as being, secondarily, a means which facilitates social and economic integration as part of the good life of an adult.

Higher education

That element of the current Helios programme which relates to educational integration was not intended to include higher education. This was not because the issue was not thought to be important, but simply from a feeling that in the first programme of work in this entire field some limit had to be set to the ground covered. Before the end of the first action programme I arranged for information on accessibility to universities to be included in the Community's official *Guide to Students*; the first results of this initiative were disappointing, only the section dealing with universities in France achieving anything like systematic information of interest to disabled students. Professor Marco and colleagues in the University of Mons showed an early interest in the European aspects of this problem, particularly as far as students with sensory disabilities are concerned. In 1986 the Commission's first action programme was able to support a seminar in Mons on 'Students with Disabilities of Sight or Hearing and Higher Education', followed up in 1990 by a conference on 'A European University for Students with Special Needs'. Apart from its intrinsic importance, the topic is another of those particularly well suited to treatment at European level, not least because of the development of major European programmes for higher education students, such as Erasmus, from which disabled students should have an equal opportunity of benefiting.

Co-operation between researchers

There is no aspect of the whole domain of disability where research is so well developed or so greatly needed as that of education. It is remarkable too that the Council of Ministers in their 1986 conclusions refer to the topics to which it was agreed that the Commission should give priority in its first activity to promote the integration of children with special needs in ordinary schools as 'research themes'. Yet there is no provision for the many researchers in the Community engaged in this field either to benefit from the programme or to contribute to it. It may be that researchers and administrators do not always see eye-to-eye; but it really will not do if administrators grumble at researchers for living in ivory towers while doing nothing to facilitate the application of their results. The introduction, as soon as it is procedurally possible, of a specific action within the programme which would enable researchers to meet together at regular intervals for the exchange of information and ideas about their work would not be costly and would be extremely productive. Indeed by reducing reduplication of effort and ensuring that the output from investment was widely disseminated the activity would more than pay for itself.

Technical assistance

I believe that we should face up to the fact that two of the present members of the Community, Greece and Portugal, need particular help in developing their systems of special education and within that their development strategies for integration. There is no need to look for political or cultural explanations for this, since the economic realities of the past are quite sufficient to account for it. The Commission already possesses the two essentials to ensure that a cost-effective programme of technical assistance in favour of these two countries could be mounted — that is, the experience of how such a programme should be designed and the contacts with experts in other member countries. It would be a great achievement if the Commission were able to persuade the Council to incorporate this as an element in the third action programme (Helios II). It is likely too that there will be before long a call for technical assistance towards the education of children with special needs in the countries of central and eastern Europe.

Education about and for disability

As well as improving the quality and promoting the integration of the basic education of all children with disabilities, there are two other developments which are needed in schools in pursuit of a positive global disability policy. One is the inclusion in the curriculum for all children of education about the realities of disability. The other is the provision for all children with disability of education about independent living.

TOWARDS A EUROPEAN COMMUNITY POLICY ON SPECIAL NEEDS EDUCATION

A final reflection concerns the idea of a Community *policy* on the educational integration of children with special needs. So far from thinking that this is an exorbitant prospect, it is hard to see how such a thing could fail to emerge, at the latest by the end of the century. Nor is this, as it were, the Commission's 'fault': it was the nature of the French initiative in 1984, their proposal for an activity not on the education of children with special needs but on their integration in the regular school, which predetermined the way things would go. Although therefore the limitations of the Treaty, unless these are modified, will mean that the form in which a Community policy on educational integration appears is a very much weaker one than can be applied to the issues of the environment and employment, yet the content need be no less substantial. In that sense, the very nature of disability itself, the implication that as a theme it can only be treated at all if it is treated in its entirety — from cradle to grave — will have led the Commission to undertake unprecedented responsibilities at the political level.

NOTES

1   'Rehabilitation' as an academic discipline appears to be medical in its emphasis as a rule.
2   It was suggested that there should be a fifth topic, transition from school to working life; but this was rejected by the Education Committee on the grounds that they had had enough of transition.
3   It is more important in a Community context than in that of OECD that all countries should be able to participate actively in a given programme; indeed, at that time it was always likely that one or another country would veto an educational activity which did not suit its own policies.
4   Variation between effective results over the country, and notably between north and south, is another problem which the Italians will be confronting in the 1990s.
5   Once in the mainstream, children with special needs can positively influence the school's whole conception of its mission, its styles and priorities, but this cannot be done from the outside.
6   Not to mention the contribution which will be made by what was East Germany and the other countries of central and eastern Europe.
7   For full discussion of categories, which also reaches a positive conclusion as to their usefulness, see Brahm Norwich, *Reappraising Special Needs Education*, Cassell (Special Needs in Ordinary Schools series), London 1990. See References below.
8   See Judith Singer and John Butler, 'The Education of all Handicapped Children Act: schools as agents of social reform', *Harvard Educational Review*, **57**, No. 2, May 1987.
9   The ATEE has over a number of years been active in the field of special needs through a working party in which Fernando Diniz, then of Thames Polytechnic, Peter Kropveld of the Zeist Seminarium voor Orthopedagogiek and their colleagues in the University of Barcelona played a prominent part.
10   The second of the plenary conferences on educational integration within the Helios programme, held in Cagliari in 1990, focused on parents and teachers.

REFERENCES

Note   For community documents on special education produced before 1982 see References to Chapter 1, and, for those after 1987, References to Chapter 7.

Community policy documents

Conclusions of 4 June 1984 of the Council and Ministers of Education meeting within the Council on the integration of handicapped children into ordinary schools (7605/84 Press 98).
Progress with regard to the implementation of the policy of integrating handicapped children into ordinary schools, Commission staff paper of 24 Oct. 1986 (Sec (86) 1758).
Addendum to the above: the situation in Spain and Portugal, 7 Jan. 1987 (Sec (86) 1758/2).
A programme of positive action at Community level concerning the integration of children and young people with disabilities into the normal educational system, Communication from the Commission (COM (87) 94 of 13 Mar. 1987).
Conclusions of the Council and the Ministers of Education meeting within the Council of 14 May 1987 concerning a European programme of co-operation on the integration of handicapped children into ordinary schools (O.J. No. C 221/1 of 8 Aug. 1987).

Commission studies and conference reports

Jørgen Hansen, *Teaching and Training the Handicapped through the New Information Technology*, Copenhagen 1984. (DE, EN, FR)

Rhys Gwyn, Report of a Commission conference on 'New information technology and the education and training of disabled persons', held at Manchester, 7–11 June 1985, Manchester 1985. (DE, EN, FR)

Richard Stowell and Deborah Cooper, *The Access of Disabled Students to and within Establishments and Programmes of Post-compulsory Education*, London 1986. (DE, EN, ES, FR, IT, NL)

Reports of international organizations

UNESCO

Review of the Present Situation of Special Education in 58 Countries, Paris 1988.

OECD (CERI)

Yvonne Posternak, *Integration of Handicapped Children and Adolescents in Italy*, Paris 1979.
The Education of the Handicapped Adolescent: Integration in the school, Secretariat paper and case studies by Aimé Labregère and others, Paris 1981.

Independent conference reports

M.-J. de Vriendt and C. Marco (eds), *Des étudiants à audition ou vision déficiente et l'enseignement supérieur* [Students with disabilities of hearing or vision and higher education], report of a conference held at Mons, 12–13 Sept. 1986, Mons 1987.

European Community Regional Secretariat of the World Federation of the Deaf, *The Education of Deaf Children*, report of a conference held at Athens, 27–29 Nov. 1987, London 1988. (EN, FR)

European Journal of Special Needs Education

Rudolf Schindele, 'Special educational support for visually handicapped students in regular schools: an analysis of its development and present state in the Federal Republic of Germany', **1**, No. 1, Oct. 1986.

Alvaro Marchesi, 'Project for integration of children with special needs in Spain', **1**, No. 2, Dec. 1986.

Graham Rodbard, 'Going Dutch! A perspective on the Dutch system of special education', **5**, No. 3, Oct. 1990.

Tony Booth, 'Integration, disability and commitment, a response to Mårten Söder', **6**, No. 1, Mar. 1991.

Ana Gortazar, 'Country briefing: special education in Spain', **6**, No. 1, Mar. 1991.

Sip Pijl and Cor Meijer, 'Does integration count for much? An analysis of the practice of integration in 8 countries', **6**, No.2, June 1991.

National Foundation for Educational Research

Seamus Hegarty and K. Pocklington with D. Lucas, *Educating Pupils with Special Needs in Ordinary Schools*, Windsor 1981.
Seamus Hegarty and K. Pocklington with D. Lucas, *Integration in Action*, Windsor 1982.

Part III

_____

Progress, Prospects and Principles

Chapter 7

The Second Action Programme, Helios (1988-91)

SETTING UP HELIOS

The adoption of the programme

It was the intention of the Commission that 1987 should be a 'hinge' year between its first and second action programmes, the first half being devoted to reporting the first programme and preparing the second, and the last six months being occupied with the process of adoption of the new activity by the Parliament and the Council. An advantage of this plan was that all the ongoing activities, such as the network of rehabilitation centres and the support for the European co-operation of voluntary bodies (European NGOs) could continue without interruption, the budget for the programme being maintained during the year of transition.

In essence this worked out as we had planned, apart from a delay of some four or five months in the adoption of the new programme. The Commission's proposal was published in July of 1987. The programme was finally adopted, not in the autumn of that year — the time at which I was due to retire from the Commission's service — but in April of 1988. This meant that my successor, Bernhard Wehrens, was faced immediately with the not altogether enviable task of seeing the proposal through the process of formal adoption. There was on the other hand some advantage in the new head's being able to play an active part in the final framing and shaping of the programme. One specific gain was that by the time it was adopted the programme had followed the fashion of the day by acquiring a name — 'Helios'.

The cause of the delay was uncertainty about the legal form of the instrument which established the programme. The result was satisfactory, a Council Decision — a more secure basis for a four-year programme than the Resolution which had adopted the first action programme.

The means for consultation

It will be remembered that for the implementation of the first action programme the Commission was advised by a Liaison Group, made up of national delegations of civil servants or experts representing typically Ministries of Employment, Social Affairs or Health. We also had an informal annual discussion meeting, over one and a half days, with the representatives of organizations of and for disabled people (the Dialogue Group of non-governmental organizations).

For the new programme it seemed to me absolutely essential that the NGOs should be involved formally in the consultation process. The principle of the participation of disabled people in decisions concerning them absolutely had to be asserted in this way; not to do this would show the Community incapable of practising what it preached. In practice too we needed the advice, at the critical times when decisions were open to influence, of those who after all knew much more about what was being discussed than anyone else. As to the ability of the NGOs to operate at the European level, that had been amply demonstrated during the first action programme.

Now, the constraining nature of a Council Decision required the setting up of a formal Advisory Committee, under the Commission's chairmanship as the previous Liaison Group had been. I therefore proposed that this Committee should be composed of two representatives of each member state, nine representatives of disabled people or their families nominated by bodies (NGOs) chosen by the Commission, and one member from each of the European bodies representing employers and trade unions.

As to the NGOs, my idea was that six of these would have the right to nominate throughout the programme, and that other NGO members of the Dialogue Group (which would continue as before) would be invited to take the other three places by rotation year by year. The six which, in my view, should be permanent members were the European wings of the World Federation of the Deaf, the World Blind Union, Rehabilitation International, Disabled People's International, the International League of Societies for Persons with Mental Handicap and the World Federation for Mental Health.

Even in the early stages of the discussions of our proposal, before I left Brussels, it was clear that there were to be reservations among the national delegations of the Social Questions Group of the Council about this arrangement, which would effectively take away from the representatives of Ministries in member states the opportunity to discuss the progress of the programme with the Commission without the presence of others. It was disappointing, though not in the least surprising, to find that the United Kingdom delegation was one of the first to express such doubts.

In the end it was again a question of a compromise, but this time one which, although offering to disabled people and their families a stronger voice than in the first action programme, fell none the less short of what should be expected of a European democracy. In the 1988 Decision two new bodies were set up. There was to be an Advisory Committee, consisting only of national representatives. There was also to be a Liaison Group, composed exactly like the Advisory Committee that I had envisaged, whose opinion was to be obtained by the Commission before consulting the Advisory Committee.

So, the diplomats of the member states won their point, in my opinion a short-sighted and ill-advised one. Certainly they had it both ways: they could hear what the NGOs and social partners had to say to the Commission while themselves retaining the Commission's private ear. This one-sided arrangement contrasts strongly with what happens regularly in the member states themselves, at least on the mainland, where social partners and organizations of disabled people are represented on steering committees of many kinds, some of them commanding very much greater budgets than does Helios. It is also interesting to contrast other procedures at Community level. In the Council of the European Centre for the Development of Vocational Training (CEDEFOP, Centre européen pour le développement de la formation professionnelle) in Berlin, for example, in the Commission's Advisory Committee on Vocational Training, and in the Advisory Committee of the European Social Fund (with a budget, not of millions, but of thousands of millions of ECUs) — in all these contexts the delegations of the national governments sit as equals, after the fashion of the International Labour Organization, with the representatives of the social partners (employers and workers); often the Commission will provide facilities for the three groups to meet separately before the formal meeting in order to review the agenda and design common positions.

Yet it would be futile to react to this disappointment merely by grumbling at the Community institutions. The true lesson to be learnt is that the non-governmental organizations of and for disabled people have a long way to go before they are considered in the Community to have a political existence in the sense in which that is enjoyed by the representatives of the two sides of industry, or for that matter more recently by the women's organizations. A first European response to that fact might be to say that it is natural and perhaps inevitable, even in a society where recognition of the rights of consumers is generally on the increase. But the American experience shows that it does not have to be so. Looking for a way ahead on this will form an important part of my last chapter where I shall also mention the encouraging progress made by the NGOs themselves during the first years of Helios.

Resources for the programme

Staff resources

In spite of the considerable growth of the programme there has been virtually no increase in the allocation of staff resources to the core team of officials responsible for it. The unit is also no longer called a Bureau but simply a Division like any other.

The experts team established by contract in Brussels to assist the Commission has however been considerably expanded, by the addition to the group of senior experts of a director and deputy director, a number of assistant experts and more clerical staff.[1] This dependence on experts under contract rather than permanent Commission officials allows for much greater flexibility in the hiring and firing of personnel. On the other hand, it puts the Commission's political control of the programme at risk, as well as making extremely heavy demands on the operational budget.

Financial resources

I had originally asked for a 50 per cent increase over the budget for the last year of the first action programme and got 25 per cent. This was not at all bad; we did however have to drop out of the programme any direct grants to housing or other environmental projects.

For the third year of the programme (1990) a concerted effort involving co-operation between the NGOs and the European Parliament succeeded in winning an increase in the annual credits for the programme of over 1 million ECUs, most of which was to be devoted to the support of the NGOs' own activities.[2]

The structure of the programme

The structure of the Helios programme has been almost identical to that of the first action programme:[3]

Policy initiatives

- follow-up to the 1986 Recommendation on employment
- presentation of new proposals in the environmental field, beginning with mobility and transport.

Co-operation and support

- extension of the network of rehabilitation centres
- establishment of three networks of local model activities (LMAs), focused respect-ively on employment, independent living and education
- institution of a 'special action' on independent living, consisting of the replacement of the scheme of grants to housing projects by the annual award of prizes for the promotion of accessible transport, public facilities and housing
- extension of the scheme of grants to support the European activities of non-governmental organizations.

Information

- launching of the first module of Handynet (Handyaids) and further development of the system
- improvements to the publication and documentation service.

As with the first programme, the interdependence of the various elements of the programme was to be essential to its effectiveness.

THE IMPLEMENTATION OF HELIOS

Policy initiatives

As well as giving an account of the progress made on the two topics just listed, I shall need to consider a political development in the wider social field which is relevant to the needs of disabled people, the Social Charter.

The follow-up on employment

At the insistence of the European Parliament the Commission had been invited to report on the implementation of the Recommendation within two rather than three years of its adoption. Thanks to the co-operation of the working party of member state representatives who worked with the Commission on this task and to the expedition of Stefanos Grammenos who as the Commission's consultant put the report together, this timetable was achieved with two weeks to spare. Addressed to the Parliament and Council the report, which appeared in July 1988, consists of twelve national reports and a comparative analysis.

The report is informative and of considerable interest. A great advantage is its structure: all the national reports and the comparative analysis follow point by point the text of the Recommendation itself; this adds greatly to the clarity and utility of a document which otherwise, given the number of issues and of countries to be addressed, would have been difficult to handle. It must however be recognized that the report contains much more in the way of updating and clarification of national initiatives and situations than it does evidence of action which was taken by the member states as a result of the Recommendation and which would not have been taken otherwise. This is no doubt partly a negative result of the short period allowed for implementation before the report had to be completed; it would however be unduly innocent not to recognize that it also reflects the freedom felt by member states to ignore a Community instrument which is not legally binding.

Another disappointment is that whereas in draft form the report ended with conclusions and recommendations, which would have been those of the Commission itself not merely of an independent consultant, these were omitted from the final version presented by the Commission to the other institutions. No doubt the Commission had its own good reasons for this, but a clear implication was that at that time the Commission did not want to force the pace of follow-up.

The Council formally discussed the report in June of the following year and its Conclusions were published in the Official Journal of the Community. It is a remarkably good document. It recognizes that disabled people 'form one of the most disadvantaged groups in the population', that they 'experience difficulty in gaining access on an equal basis to employment and vocational training' and that 'their unemployment rate is appreciably higher than that of the population as a whole'. While stressing the essential primacy of 'general policies based on economic growth and job creation' it accepts that 'success of such policies does not necessarily guarantee equal opportunities for disabled people'. Special measures are therefore needed, aimed at 'improving the situation on the labour market for disabled people'.

This responsibility of the Community towards disabled people is firmly set in the context of fundamental policy aims, another excellent thing about these Conclusions: 'all citizens of the Community must without exception benefit' from the achievement of 'the internal market, including its social dimension'. Discrimination against disabled people in regard to access to employment and vocational training is unacceptable for the best of reasons — because 'no citizen of the Community' should suffer it.

The Council is also surprisingly honest in its assessment of how little the Recommendation itself has in reality achieved. It has, we are told, 'contributed to a review' and 'encouraged new measures' in accordance with its spirit. Even more disarmingly, 'it has offered a Community reference framework for national measures that were being prepared when it was adopted'. It would be difficult to find words which demolish more skilfully than that any faith we may have in the effectiveness of *non-constraining* supranational instruments in the social field. Neither those countries who have recently legislated on the topic nor those who are just about to do so will alter one word of their law or draft because of them; nor will such instruments persuade a country which otherwise was not intending to legislate to do so. Only those countries which happen, at the moment when the international instrument is adopted, to have perceived the need for new legislation on that very topic and to be in the early stages of plotting out what that should comprise may be influenced by it. Of how many countries — out of the twelve at present in the Community — will that be true in any instance? And of what use is that proportion of 'hits' to a Community which is committed to developing the social dimension of European integration?

Yet the overall effect of the Council Conclusions of 1989 is encouraging. The Commission's original insistence that there is a need both to eliminate negative discrimination and to implement policies of positive action is reinforced. The member states are invited to involve the social partners and the representatives of disabled people in 'defining and implementing' the necessary measures. Above all the Commission is given a threefold charge. The first two elements concern the intensification of actions already under way, the exchange of experience on 'occupational integration' within the Helios programme, and financial support to the same end by means of the European Social Fund. The third invitation is for the Commission to do something new, and is therefore far the most important of the three:

> The Council invites the Commission to submit to the Council, on the basis of an evaluation of the results of the implementation of the Recommendation, proposals in the field covered by the said Recommendation which will ensure better coordination and greater consistency between the measures introduced by the member states.

While it might be going too far to say that that text has no meaning unless it is intended to invite the Commission to introduce a draft Directive on the employment of disabled people in the Community, it is evident that, had the Council intended such an invitation, there would have been no need to express themselves more forcibly than they actually did.

So far the Commission has not responded directly to this invitation. This is not to say that it has no intention of doing so — the problems resulting from the smallness of the core team of officials in the Commission's service concerned with disability must never be forgotten. Nor does it mean that nothing has been done. No one could accuse the Helios programme of not playing its part in organizing exchange on economic integration; there has too been an important development in the Social Fund. Both these points are dealt with later in this chapter.

The Commission has also responded to the concern of the Council Conclusions with information. A first idea, that it would be possible to develop quite quickly an employment module of Handynet, was frustrated, as we shall see, by the relatively cautious approach of the member states to the development of that project. Much more successful has been a third but more effectively targeted and resourced essay into the difficult territory of employment statistics. For this the Helios Division and the Commission's Statistical Office in Luxembourg have co-operated in entrusting the work to the researcher in the best position to undertake it, Stefanos Grammenos. The first part, comprising national reports and a synthesis for six member states (Germany, Greece, France, Luxembourg, Portugal and the Netherlands) was completed in the autumn of 1990, with much better results than anyone had expected. The second phase of the work, covering the other six countries, is being completed in the course of 1991.

Useful as these developments are, it is obvious that they do not constitute a response to the Council's third invitation to the Commission. Given the preoccupation at the policy level with the proposal on mobility, and the need during 1991 to make the best of the last year of Helios I and both plan and have adopted its successor, it may well be that the two or three officials of the Division in the Commission's service responsible for all this will not be able to implement this response until the third action programme (Helios II) has got under way. Meanwhile the mobility initiative is highly relevant to employment needs, and is indeed seen by the Commission as at least a partial response to the Council's third charge.

The Social Charter

It is above all with Jacques Delors, President of the Commission, that is associated the belief that economic integration cannot be promoted without a 'social dimension'. What that means became clear when the Greek Commissioner responsible for Social Affairs, Vasso Papandreou, presented in 1989 her proposal for a Community Social Charter. Even here it is necessary to record, without bitterness, a significant disappointment, at least for those with the interests of all disabled people at heart. What was originally entitled a 'Community Charter of Fundamental Social Rights' had become by the time it was adopted by means of a Council Declaration (only the United Kingdom abstaining, it will be remembered) the 'Community Charter of Basic Social Rights *for Workers*'. At first it had looked as if the Community was about to achieve a major sortie from the economic limitations to its competence which had besieged it for so long, but it was not to be. The restriction of the Charter to workers is all the more surprising for the fact that the proposals are by no means confined to major funding and constraining legislation. At all events, the limitation is of vital concern to the world of disability, and I must return to this point in my last chapter (p. 183).

Meanwhile, let us see what the Charter, and the action programme to implement it presented by Commissioner Papandreou later the same year, have to offer to disabled people. There is some good news here. 'The disabled' have a section devoted entirely to them. Certainly, the Charter itself speaks only in general terms of 'the fullest possible integration' and of the relevance to this of vocational training, 'professional insertion', and the improvement of accessibility, mobility, the means of transport and housing. Yet the inclusion here of environmental as well as directly occupational elements is extremely encouraging.

The Commissioner's action programme has a lot more to say. At the level of principle it recognizes that the social and economic integration of disabled people 'is not only a question of justice but also an economic issue', and identifies the true significance of the Helios programme as a basis for 'coherent overall policy'. At the practical level, it calls for a Council Decision to enable the development of the Handynet project and another to establish a third action programme. But its most important element concerns immediate policy development: the Commissioner gives notice of her intention to bring forward a proposal for a Council Directive 'aimed at promoting the travel conditions of workers with motor disabilities'. In view of the importance of freedom to travel if disabled people are to be able to attend vocational training and to work, it is argued that this initiative on mobility can be seen as the Commission's response to the third invitation made by the Council in their 1989 Conclusions on employment described in my previous subsection.

Although the Commission had already expressed its intention to make policy proposals on transport for disabled people, in its 1986 proposal for the Helios programme for example, the very specific mention here in the Social Charter action programme constituted a major step forward in the implementation of this idea; though the mention of 'workers with motor (as distinct from other) disabilities' is a surprising and disquieting qualification, the text promises some substantial reward for the political and technical investment made in this domain. Nor does the restriction of the Social Charter to workers add to this specific proposal any problems which were not already inherent in it.

Before describing the progress made in preparing this mobility initiative, I must point to a section of the Social Charter which is not devoted specifically to disabled people but which threatens to be very bad news for them over the whole field of environmental improvement. My fears that the poor formulation of Article 118A of the Treaty under the Single European Act would work out to the detriment of disabled people have turned out to be only too well founded. The Article, it must be remembered, calls for Directives from the Commission to promote the health and safety of workers 'especially in the working environment'. As I feared, this has been interpreted, by a decision which it will probably be impossible to reverse, in the restrictive sense, that is to say as if the word 'especially' was not there. In both the Charter itself and the action programme to implement it, the whole section on this topic is headed simply 'Right to health protection and safety at the work-place'. The narrowness of this interpretation is reinforced by the fact that another major section under the heading 'Living and working conditions' deals only with questions of labour law and does not treat living conditions at all. The effect of these two sections is to undermine much of the promising link made between environmental improvements and employment in the section on disability.

The initiative on mobility

Although much of the preparatory work needed for the Commission's policy initiative on mobility and transport for disabled people had been completed in the course of the first action programme (see Chapter 2), there were still a few loose ends which needed attention. The results of the work done on all the different kinds of transport and personal movement had not been fully and logically set out; the issue of a possible European Travel Card was still in the air; no strategy for the adoption and implementation of a Community instrument had been set out.

Accordingly, in 1988 the Commission contracted with ERICA for the completion of a report on these points, and Eirlys Roberts, ERICA's president, invited me to undertake the work.[4] It was agreed that the opportunity should be taken to include also in the report a section which would carry forward the work done on the next environmental theme to be treated by the Commission at policy level, the accessibility of public buildings and facilities.

The three sections of the report which concern mobility aim to deal with the three loose ends which had been identified. The first consists of a synthesis paper which in brief concludes with recommending to the Commission this strategy:

– Community action should consist of interdependent technical and policy-oriented activity
– the policy action should take the form of a draft Directive, referring to any or all of Articles 48, 8A and B and 118A of the Treaty[5]
– by means of a phased rolling programme the Commission could develop a framework Directive into a series of precise objectives and standards; at the same time a European Code of Good Practice could be prepared and published and a European Travel Card instituted.

The second section of the report comprises a detailed European Code of Good Practice to Promote the Mobility of Disabled People. The specific sections, each of which is preceded by a set of policy foundations (see Chapter 5), cover these areas:

– public transport: accessibility and concessions
– special services (door-to-door transport and similar systems)
– private vehicles
– street mobility: pedestrians and wheelchairs
– supporting actions: information, training, participation and research.

Having drawn on all the work done by the Community, the European Conference of Ministers of Transport and the Council of Europe, as well as numerous national reports, regulations and information brochures, I was able to submit the draft of the Code for discussion by meetings of experts in four countries and to individual experts for written comment in four others.[6] In addition, through the good offices of Dr Mary John, I was able to receive comment on my draft from representatives of disabled women in the Community.

In the third section I presented a completely new detailed plan for the institution of a European Travel Card for disabled people. The essential provisions were these:

– The setting up of the Card system should be mandated by the Council, and the detailed proposal presented by the Commission to the Council as a draft Regulation, following consultation involving national representatives, members of associations of and for disabled people and in the field of transport, and the European Conference of Ministers of Transport.
– Criteria of eligibility to hold a Card (and to enjoy the specific benefits indicated on it) will be established at Community level; Cards will be issued to eligible members of voluntary associations of or for disabled people authorized to do so

by national authorities; Cards will be authorized and produced by the Commission who will send them direct to the 'licensed' associations in member states.

- On each Card will be printed, in all the Community languages, its title and a statement authorizing the holder to receive the benefits and services indicated on the Card; these benefits will be indicated by means of pictograms, and the holder's area of disability will be indicated by a two-letter code.
- Depending on the nature of the impairment, Cards will be issued permanently or for a stated duration according to principles laid down at Community level.
- Together with the Cards, information sheets will be issued which explain the actual rights and services currently available in the country or countries to be visited.

Of these provisions, the last is among the most important. For many years to come (to say the least) the rights and services available to people with different disabilities wanting to travel will vary enormously from country to country in the Community. This has two vital implications. The first is that no European Travel Card must pretend to offer more than what is available to nationals with a given disability in the country concerned. The second is that a Card is useless or worse (in the sense that it might raise false hopes) unless it is linked to an up-to-date service of detailed information about the facilities and rights which actually exist in a given country, and unless this information is available to disabled travellers *before* they set out on their journey.

The scheme was developed by means of a questionnaire asking for both overall and detailed response to a first draft of a proposal for a European Travel Card of this kind. This was sent to over a hundred of the Commission's established contacts, all of them with experience in working at the European level. These were in fact the members of the Commission's principal networks at the end of the first action programme — the leaders of the district projects, the directors of the centres in the rehabilitation centres network, the RI national secretariats, the NGOs in the Dialogue Group, members of the Handynet 'family' and experts who had worked with the Commission specifically on mobility questions. There was a very high response rate of over 85 per cent, and of these another 85 per cent were entirely or largely positive in their general response to the proposal; only 4.5 per cent were opposed in principle. In detail on the other hand numerous comments, criticisms and counter-proposals were made, so that the scheme as finally presented in the report is a considerable improvement on the draft. There is a clear lesson here as to value of consultation if it is taken seriously; it is also evident that this kind of distillation of informed and representative opinion would have been impossible if the exchange activity of the first action programme had not established the various networks capable of delivering it.

The report was delivered early in 1989 and I had the opportunity to present its results at an international conference on 'Transport without Exclusion' organized by the French Ministers of Transport and for the Disabled in Dunkirk in December of that year. In 1990 the Commission was able to start active work on the preparation of the proposed Directive on mobility and transport for disabled people. Work is therefore at a delicate stage, and no one would want to prejudge, still less prejudice, the outcome. None the less it is important to understand the difficulties which the

Commission has to face in a task which might at first sight seem relatively simple but which is anything but that.

The unique responsibility for bringing forward formal Community proposals, including the choice of instrument to be proposed, is a jealously guarded privilege of the Commission, but by no means always an enviable task. Of the Articles in the Treaty suggested in the ERICA report, the case for choosing 118A is strong, since it is both relatively specific and allows adoption of Directives by means of majority vote in the Council.[7] That this restricts the benefit of the Directive to workers has to be accepted as inevitable at the present stage of development of the Community; the strategy here should be both to define 'worker' for the purposes of the Directive as widely as possible and to offer the Council a Declaration, for adoption at the same time as the Directive, expressing the political will to ensure that disabled people who could not be defined as workers benefited also from the measures undertaken and the services provided. I return to this point in Chapter 8 (p. 182).

More serious, as I have already suggested, could be the effect of the narrow interpretation of the expression in Article 118A 'especially in the place of work' as if the word 'especially' simply was not there, since this means that the Commission may have to argue against opposition that travel to and from work or training can and should be regarded as an essential extension of the work-place where disabled workers are concerned. There will also be a question of what modes of transport can be included, given the limitations of the notion of travel between home and work; the exclusion of air travel seems only too likely.

We can see therefore that the problem which the Commission has to face takes a classical form. An instrument covering all forms of transport, all purposes of travel and all disabled people might be a possibility, but it could not possibly be anything as powerful as a Directive; any constraining instrument on the other hand must be based on the precise text of a specific Article in the Treaty and therefore suffer whatever limitations of scope that may imply. Getting such a Directive through will involve disappointment, but would successfully elevate the whole question of the needs and rights of disabled people to a political level never before attempted or even imagined. The Commission's proposal for a Council Directive, as it was finally presented in February 1991, reflects a recognition of these possibilities and limitations.

Other policy areas

I have mentioned that the 1989 ERICA study on mobility for which I was responsible contained a fourth section which covered the topic of what is intended to be the second of the Commission's policy initiatives in the environmental field, the accessibility of buildings and facilities intended for public use.

The definitions of accessibility, of the kinds of buildings and facilities to be considered and of the various agencies and persons to be involved, have already been set out in that part of Chapter 5 which deals with this topic. The 1989 report endeavours to assist the Commission towards the active preparation of a draft Directive or other instrument on this theme in the future by analysing the key issues and recommending a strategy for confronting them. This would involve the backing up of a policy initiative by means of intensified exchange activity and the development of a European system of data bases on access.

Meanwhile progress was also made early in the Helios programme in the preparation of the third environmental theme, housing and services to the home, by means of a European workshop to follow up the 1987 study prepared for the Commission by the Housing Research Institute in the Netherlands.

It must be admitted that the timetable I envisaged in 1987 for the policy development component of the Helios programme, involving the preparation of a draft instrument every year, was much too optimistic. Unless and until there is a substantial increase in the core team of officials working on disability in the Commission's service, the notion of one policy initiative per programme — that is, every four years — would be more realistic.

Co-operation and support

The network of rehabilitation centres

The development of this network has followed closely the lines envisaged in the Commission's 1987 programme proposal.[8] The only apparent anomaly is the very different way in which member states have responded to the opportunity to reselect the centres recommended to the Commission for membership. France, the Netherlands and the United Kingdom have not retained any of their former members; Denmark and Ireland have made no changes or additions.[9] One less fortunate consequence of those changes which have been made has been the loss to the network of some prestigious institutions with world-wide reputations.

In the Commission's experts team Louis Van Amelsvoort, although with no more resources than were available for the network in the first programme, is able to run an extremely active and intensified programme. The structure of meetings which allows five thematic seminars and one plenary conference every year is a great advance on anything done before — a good example of how one can do things better if one has the chance to apply the lessons of experience. The study visit programme is maintained at the good level of over 20 group visits a year and there is an increase in the number of individual secondments for intensive professional training.

The participation for the first time of centres concentrating on the training of deaf students and the increase in the number of centres concerned with visual disability (from one to five) and mental illness are well in line with the Commission's programme expectations; the new seminar structure makes it possible to give due attention to what is specific to these problems (for example, the seminar on the training of young people with hearing disabilities in Valencia in 1990). It is interesting that of the present 50 network members no fewer than 22 claim to be concerned with 'all disabilities'. Of the others, 22 are specialized in one broad category of disability (6 on mental handicap; 5 each on physical and visual disability; 4 on mental illness; 2 on hearing impairments). The remaining 6 centres deal with more than one category but not all.

Although there is still the problem that major categories of need are by no means represented from every country, this deficiency is at least to some extent met by the growth of the 'outer network', the idea of which had already been established in the first programme. Indeed the involvement of the outer network, comprising at least another 50 centres, is perhaps the most important advance made by Helios in the history of this network. Professionals from outer network centres regularly take part in seminars and study visits and in this way the dissemination effect of the network is greatly increased. The national network of centres concerned with psychiatric disabilities which is animated by the psychiatric hospital of Thessaloniki in Greece is one among a number of good examples of the effective operation of the outer network at national level.

There is finally a close co-operation, as we should expect, between the network centres and the local model activities (LMAs) concerned with the employment of disabled people. Representatives of these LMAs can participate in the seminar and study visit programme of the centres network; of the major joint seminar in January 1990 and of the 'attention plan' for the economic integration of women I shall have something to say in the next subsection. Priority is also given to innovatory structures of training and employment; a seminar held in Rome in the autumn of 1990 focused on the co-operative movement and included a comparison of how this has developed in Italy and elsewhere. The question of integrated (mainstream) training, though by no means neglected by the network, may need more attention in the future and this could offer an excellent opportunity for a link-up between the centres network and the educational element of Helios.

The local model activities (LMAs)

It will be recalled that the 80 LMAs are organized into three theme-based networks, the Commission's original idea of a fourth network devoted to the co-ordination of all local services having been abandoned in order to avoid overcharging the system. There are 32 LMAs in the network concerned with economic integration (employment and vocational training), 27 in the social integration network (focus on the environment and co-ordination of services to promote independent living) and 21 in the educational integration network (development of mainstreaming).[10] General management of the LMAs is undertaken in the experts team by Claudine Van Lierde who had been a leading member of the Interact team in the first action programme.

The *education network* has the organizational advantage of a relatively small membership, and the substantial asset of the prescription in the annexe to the Council Conclusions of 1986 of four major annual themes which would facilitate the concentration of the exchange activity on issues known to be prominent in the minds of practitioners and policy-makers. We have seen in Chapter 6 that while the education LMAs got off to a good start, it was not possible to launch the thematic work until the Rotterdam conference of October 1989. By then, the timetable required two themes to be treated at once (the classroom situation and co-operation between special and integrated systems), to which — as if that were not enough — the Dutch added a third (transition).

Three different kinds of product emerged from Rotterdam. The first was a considerable amount of useful evidence and opinion about the state of mainstreaming in the member states; the most significant points of this kind have been set out already in Chapter 6.

Secondly, there was the acquisition of a new level of understanding about the extent to which convergence of approach and objectives in member states offered any foundations on which a European policy could be built. On this point the Commission took a positive view, so much so that it presented a draft Resolution on the Rotterdam themes, which the Council duly adopted in May 1990. While in content this did not add a great deal to what was already known and agreed, it did represent some modest progress of a political kind; a Resolution is not by any means a powerful instrument but it is stronger than any expression of will which the Council had permitted itself on this subject before.

Thirdly, there were inevitably lessons to be learned from the Rotterdam conference — the first event of its kind at Community level on this topic — about the most effective ways of working on educational integration at Community level. In the past, all the Commission's conferences in the first action programme had been paid for fully by the Commission. For the education integration themes in the Helios programme, on the other hand, it was from the beginning proposed that costs would be shared between the Commission and a 'volunteer' host country; in 1989 this meant both the Dutch Ministry of Education and the city of Rotterdam. Apart from relieving pressure on the Commission's budget, this method has the additional advantage of ensuring more commitment and therefore more dissemination in the country in which the conference takes place; by a process of simple rotation, all the member states could be involved in this way within the compass of three four-year action programmes, and this would make a significant contribution to the solution of that most intractable of all problems, the effective communication of the results of European work in the member states. However, joint funding has the possible disadvantage that the influence of national or local priorities may lead to some conflict of objectives between these and the requirements of the Community programme which only the Commission is in a position to defend. It could be said that in 1989 this defence of the European interest was less than total.

In particular, although the LMAs were represented at the conference and there was a presentation of their work, their level of participation and active contribution fell far below that which was envisaged when the programme was originally designed. It is quite normal for national officials and academics who have not themselves previously been directly involved in the LMAs to have little or no idea of what they are for, except (at best) in their own country; the Commission has to counteract that deficiency as powerfully as it can or else the LMAs will be undervalued — an extremely dangerous outcome, as we shall see, threatening the whole structure of the action programme approach to Community endeavour.

It is equally significant that although the Arion scheme organized by the Commission's Education Division offers a good number of places each year for subsidized group study visits of educationists concerned with special need (recognized as one of Arion's priority themes) it was not possible at Rotterdam to include the results of this activity as one of the conference inputs.

Still more important was the evidence of Rotterdam on the significance of research, to be seen as an essential element in an educational activity in a sense in which it is not when themes such as employment and the environment of independent living are at issue. The inclusion of a scheme of exchange and co-operation between researchers would ensure substantial progress on educational integration in the third action programme.

In one sense the LMAs on *independent living* are less easy to handle than those on either education or employment, since the topic is in itself unwieldy, comprising as it does transport, public access, housing and home services, and the local means for co-ordinating all these. In turn too this implies a greater divergence between the priorities and structures of the individual LMAs themselves. Important progress has however been made both in learning how to operate such a network effectively and in drawing from it conclusions which bear on policy.

Mary Kyriasopoulou has turned the difficulty posed by the vast scope of the topic and the divergence of the approaches of different LMAs to good account by encouraging the formation of small groups of four or so active people from LMAs in different countries to work together on a topic which they have identified as of common interest. Group study visits and seminars can then focus on this subject, the small group being able to work far more intensively on it than would have been possible for the network all together. The strategy therefore involves better results achieved by easier (and cheaper) means. On the other hand the network is not to be allowed to split up into a number of separate sub-networks; the product of the work of the groups will always be brought to the centre, and each year new groups will be formed to open up or follow different topics.

A second result of grappling with the problems of local co-ordination over this wide area has been the intention to involve in the programme the European and international associations of local authorities. This development had in fact been started successfully enough towards the end of the first action programme, and in view of the close relations already existing between the various associations and the Commission in the social and economic fields there should be no difficulty in reviving it.

As to policy implications, what seem to me the two most prominent to emerge to date are closely related to each other. The first is the observation on the part of Kyriasopoulou that those working at the grass roots in the LMAs are constantly expressing how their ability to achieve good standards of service is limited by financial constraints and administrative or legal difficulties. In other words, it is not simply a question of those at the centre and leadership of the programme looking to the LMAs to provide data on which policy development can be founded (if that is indeed what is expected of them); there is also a force operating in the opposite direction, the LMAs looking to the decision-makers to provide policy developments which will make their task less impossible. This demand is a familiar one enough on the national scale, naturally; the point here is that we are not dealing with the national level but the European one, and that the decision-makers whose intervention is being sought are the Community institutions.

The other key policy factor which was highlighted early in the operation of the LMAs on independent living is the fundamental importance of promoting the influence and advocacy of the disabled people themselves. Indeed this theme was given prominence during the programme's first independent living seminar in Brussels in December 1989, by means of an address given by Mary van Dongen of the Netherlands Gehandicaptenraad. As well as giving an account of the setting up by disabled people of a European Network on Independent Living (ENIL) at an encounter in Strasbourg in April of that year, van Dongen outlined the progress of the independent living movement in the Netherlands, and proposed this as a model for similar developments throughout the Community. In view of the importance which I attach to this theme in the last chapter, it is worth stressing here its emergence as a key issue so early in the exchanges between disabled people and professionals working at the local level.

With the LMAs on *employment and vocational training* we are back with a theme where it is not difficult to maintain concentration at the level of ideas; on the other hand, the co-ordinator in the Helios experts team, Clemens Russel, has to contend with a large network of 32 members. One of the most fascinating aspects of the messages which emerge from this activity is the interest shown both in innovation and in the best tried traditional strategies. New developments in telework in one of the Irish projects, at Tullamore, County Offaly (successor to the previous Midlands district project), has inspired interest and visits from a number of other LMAs, especially in the south of Europe. Interest has also, for example, been shown in the management and productivity of co-operatives, as well as in the struggle for an equal opportunity for disabled women. Indeed this theme has evoked the invention of a new method of network operation, the 'attention plan'. This enables the co-ordinator to call on all the LMAs in his network to explore the reality of a given problem in their locality by responding to a set of common questions and to report back at a plenary meeting by an agreed date. Yet on the traditional side, it is interesting to note an increasing demand for sheltered employment places in Germany, and a new interest in the usefulness of employment quotas in Denmark.

In co-operation with the network of rehabilitation centres, a major effort was made to focus the contribution on this theme to European policy development, by means of a joint seminar of the two networks held in Brussels in January 1989. Keynote speeches on assessment, placement, working situations and sheltered employment were made by Russel himself, Van Amelsvoort, Grammenos and Tina Bertzeletou of CEDEFOP in Berlin; the principal existing texts of the United Nations, the International Labour Organization, the Council of Europe and the Community were also used as a basis of discussion. How much influence this discussion will have on European policy makers remains to be seen, but there is no doubt of the value of it to the participants.

Russel is much concerned at the restraint, even timidity, which he finds among people in employment circles in many countries, the result perhaps of a fear of returning recession and unemployment. He is also dissatisfied with the level of participation of disabled people in the study visits and other elements of the network's programme; the idea of a 'quota' to make this obligatory is being discussed. In co-operation with Grammenos, a major effort has also been made to elicit from all the LMAs accurate data (including statistics) concerning those in need and the effectiveness of the services available. In consequence, by the end of Helios I there will be a corpus of fresh information of a uniquely precious kind to set alongside the more general surveys of Grammenos and others. It is not easy to imagine what more the policy-makers could want than this.

I can refer to the other elements of the Helios programme more briefly. This is not because they are less important than the LMAs. People are constantly wanting to attribute to one or another of the exchange and information activities of the programme more importance than to all the others, and this is always wrong. The only action which has precedence is that undertaken by the Commission at policy level. The activities I shall now mention are vital to the whole balance of a programme which has been designed with such ideas as balance and coverage very much in mind.

The special action on independent living

The scheme for the presentation of awards for environmental projects was launched in 1988 and the first set of these awards was presented by Princess Juliana of the Netherlands in Brussels in December 1989. The aim was to have one award for each member state in each of the three main categories of project — mobility and transport, access to public facilities and housing. Considering this was a first endeavour at something never before attempted, the rate of successful participation was most encouraging. There were ten prize-winning projects for transport and for housing, and nine for public access; the great majority of the projects were able to contribute imaginatively to the exhibition, and a number of videos were also presented.

All the practical arrangements, including the meetings of the jury of experts from all Community countries, have been entrusted by the Commission to the United Kingdom secretariat of Rehabilitation International, the Royal Association for Disability and Rehabilitation (RADAR), whose director until 1990, George Wilson, continues to give it his personal attention.

Convenient as Brussels is from many points of view, the Borschette meeting-room building of the Commission does not offer the best possible site for an event where publicity is imperative. The choice of a hotel in Brighton for the second set of awards, due in December 1991 for projects submitted in 1990, aims to give a better opportunity to display the excellent examples of good European practice made available. By the end of the programme the accumulation of data on some 50 projects in all three domains will offer valuable material both for direct technical application (including the training of architects and other professionals) and as a basis for policy development both in the member states and on the part of the European institutions.

Support for non-governmental organizations

As was to be expected, this element of the programme has continued to develop in quality and scope without the need for major modification.[11] The increasing demand which the success of the activity has inevitably evoked and the predictable inability of resources to keep up with this has inevitably led to some tightening of criteria, but in spirit the Commission's support remains what it always was and the autonomy of the associations is fully respected. The formation by a number of leading NGOs of specifically Community sections where these did not exist before is moreover a useful step forward.

Among developments of particular importance has been the first endeavour, undertaken by means of a seminar organized by Eurolink Age in Florence in March 1989, to grapple with the problems of ageing and disability.[12] This was particularly timely in view of the new action programme on ageing being developed by the Commission at that time, and of the decision to create a European Year of Elderly People in 1993. It is to be hoped that the draft European Code of Good Practice on Disability and Ageing will establish a sound basis for policy development in this domain.

Most important of all has been the progress made at the political level, progress brought about by the NGOs themselves but in a framework offered by the Commission. A skilfully organized campaign on the part of the European Community Regional Secretariat of the World Federation of the Deaf engaged the co-operation of nine other leading NGOs in persuading the European Parliament to vote an additional sum of over 1 million ECUs to the Commission's budget for the Helios programme in 1990.[13] A further campaign the following year helped to secure the maintenance of the budget at this level against an attempt on the part of the Council to cut it severely. These successful interventions represent a breakthrough in the ability of European organizations of disabled people to operate the Community democracy in their interest, by no means an easy task.[14]

In 1990 also the NGOs further strengthened their position by forming an independent group 'NGOs in Consultation', under the first chairmanship of Tony Lumley, secretary-general of Mobility International. With this reinforced facility for exploring common positions in advance of formal meetings with the Commission, and for planning other initiatives in relation to the European institutions, the European NGOs of and for disabled people can be seen to be pursuing empowerment very much in the way recommended in this book.

In the section on the LMAs I mentioned the creation by physically disabled people meeting in Strasbourg in 1989 of a European Network on Independent Living. This has also been a development full of promise. We may well see the interests of those with motor disabilities as well represented at European level in the future as those of sensorily disabled people already are. The formation of a European Confederation for the Employment of Disabled People is another encouraging initiative.

Arts and sport

The activity in these spheres which we initiated in the first action programme has been considerably reinforced by the allocation on the part of the Commission of increased resources and the setting up of a separate experts team to co-ordinate the co-operative work.[15] On the side of the arts, for example, a new non-governmental organization has been formed known as EUCREA (European creativity; its formal name is Association européenne pour la créativité des personnes handicapées, or European Association for the Creativity of Disabled People). Recent developments include the setting up of a European Alternative Arts Centre in Liège, a theatre festival and exhibition of paintings, both involving mentally disabled people and held in Belgium, a seminar on music and movement in Vejle in Denmark and a symposium on creativity and disabled persons in Greece. Also associated with the programme are a workshop in Hanover which has brought together artists from five Community countries to work with blind people, and the celebrated Oiseau Mouche company of mentally handicapped actors centred on Lille. 1989 also saw the completion of an important study commissioned during the first action programme and undertaken by the Hester Adrian Research Centre in Manchester on the promotion of creative activities for people with profound mental retardation and multiple impairments.

Information

Handynet

Progress in the implementation of the European Community multilingual computerized information system (Handynet) has been sufficient to ensure the development of a project with enormous potential but whose whole future at one time looked in doubt. That the advance has been slow is no more than should be expected for an endeavour whose considerable technical difficulties are exceeded by the political problems it excites in the member states.

By the middle of 1990 very nearly all the member states had signed the convention with the Commission for their active participation in the implementation of Handyaids, the first module of the whole system.[16] The sole exception was Germany where a complex set of difficulties has made agreement to the Commission's proposal particularly difficult. Based on the Commission's specially devised nine-language thesaurus (Handyvoc), the register of technical aids available in the Community and directory of the bodies responsible for their production and distribution which constitute Handyaids are now able to prove their usefulness for all to see.

Although the Council in its Decision of December 1989 did not give its agreement in principle to the development of other Handynet modules, it is not over-optimistic to suppose that these will be accepted once Handyaids has proved its practicability and usefulness. Among the first of the new modules to be ready will probably be that on computer softwares for special needs education, but there will be many other candidates and the Commission's chief problem is likely to be establishing priorities among them.

Publications

Early on in the Helios programme it was decided to amalgamate the rehabilitation network journal and district project newsletter which had been appearing during the first action programme. The new periodical, known simply as *Helios*, is published in all the Community languages and covers all aspects of the action programme.

The publication in a number of languages of studies directed by the Commission's Bureau, which had been a prominent feature of the first action programme, has been discontinued in Helios.

The media

It has for a long time been realized that there is need a Community action to promote public awareness of disability problems, achievements and potentials, as soon as the resources to do this could be found. The start which we made with this in the first action programme had to be abandoned when it proved impossible to replace Charles Humblet in the Commission's core team. However within the Helios programme the Commission has reopened discussion of this topic, and there is hope for concerted action on it in Helios II, due to start in 1992. A good start was made by the organization in May 1990 of a European conference on 'The Portrayal of Disabled People through the Mass Media' at Val Vibrata, one of the Italian LMAs.

Other initiatives relevant to disability

The European Social Fund

Since the start of the Helios programme in 1988 there have been two important developments for disabled people within the European Social Fund.[17] The first is a number of quite novel interventions on the part of the Fund in favour of the deaf community, a consequence of the success of the European Community Regional Secretariat of the World Federation of the Deaf in encouraging the European Parliament to adopt a Resolution in June 1988 in support of the official recognition of sign languages. One of these projects concerns the training of deaf youth workers in north-west England; the second is for the setting up of a centre for the training of sign language interpreters in Greece; the third consists of a large grant in support of the advanced training of teachers of British Sign Language in the University of Durham.

Of much wider implication has been the development of a major Commission proposal for a programme to support the full participation of disadvantaged persons in the economic opportunities of the free market from 1992 onwards. Known as the Community Initiative, it comprises three actions, one of which, Horizon, is above all concerned with disabled people.[18] The central aim is to reduce unemployment by means of training and job-creation initiatives. A relatively large budget is foreseen which may be devoted to the direct support of activities in the poorer regions of the Community, and to multicultural exchange programmes provided one of the partners consists of or includes a poor region. Although everything will depend on the quality of projects encouraged and presented by the member states, Horizon offers the prospect of a return to the good days of the 1970s when disabled people were a named priority category within the European Social Fund — and perhaps something more than that.

Research and development

Within the programme of the Directorate-General responsible for research and development in new technologies of information and communication, the European Parliament voted 10 million ECUs in the budget for 1991 for a new action on 'technology for the socio-economic integration of disabled people and the elderly' (TIDE).

Within the programme on advanced informatics in medicine, which is expected to run for three years from May 1991, disabled people and the elderly are also mentioned specifically as target groups; they continue to be so in the concerted research activities of the biomedical and health programme.

IMPLICATIONS FOR HELIOS II

Obviously, it is too early to attempt any global evaluation of Helios. The Commission will present its own evaluation in due course, greatly assisted in this by the very substantial reports which are already being produced by the Helios experts.

That the Council will approve the adoption of a third action programme (Helios II), to start in 1992, was put beyond all doubt by the outcome of a 'political debate' of the Ministers of Social Affairs which took place in September 1989. In the published Conclusions of this discussion, the President stressed the need for 'a global policy to co-ordinate all measures affecting the daily lives of handicapped persons' and 'account to be taken in the different Community policies of the specific needs of the handicapped'. There should be 'a procedure for following up and giving impetus to these actions' and 'the Commission should be able to make proposals on these points'.

Whatever may be the effect of the evaluation which the Commission itself makes of Helios I, there are a number of elements of it which it is probably safe to say will be continued and developed without any major modification during its successor. The crucial series of policy initiatives is the most obvious of these; the programme of grants to support the European co-operation of NGOs is another.

We should hope too that there will be additional resources within the Commission's own services to make it possible to develop some useful actions which it has been simply impossible to cover so far. One of these might be the topic just mentioned of the presentation of disability in the media. Others would be the initiation of more active liaison with other activities of the Commission so that disabled people get all the benefit from these that they should. Important examples are the many programmes of research and development in the field of new technology, and a number of the activities of the Task Force on Human Resources.[19]

As for Handynet, apart from determining priorities of content, the Commission's main problem will be fostering the technical developments and political will in the national systems needed if the member states are able to respond to the succession of proposals for new modules which are likely to emerge from Brussels. The Commission has for a long time been clear and consistent about its main objectives for Handynet and it is hard to imagine any fundamental change of position on this.

It is to be hoped too that the annual awards for environmental projects which constitute the special action on independent living will be at least maintained, with whatever modifications of content or organization are suggested in the light of experience. Better still would be an increase in the budget for the programme sufficient to revive the Commission's original intention to run, in addition to these largely symbolical awards, a scheme of substantial direct grants to projects about to be launched or in the early stage of development. There is no doubt that this would give much more weight to this element of the programme. The availability of 'real money' would stimulate competition within and between member states in a way that courtesy awards simply cannot do, as well as giving more solid proof of the value which the Community attaches to this whole domain.

Coming to the networks of rehabilitation centres and local model activities (LMAs) we find ourselves confronted with questions, even perhaps doubts, which I believe to be of the greatest interest and importance. Networks of this kind are costly in staff and in cash terms — if, that is, any serious effort is made to operate them in a dynamic way. There need to be study visit schemes, and programmes of seminars and conferences, and a great deal of information in print form as well as final reporting. Anyone who has not worked at European level can have no idea of what has to be added to the normal weight of that, in terms not only of cash cost but of time consuming process, when one is obliged to work in nine different languages, something which no other supranational organization is doing or has ever done. Apart from the organization of all this, network members need a constant service of professional advice and support, and this implies the services of adequate staff of high quality, evidently an extremely costly provision.

So the question must be asked: is it worth it? Without these networks, the Commission's whole programme would appear at first sight far less vital and rich. We can observe too the concern of those who are promoting the setting up of a new Community action programme concerned with ageing that if the money is not found to enable this to include a network of model projects the whole action will not amount to very much. Yet we shall need stronger arguments than these if we are to convince the European decision-makers that the continuation or development of the network elements in Helios II is clearly justified and necessary.

Let me say at once that I believe that it is. To explore the point we need to ask ourselves again what the networks are for. To this the basic answer is simple enough: they are intended to influence practice directly and policy indirectly. Let us look at these two aspects in turn.

Networks enable *and inspire* those involved in the everyday problems of disability to learn from each other's experience. This is because, if they are energetically and sensitively managed, they enable the essential human processes on which authentic learning depends to take root and flourish — processes such as seeing one's own work with new eyes, becoming receptive to new ideas, the development of skills in distinguishing what in other situations is relevant and applicable to one's own, the willingness to impart knowledge and understanding as well as to receive these (i.e. to give to the system as well as take from it).

The people we are talking about are of course the many kinds of professionals and voluntary workers who are directly engaged at different levels of professionalism and responsibility, whether in establishments or the open community, in working for the improvement of the quality of life of disabled people. Included in this of course are all the families and friends of disabled people, and all the disabled people themselves, whether they are working for others with disabilities (for example, in the independent living movement) or simply building their own quality of life. They are what the French call 'les hommes du terrain', the people at the grass roots.

There is no doubt that these people are directly and effectively touched by the networking process. I have plenty of cogent evidence of that myself; the Interact experts of the first action programme and the Helios experts have evidence in abundance. Moreover, very many of such people are, directly or indirectly, so affected: it is not that we are thinking merely of the directors of centres and leaders of projects; those significantly involved are to be numbered in thousands rather than hundreds. Provided quality in the operation can be guaranteed, increase in the number of centres or localities in the networking activity will give a full equivalent increase in the achievement. In principle, therefore, the more networks with the more members, the better. In practice, of course, the number is limited by the amount of work that can be done by a central team in terms of organization, reporting and so forth.

Since networking is, at the practical level, effective in its own terms, the value that anyone assigns to it will depend on the extent to which he or she values grass-roots practical improvement; put another way, it depends on the value he or she assigns to people working, at various levels, in direct contact with everyday problems, to their aspirations and to the work they do. Those who have had little or no experience of bureaucracy or the diplomatic and political processes may be forgiven for supposing that everyone assigns a high value to these things and these people.

Alas, it is not so. The conclusion is this: as far as concerns the first of the two purposes of network activity, the bringing of direct influence to bear on practice, the value which is attributed to this will depend on the value system of whoever is making the valuation. It is not even going too far to say that a person's whole vision of Europe is engaged when this issue is being addressed.

Looking now at the indirect influence which networking may have on policy, it is evident that this could take effect at either one or both of two levels, the national and the European. At the national level, there is of course already evidence of such influence but its extent is in my judgement disappointing. It is not always clear that member states know how they intend to apply the experience of their network members in the national situation or that they are able or willing to find the resources to see that any such application comes about. Nor is it always clear either that the civil servants directly involved in co-operation with the Commission in the implemen-tation of the European programme have the ear of senior colleagues in influential positions at home, or that those European parliamentarians who are well informed and enthusiastic about the Community activity in the field of disability are able to carry this message back to their own national parties.

Nor, it seems, would the addition of a substantial input of money from the Com-mission in support of the day-to-day costs of participating centres or localities, if it were possible, make much difference to the attention which national authorities would give to what was happening from a policy point of view.

Certainly some progress in this matter could be made and should be attempted. Before any networks were set up it could be made clear to the national representatives that one of the objectives was to provide evidence of good practice as a basis for national policy development. More detailed criteria for selection of network members could be imposed by the Commission, and the member states could be bound to use relatively open selection procedures, involving statutory and voluntary bodies which would then participate in monitoring the progress of the networks at the national level and in devising national strategies of dissemination of their results.

In this way, over time, the networks would acquire a reputation for relevance and seriousness among national decision-makers, and their direct contribution to national policy development would grow. But it would not be a quick process, and would be unlikely to work equally well in all countries. Yet in the end this is not a fatal objection to the value of the networks, since they can make a vital and unique contribution to the development of European policy, which when expressed in the form of Community policy instruments (wherever possible of a constraining nature) influences national policies far more effectively since the instruments bear on all the member states equally and at the same time, as well as entailing the obligation of the national authorities to report to the European institutions on all they have done by way of implementation.

To appreciate the importance of this contribution, we need to consider the various means by which the Commission can gather data and opinion as a foundation for its policy proposals. I suggest that there are four of these:

1. Previous policy instruments of international organizations on the given topic, for example resolutions or conventions of the United Nations, the International Labour Organization, the Council of Europe and the like. As a general rule I believe that this is a recourse of very limited use. These documents, entirely valid in their own terms and appropriate for their own purposes, were developed in a totally different political context and aimed at a different membership of countries. As check-lists of ideas to ensure that significant points have not simply been forgotten they can be useful at one stage or another of the preparatory process of a Community initiative, but it would be fruitless to rely on them for more than that. What I say here does not of course apply to the special case of the European Conference of Ministers of Transport.

2. Commission studies and consultants' reports. These are obviously an extremely useful and flexible resource, as the Commission can both time and design them to suit its precise policy needs, and to fill whatever gaps exist in the available knowledge and understanding of the subject. Because of this ad hoc 'customer' character they are highly cost-effective, and it is indeed unlikely that a policy proposal reliable as to content can be devised at European level without resort to one or other of these.

3. Study of analytical reports of network activities. Again this is, surely quite obviously, a precious source of knowledge and understanding that gets under the surface of all the sometimes blithe generalities of international discourse. Its unique quality is that it brings to light not only the reality of everyday solutions to everyday problems, but also the many situations where no solutions can be found — and the reasons for this. This is the 'grass-roots dividend', something which only networking can reliably and consistently deliver, something particularly appropriate to the down-to-earth style which always characterizes the Community when it knows where it is going.

4. Consultation of networks and other collaborators. When the Commission has a discussion document or first draft of a policy proposal ready for the consultation process the existence of active networks means that it is always able immediately to call on the opinion of disabled people and professionals in all the Community countries who are both in close touch with everyday realities and yet used also to thinking and feeling at the European level. This mode of consultation is quite

out of the class of any other where the task is to design a policy proposal which responds to needs of people in twelve countries with their different cultures and economic and political situations.

Nothing could be clearer to me than the fact that of these four possible sources of inspiration, facts and understanding it is the three that are Community-based which can make an authentic contribution to a Community initiative. Of the four, the third depends entirely and the fourth to a very large extent on the existence of co-operative networks of centres or localities. My conclusion is that on the grounds alone of their value to the development of Community policy the networks perform a function that is vital to the Community and therefore well worth the cost in staff and cash.

Returning to Helios II, there may well be good reasons for redesigning the networks, rethinking their size, number, interrelations and thematic content in the light of experience. At least I should hope that both establishments (such as centres of rehabilitation and training) and localities will still be involved. Indeed, new elements may need to be added. As Armand Maron has pointed out to me, there is no reason in principle why the topics of prevention and medical rehabilitation should not be included in the programme if that is found to be practicable. Any thought of eliminating the networks from the programme would in my opinion cripple it fatally.

NOTES

1 The director is Armand Maron, former director of the Belgian Fonds national de reclassement social des handicapés, and the deputy director Cristina Louro, former director of the Gulbenkian Centre for children and young people with cerebral palsy in Lisbon, a member of the rehabilitation centres network. From the previous Interact team, Claudine Van Lierde has taken responsibility for the local model activities; during the programme, Danielle Rimbert was succeeded as co-ordinator of the Handynet project by Josiane Pierre from the Mulhouse rehabilitation centre, and Lieven Joniaux left to become first head of the experts Team Creativity and Sport. Louis Van Amelsvoort, previously on secondment to the Bureau from the Dutch Ministry of Social Affairs, took over charge of the rehabilitation centres network.

2 The allocation to the programme for 1991 was about 7½ million ECUs. For the successful campaigns about the budget, see p. 164 above.

3 Compare Chapter 2, p. 18.

4 Two of the earlier Commission studies on mobility had also been entrusted to ERICA (see References to Chapter 5).

5 For Article 118A see p. 157. Article 48 concerns the free movement of workers, and Articles 8A and 8B the creation of the free internal market.

6 The meetings were organized in co-operation with the RI secretariats in the four countries (INSERSO in Spain, the Gehandicaptenraad in the Netherlands, CNFLRH in France and RADAR in the United Kingdom). The four individual experts, each of whom consulted organizations of disabled people in their own country, were Miguel Gerez, John Fredericksen, Hans Aengenendt, and Paola Vulterini in respectively Belgium, Denmark, Germany and Italy.

7 Important, above all, because a Commission draft Directive is likely to encounter opposition, notably from Denmark, Germany and the United Kingdom.

8 For rehabilitation network members, see Appendix 2C.

9 Nor has Luxembourg, but this involves only one centre. Spain (one new member added)

and Portugal (no change) have naturally not dropped any of their former centres since they only joined the network in 1986–7.

10   For a list of LMAs, see Appendix 2B.
11   Appendix 2A contains a list of the NGOs which are members of the Commission's Dialogue Group; other NGOs may also be eligible for financial support within the programme.
12   I was invited by Age Concern to act as a chairman and rapporteur of this seminar; see References below.
13   DIP and AEH were not involved.
14   ECRS was also responsible for a survey of deaf people in the European Community, commissioned during the first action programme and published in 1990; see References below.
15   For this unit, see n. 1 above.
16   For the list of national Handynet data collection centres, see Appendix 2E.
17   Unfortunately these do not include a decision on the part of the Fund to recognize activities related to sheltered employment.
18   The others are NOW (equal opportunities for women) and EUROFORM (new qualifications).
19   These could include Arion (exchange of educationists), Erasmus (university exchange), Lingua (language learning) and the various actions involving young people.

REFERENCES

Note References to Community documents produced after 1987 on employment or on environmental topics (transport, housing, etc.) are given at the end of Chapter 5.

Community policy documents

Proposal for two Council Decisions establishing an action programme at Community level to promote the social and economic integration and independent living of people with disabilities (COM (87) 342 of 20 July 1987).
Council Decision of 18 Apr. 1988 establishing a second Community action programme for disabled people (Helios) (O.J. No. L 104/38 of 23 Apr. 1988).
Commission Report on the application of Council Recommendation 86/379 EEC of 24 July 1986 on the employment of disabled people in the Community (COM (88) 746 of 15 Dec. 1988).
Commission Report to the Council on the establishment of the Handynet system (COM (89) 450 of 27 Sept. 1989).
Council Conclusions of 29 Sept. 1989 concerning a global European policy to assist the handicapped and disabled (8773/89 Press 165).
Council Decision of 18 Dec. 1989 concerning the further development of the Handynet system in the context of the Helios programme (O.J. No. L 393/35 of 30 Dec. 1989).
Resolution of the Council and of the Ministers of Education meeting within the Council of 31 May 1990 concerning the integration of children and young people with disabilities into ordinary systems of education (O.J. No. C 162/2 of 3 July 1990).
Commission Interim Report on the implementation and results of the Helios programme promoting the economic and social integration of disabled people in the European Community. Period 1.1.88–30.6.90 (Sec (91) 299 of 25 Feb. 1991).
Commission proposal for a Council Directive on minimum requirements to improve the mobility and the safe transport to work of workers with reduced mobility (COM (90) 588 of 25 Feb. 1991).

Commission studies

James Hogg and Judith Cavet (Hester Adrian Research Centre), *Occupational and Leisure Activities for People with Profound Mental Retardation and Multiple Impairments*, Manchester 1989.

Lesley Jones and Gloria Pullen, *Inside We are all Equal — a social policy survey of deaf people in the European Community*, Durham 1990.

Report of independent seminar sponsored by the Commission

Patrick Daunt, *Age and Disability — a challenge for Europe* (with French parallel text: La Vieillesse et l'invalidité — un défi pour l'Europe), report of a Eurolink Age seminar held at Florence, Mar. 1990, London 1990.

United Nations

Disability: situation, strategies and policies, United Nations, New York 1986.

Report on National Legislation for Equalization of Opportunities for People with Disabilities: examples from 22 countries and areas, UN Centre for Social Development and Humanitarian Affairs and Rehabilitation International, Vienna 1989.

Peter Mittler, *Towards the Year 2000 — from awareness to action*, paper commissioned by the Disabled Persons Unit, UN Centre for Social Development and Humanitarian Affairs, Vienna 1990.

Chapter 8

Prospects and Principles

PROSPECTS

If we are to consider the possibilities for a substantial improvement in the situation of disabled people in the European Community over the next decade or two we shall find that there is no place for either pessimism or optimism.

That pessimism would be wrong is demonstrated by the progress that has been made since the 1950s and 1960s in terms of legislation and facilitating measures, the development of official agencies, the growth in the range and effectiveness of voluntary organizations, improvements in the attitudes of professionals and the general public and increased participation and self-determination among disabled people. Moreover, in spite of the economic restraints which have characterized the last decade, accompanied as they have been by a tendency to promote competitive over co-operative motivations and to foster the confusion between the making of money and the creation of wealth, progress in many fields and many places continues.

On the other hand where progress in the domain of disability is concerned nothing may be assumed, and to speak of the need for an ongoing struggle is never an exaggeration. In many countries there have, in real terms, been cuts not only in benefits but also in services; where there are so many examples of progress actually being reversed it would be absurd to indulge in optimistic complacency. Most significantly, in all the Community countries policies of deinstitutionalization depend on the transfer of resources if standards are not to decline, and this offers opportunities to the budget-cutter which may be irresistible. And it would be a fatal error to suppose that we can largely rely on an imminent increase in the general prosperity, as a result of 1992 or the peace dividend or whatever. It may be true that *potentially* an economic upsurge could be of more benefit to disabled people than any other development or initiative, but we must not be deluded by any supposition that this would happen automatically.

Nor is there much evidence that national governments are willing to think in terms of a national comprehensive plan to meet the needs of disabled people; too often they seem to prefer to respond to pressures in an ad hoc way. As for the development of European policy, some at least of those close to the scene do not believe there is any significant commitment to this idea among the national authorities. The Commission's experts are well enough aware that those working in the field in the member states need a stronger political framework than is generally available. Sometimes, disabled people and their allies seem to lack the political skills necessary for progress at this level; leaders in the militant movement recognize the serious need for training in advocacy.

Before however exploring what I believe is the need for new alliances, I must explain what I regard as the aim of all effort to improve the situation of disabled people.

The general aim

The objective of independent living is rightly regarded as so important that there is a danger that we should be led to the mistake of thinking that it is the global aim. That this is not so can be seen as soon as we take a cradle-to-grave viewpoint: independence is evidently not a dominant objective for young children — preparation for it may well be, but, as we have seen in Chapter 6, the preparatory aspect of childhood should not be overstressed. The importance of independence in old age is also not a simple question. Indeed, there is not even need to look merely at the beginning and end of life to discover that independence cannot be promoted to the top of the pyramid of aims and objectives — for everyone, the relation between happiness and independence is far too complex, even ambiguous, for that to be possible.

At the Eurolink Age seminar on 'Disability and Ageing' which took place in Florence in March 1990 we concluded after some discussion that the overall aim should be the promotion of a *good quality of life* for all people with disabilities. Its superiority over independence in the hierarchy of goals is confirmed by the fact that individuals may vary in the degree to which they want to be independent but not in their desire for a good quality of life. As Patricia Rock has pointed out 'the concept of independence is a self-defined one which varies from person to person'.[1]

Of such a good quality of life we were able to identify these components:

- *autonomy*: the freedom to choose a preferred way of life
- *independence*: the opportunity to make one's own practical decisions; encouragement not to be over-dependent in everyday matters
- *integration*: acceptance by society as a fellow citizen and member of the community, with full political as well as social rights; freedom from marginalization
- *respect*: recognition of the value of one's identity and role, and of one's contribution to the lives of others
- *ownership*: the possibility to keep one's own personal possessions and retain control of one's own finances
- *social involvement and communication*: access to regular, free social contact and communication with others, including family and peers; freedom from isolation
- *activity and mobility*: access to a range of useful and interesting occupations, of educational experiences and cultural, leisure and self-help activities; encourage-

ment and support in undertaking these; availability of an accessible environment, including transport
- *privacy*
- *tranquillity*: freedom from noise and disruption; continuity of place and environment.

Of course this analysis is imperfect and could surely be improved in many ways. Apart from anything else it reflects the context from which it is derived — a seminar on disability and ageing. Because of that it understates the need for personal development, and there are probably other points of emphasis appropriate to elderly people rather than to others; in spite of the context on the other hand, there is no mention of protection from exploitation and abuse, or indeed of the whole medical domain.

For all these deficiencies, I believe the analysis has some general and particular merits which would justify using it as a basis for further work. A great advantage of a 'shopping list' like this is that it both helps us to clarify some of our generalizations and (more importantly) leads us quickly in the direction of genuinely individual applications.

At the general level we can see that, while the global aim is indeed appropriate to everyone without exception, the relative importance of the particular components will tend to vary according to age-groups and to kinds and levels of disability. Of course the general warning about generalizations must apply here, their usefulness in the construction of conceptual frameworks, problem maps and planning parameters never being allowed to translate itself into individual prescriptions.

In fact the list itself protects us from that danger, above all in its insistence that *there is no one to whom all the components of the aim do not apply*. From that powerful starting point, the list actually requires us to explore authentically individual life-plans which take into consideration the desires and aspirations of the individual quite as much as what is perceived as feasible or regarded by others as normal or meritorious.

It is true that thinking more specifically about the needs of children would make us want to modify and perhaps add to the list of components and what is said about them. But the general effect of the list will be to support the approach which I have defended earlier on, I mean the view that the lives of children should be seen as primarily an end in themselves and only secondarily as a preparatory means to adult life.

The list as it stands has, I suggest, also some particular merits. Above all it endeavours at least to postulate one possible statement of the relation between autonomy and independence. If this is more or less correct, then it would carry the important implication that autonomy includes the possibility of choosing a life-style in which independence is not all that prominent. A second merit is the demotion of another false pretender to the title of overall aim — integration. Evidently integration is an enormously important component of a good quality of life as a general rule; just how important to each one of us must be an issue in which there is plenty of room for personal choice and for variation of choice at different times in our lives. We need to beware too of the danger implicit in integration as a one-way process, stressing the need for disabled people to adapt to the given environment and so overlooking the need for the environment itself to be adapted so as to be accessible to disabled people.

To place independent living and integration in a correct relationship with the global aim should help to protect us from the mistake of thinking that the life-styles desired and eloquently proclaimed by some are necessarily desired by all or desirable for all, and from the proliferation of new and perhaps inflexible orthodoxies. This does not on the other hand mean that we should underestimate the importance of social integration and independence.[2] We should hope to find them, as it were, on every-one's list, and it would be entirely appropriate for them to appear at or near the top of the list of objectives of some organizations of disabled people.

Reservations about independence do not either imply a failure to recognize that many disabled people, for any of a variety of reasons, may be inclined to under-estimate their own independent potential and need a good deal of positive encourage-ment if they are to put this to the test. Nor is it at all strange that independence as well as integration have been and are so prominent in the programmes of the European Community, including above all Helios. For reasons explained in Part I, Community action in the disability field has focused — not exclusively but largely — on the economically active adult population. As the Community's attention is drawn increasingly also to the needs of children and elderly people, so we can expect to see, at least as far as the concept of independence is concerned, some shift of emphasis.

Before leaving this discussion of the aim I need to mention the idea of 'equality of opportunity' which also figures prominently in the discourse of politically active disabled people. I shall discuss this in the next main section of this chapter under the heading of 'Principles'.

The notion of empowerment

'Empowerment' is a term which we hear of more and more in the discourse of disabled people and their allies. This is not surprising, particularly in view of the recent achievement of the militant movement of disabled people in the United States already described (p. 51). The proof of effective empowerment is the ability to influence the political process in favour of a given aim — in this case the achievement of a better quality of life for all people with disabilities of whatever kind and severity.

We have seen that the economic, social and educational issues which I explored in Part II are relevant to all kinds of disability. It would seem quite obvious that if the representatives of people with every kind of disability are to influence the political process in the fields of employment, environmental accessibility, education and ben-efits they should combine their forces in order to do this, since evidently their political weight if they are all working together is vastly greater than the addition of all that they could achieve separately.

The setting up of this co-operation, at local, national and European levels, could be attempted by either one of two means. The various organizations of disabled people (of those with mental, motor or sensory disabilities, for example, but also more specialized associations of those with such impairments as spina bifida, muscular dystrophy, multiple sclerosis, epilepsy) could retain their independence for all the purposes of basic membership and allegiance and for many services of support and advice, but then come together at regular and appropriate times to discuss common problems, seek for common positions and plan common political action. This is the model which the European Commission has fostered at the European level, and the evolution of which we followed in the last chapter. Alternatively, a group which has taken the lead in militancy and advocacy, no doubt in fact therefore a group of physically disabled people, could open its doors to all disabilities, perhaps at the same time claiming that it alone can represent the whole world of disability in an effective and authentic way.

I have argued in Chapter 3 that of these two alternatives the second is inadequate and that it would be better for all concerned if it were abandoned. I hope that this is even more evident now that we are concentrating on the precise and urgent issue of political influence — influence, that is, not only by means of consultation in the lead up to new measures but also throughout the process of implementation. I do not believe that an organization established by and for physically disabled people could ever accommodate as full and equal members deaf people, or people with mental handicaps, or users of mental health services, to mention only the most obvious difficulties, without having to adapt its own style and goals in such a way as to make it incapable of pursuing effectively the very ends for which it was first set up.

It must be admitted that the first alternative makes tough demands on the militant organizations of physically disabled people, demands at one and the same time on their altruism, their solidarity and their flexibility. It cannot be easy to lead a struggle for equality without becoming something of a purist, and harder still to have to concede some of this allegiance to absolutes in favour of those compromises which co-operation may require. They would need to abandon any pretension to be the only authentic voice of disability ('disability' here in the wide sense, of course). They would have to recognize and respect the difference of styles and positions of other organizations, and accept them as equals. Coming to terms with the fact that the representatives of the community of deaf people might have very different views on educational integration would be one necessity, but not perhaps the most difficult to adjust to. What might be much more difficult would be accepting that, in organizations of mentally handicapped people, for example, or of users of mental health services, there may be a continuing role for family members or professionals of a kind which would not usually be found or welcomed in organizations of physically or sensorily disabled people. But to fail to accept this would be to engage in conflict with a reality which is not contingent but will abide whatever anybody says or does.

And, on the other side, and in spite of the validity of those roles I have just mentioned, the national and international associations concerned with mental disabilities — using the term here to cover both intellectual and psychological problems — will need to adjust and evolve, so as to be able to demonstrate beyond all doubt that they are, *or can operate authentically as*, organizations 'of' not merely 'for' disabled people. This would mean promoting this aspect of their work to a much higher position than I believe it typically enjoys, and therefore devoting more resources to it. I am convinced that this is possible and the right way ahead. To illustrate that confidence: no doubt it is true that family members can be bad at promoting the autonomy and self-advocacy of a mentally handicapped person (they may be over-protective, over-anxious, inclined to underestimate potential and so forth); equally, it is evident that some family members are extremely good at this, and where this is so likely to be better than any one else. And, since representative empowerment entails leadership of the 'all' by the 'some', that is good enough. At the same time, I suspect that if this evolution is to happen to any significant extent, far more encouragement and incentives in its favour will have to be afforded to the associations concerned from official sources.

Patterns of representation

That the implications of what I have just argued need not be so revolutionary or exigent can be shown by means of a simplified model. Let us suppose that five major organizations of disabled people agree that they will preserve and respect each other's independence, but will work together, both regularly and as occasion demands, to explore common positions and plan interventions in the political process.

The five organizations might be the leading associations of people with motor, visual, auditory, intellectual and psychological disabilities. The group might call itself something like a National Council of Disabled People, the idea of federation being important for its stress on non-intervention in the styles and priorities of the member associations. The Council could include among its ground rules these provisions:

- at all Council meetings each association could be represented by two people, each of whom must be disabled according to the definition of the association concerned
- each representative could be accompanied by a companion, who might be a professional (signer, nurse, therapist, doctor, social worker, teacher and so on) or a personal friend or family member
- in addition to the expenses of members and their companions, all companions would be paid a fee for their service to Council meetings
- the chairmanship of the Council would rotate among the member associations annually or biennially; the secretariat would either rotate or be located with one member association, the expense being shared
- the Federation would be open to new members, notably associations of people with specific disabilities but also associations with 'horizontal' definitions (of elderly disabled people, for example, or of disabled women).

What would the Council do? Its main task would be to develop political skill and effectiveness. One might hope that this would include the recognition that whereas bitterness can be productive, sourness almost never is; also how to be nice to one's friends and concentrate one's attack on — well, not enemies exactly — let us say the right target.

Such a Federation should soon be able to assert its rightful claim to represent, within reason, all disabled people, and to reinforce that claim rapidly by the addition of new member associations. What we might then hope to see would be something very much tougher than we have ever seen in the countries of the Community. I actually believe that European disabled people have been patient too long; I also believe that those forces in society which feel more comfortable when disabled people are maintained at (or reduced to) the level of recipients of charity are more likely to gain in influence than to lose it in the next decade. In other words we are confronted with a world where those who do not fight for their rights will get nothing worth having.

As to rights, see p. 184 below. As for fighting, without actually intending incitement to riot, I do mean something more than mere words. It could be instructive for a start to see some wheelchairs on the London Underground and let the authorities work out what they were going to do about it. Massive solidarity of the kind the Federation I have described would express could not fail to make an impression on the public, the media and the political institutions, and if that impression were sometimes underlined by acts of cheerful obstruction so much the better.

All this implies of course the rejection of the view that prominent activism about disability as such is stigmatizing — a recipe for doing nothing if ever there was.

Levels of representation

The federal approach that I have just described can apply equally well to local, regional, national, European and international levels. Of these there are two, the national and the European, about which there are some specific points to be made. What applies at the national level might also apply lower down, above all in federal states; and what is said for the European Community might have some application in international contexts too.

On the national scale there would be two basic points of a constitutional kind to which I suggest priority should be given. The first would be to campaign in every country for the creation of a Ministry for Disabled People which would be independent of other ministries, have the support of its own civil servants and control its own budget.[3] In all other relevant Ministries there would be a unit concentrating on the problems of disabled people (including of course disabled children, young people and elderly people) on all issues for which that Ministry was responsible; the units in the British and French Ministries of Transport would be models for this. These units would include in their responsibilities the consultation of the organizations of disabled people and the bringing together of them with representatives of professionals and the two sides of industry. The senior civil servant of the Ministry for the Disabled would preside over a committee of the heads of all those units.

The second constitutional goal should be to achieve statutory recognition of the right of the Federated Council to be consulted by the Ministry for the Disabled, above all whenever legislation is in preparation. On that basis the Council would be able to set about its main practical work – the achievement over time of a coherent and comprehensive set of statutory measures to guarantee the best possible quality of life for disabled people, based on a declaration of their rights and culminating in a social charter for the implementation of these.

At the European level the critical development would be the setting up in the framework of the European Parliament of a Forum of Disabled People in the European Community; the precedent already exists in the women's sector. This would be constituted exactly in the same way as the Federated Council just described, except that the member organizations would of course be European not national associations of disabled people; thanks to the Commission's action programme an impressive number of these not only already exist but are active and experienced in European problems and styles of work. As well as having formal rights of consultation granted by the Parliament, the Forum and its secretariat could be called on for information and advice whenever this was needed by a parliamentary commission or an individual member, and would maintain close contact with the Parliament's All-Party Group on Disablement which the British MEP Derek Prag has convened so faithfully for a number of years.

At the same time we should hope to see development in relation to the European Commission too, on the lines that the Commission itself originally set out in its 1987 proposal for what became the Helios action programme, as I have explained in Chapter 7. That is to say, the formal Advisory Committee working with the Commission in all future action programmes to promote a good quality of life for disabled people would consist of representatives of the European organizations of disabled people as well as of the social partners and the governments of the member states.

Since this book is above all concerned with the 'European Response' to the needs of disabled people, it will be fitting to end this section on 'Prospects' with a look at how European empowerment as I have just described it could best be used in order to promote the aim.

The European way ahead

It will be recalled that both the first action programme and the Helios programme of the Commission have consisted of three interrelated elements, the development of a series of policy instruments, the operation of a number of activities of technical co-operation focusing on networking, and the creation of a multilingual computerized information system (Handynet).

The direct effect of the activities of information and co-operation is to enable disabled people, their families and the professionals who work for and with them to improve the quality of their technical work and the effectiveness of their political efforts by becoming better informed, by learning from each other's experience and by being inspired by each other's aspirations and achievements. Exchange programmes are often criticized on the grounds that they are merely means for subsidizing unnecessary foreign travel on behalf of those who are not short of resources anyway. This cannot be said of the Commission's programmes in the field of disability, which focus on the exchange of experience between disabled people, voluntary workers and professionals working at local level, engaged directly in teaching, caring or rehabilitation, or representing disabled people in European organizations which have the greatest difficulty in finding any funds at all for their work.

Moreover it must be remembered that someone who has had a meaningful and useful European experience will carry the benefit of that for a number of years, so that the wastage of the learning acquired is relatively slow; meanwhile more and more people have their turn to participate so that there is a real and continuing accumulation of programme benefit. Obviously this effect is greatly increased in so far as those engaged in the exchange activities are themselves effective multipliers of ideas.

Indirectly, all this activity of co-operation will, as was noticed in Chapter 7, have some positive influence on those in member states who are responsible for policy development, but it would be unwise to set too high a value on that influence and fatally mistaken to count on it as an adequate means for having an impact on national policies. The representatives of ministries more or less directly engaged in the programmes typically make a most valuable personal contribution to it; how far they are able to influence senior colleagues at home is a very different question. It would be surprising if, given their schedules and priorities, the latter were to regard the results of European co-operation as anything other than marginally useful to them.

These results are on the other hand quite vital for another purpose; the European Commission itself absolutely must be able to draw on them for the preparation of its policy proposals, for the simple reason that European proposals need European data — not only 'cold' data such as statistics but the results of European discussion and exchange. And it is clear from what has just been said about the necessarily limited impact of this co-operation on the national processes of decision-making that it is the framing of proposals for European policy instruments which should become in the future the top priority for the Commission's work.

Wherever possible, these would be constraining instruments; these establish legal requirements which are superior to national law, and in pursuance of which national laws and regulations have to be adapted. Since on many issues (transport and access are good examples) there will be the need for precise European standards, the best procedure might be the laying down of common binding policy foundations by means of framework Council Directives on the various topics, followed by the adoption over time of detailed Council Regulations establishing the precise objectives and standards; these Regulations should be formulated by working parties mandated by the Directives and presided over by the Commission.

Flexibility might well on the other hand be needed in achieving the coverage which the reality of needs of disabled people actually requires — that is unless and until the Treaty is further extended to include in its scope social issues at present excluded. For example, under the present Treaty provisions, it might be legally possible to introduce legislation on many issues for disabled workers, those disabled people who are not defined as workers being for legal reasons excluded. Since this would include not only all disabled elderly people, all disabled homemakers and all those on full disability pensions and thus off the labour market, but also probably all those engaged in adult training centres (or their equivalent) and even sheltered workshops, the size of the problem must not be underestimated.

Following the precedent set by the Directive on the Education of the Children of Migrant Workers, the only solution in the short term would be for the Council to make, in parallel with each Directive, a formal Declaration of political will to afford to disabled people not recognized as workers the same rights, services and facilities as were prescribed by the Directive itself. This would of course only be a second best; those covered only by the Declaration would not for example have any legal redress before the Court of Justice at Luxembourg. But it would not be useless either. Such a Declaration would greatly strengthen the position of the concerned pressure groups at home, and would be bound to have some immediate direct effect. It would moreover have a secondary use in highlighting very precisely and publicly the deficiencies of the Treaty in the social field.

Even given this kind of flexibility in the handling of Directives, it must be recognized that there may be some themes on which a Recommendation, carrying only political and no legal force, is all that could be attempted. It should be remembered too that a Recommendation could be conceived as the first step towards a Directive, as we hoped would happen with the 1986 Recommendation on Employment. Where reluctance on the part of member states is evident, their own failure to implement a Recommendation could be the only evidence capable of persuading them to accept the need for a Directive.

It is for this reason that special importance should be attached to the bringing forward as soon as possible of draft legislation on the topics of employment and vocational training. Nor have I any personal doubt that this should include provision for a Community employment quota system as demanded by the European Parliament, with a massive majority, in 1986. The arguments in favour of this controversial opinion have already been set out in Chapter 4 (p. 67). It follows of course from what I have already said about the demands which the preparation of policy instruments makes on the Commission's core team, that to do both this and present the foreseen series of policy proposals in the environmental field would require an increase in the Commission's resources of official staff.

Progress at the political level on specific major issues affecting the lives of disabled people should not be seen as an alternative to the establishment of a European Social Charter which would be applicable to all citizens, unlike the 1989 Charter which, as we saw in the last chapter, is of benefit only to those defined as workers. Work on the preparation of an all-embracing Social Charter should go on in parallel with the series of policy proposals for disabled people, and the two actions should complement and reinforce each other.

There will naturally be powerful opposition to each and every policy proposal of the Commission in the domain of disability, above all if constraining legislation is involved. The member states will try to defend the position that in so far as disabled people can compete on the labour market their needs are secured by mainstream employment measures, and in so far as they cannot then their needs belong to the 'soft' social area in which the Community has no competence. That the first of these points is invalid is of course demonstrated by the whole history and present development of specific measures on the employment of disabled people in the member states themselves; and once that first point is disposed of at the level of principle we need not be too anxious about the second. None the less, even in the employment field where Community competence is generally conceded, the resistance against Commission proposals will be obstinate and even bitter, and recent experience shows that, unless there is a change of regime, this will be above all the case on the side of the United Kingdom. The oft-repeated view of British Ministers, that Community activity in fields such as this should be restricted to the exchange of information and experience, 'owing to the diversity of circumstances and traditions in member states',[4] reflects only too well the will to defend that diversity at the expense of European integration.

It will also be necessary to combat the familiar argument that specific measures actually increase marginalization, a point of view which appears attractive at first sight but which whenever it is applied in practice is likely merely to undermine the effort to do anything relevant to disabled people's actual needs. Yet in the end it is at this political level that the whole of the Community's effort to promote a better quality of life for disabled people should and will be judged. There is much here at stake, because what the Community might achieve for disabled people by this means simply cannot and will not be achieved by any other means; the potential of the Community in this field is something unique. The overcoming of Council resistance will call for solid support from the European Parliament, more aggressiveness on the part of the representative organizations of disabled people, and considerable courage and persistence from the side of the Commission. Of these, the first is virtually assured, the emergence of the second can reasonably be expected, and the third is at least to be hoped for.

PRINCIPLES

I want now to suggest that everything we do in relation to disability should be founded on two complementary principles, with the second of which are associated two further guiding concepts, both of which are also of universal application. The two principles are concerned with *rights* and *equal value*, and the two guiding concepts with *relativity* and *individualization*. More specifically, the four notions are:

1. The principle that all measures should be founded on the explicit recognition of the *rights* of disabled people.
2. The principle that all people are to be regarded as of *equal* value, in the society and to the society.
3. The guiding concept that all progress is *relative* to the potential and possibilities of individuals in their particular circumstances.
4. The guiding concept that priority should at all times be given to the provision of services which meet *individual* needs.

Rights[5]

When introducing the 1986 Recommendation on Employment, the Commission was successful in insisting that this should be explicitly based on a recognition of rights. The preamble includes this clause: 'Whereas disabled people have the same right as all other workers to equal opportunity in training and employment . . .'. The formulation may not have been the strongest possible, but at least the reference to rights is there, and the statement of it was thus able to be repeated in the preamble to the Decision which established the Helios programme.

Of course there was some discussion of the point, and, as usual where rights are concerned, a particular dislike of any mention of them among official United Kingdom representatives. In order to explain why opposition to the mention of rights is often so successful, I need to introduce the reader to what I call Catch-23. It will be remembered that Catch-22 in the book of that name designates the trap sprung by means of two official statements or positions, neither one of which looks or is threatening on its own, but the combination of which is quite devastating.[6]

Catch-23 goes like this:

- First statement of position: 'We can only properly speak of rights when these are enshrined in law.'
- Second statement of position: 'Legislation is not the answer to our problems.'

We can see that Catch-23 is even more insidious than Catch-22. While the first statement looks relatively harmless — one of those typically mandarin remarks which does not really affect anybody — the second looks positively engaging, since it appeals to our suspicion that legislation is a blunt and ponderous instrument, to our tendency to associate it with bureaucratic delay and the jargon (not to say the fees) of lawyers, to our preference — particularly if we are British — to think of ourselves as practical chaps who prefer pragmatic (blessed word!) solutions to the claptrap of the high-minded and the mumbo jumbo of jurists.

Of course when we put the two statements together we can see the trap for what it is: since the first statement is clearly universal and the second one can be applied blandly to any circumstances whatever, the implication of the two in combination is that no one has, or can have, any rights at all. But of course Catch-23 works, like any other trap, by not letting people see it; the moment the total implication is perceived the Catch loses its power because it is obvious that it negates too much. So what the operators of the trap do is articulate, in any given situation, only that one of the two statements which is sufficient for the purpose of ensuring that any initiative to establish the rights of disadvantaged people in law is suppressed at an early stage. That campaigners for a fair deal are so easily outmanoeuvred may seem astonishing but is not perhaps untypical.

Once we have perceived the trap we can proceed to demolish it by pointing out that the second statement (that 'Legislation is not the solution to our problems') only gains credence by means of a deliberate confusion between the proposition that legislation is not sufficient for a solution (as is commonly true), and the proposition that legislation is not necessary to a solution (which, if the first statement is correct, is evidently untrue). Once the second statement has been demolished in this way we can turn the first one against its promoters: if we may only speak of rights once these are established in law, then what we must do is precisely that.

The idea that disadvantaged groups in our society will ever get a fair deal until their equal rights are legally guaranteed, for the whole range of services and sectors within which the disadvantage operates, is so contrary to common sense and to the universal experience of human conduct that it can only be tendentious. If we hear it being proclaimed by someone who pretends to have the interests of disabled people at heart we may be sure that he or she is unwilling to make the sacrifices of economic and other privilege which an authentic endeavour to better their quality of life must entail.

Equal value

When setting out my ideas about educational values in 1974 I defined the 'equal-value principle' in this way: 'the education of all children is held to be of equal value'.[7] Later in the same book I argued that this attribution of equal value should be accorded not only to the education of all children but to all children themselves.

I made it my practice to apply this principle as best I could in all the work on the theme of equality of opportunity in education in which I was engaged in the Education Division of the Commission between 1974 and 1981. But it was when in 1982 I became responsible for the Community's first action programme on the social integration of disabled people that the application of that principle at the European level became for me of paramount importance. The whole tenor of my experience in the six years that followed confirmed for me the validity of the principle and its relevance over the whole range of sectors and services which contribute to a better quality of life for disabled people.

In 1974 I derived the equal-value principle from a *familial model*:

> The family is a given, *the* given, equal-value system. Without being at all blind to the failures and anguishes of family life, we know, indeed we all universally assume, that it is the function of the parents, the managers of the family, to value all the members, the children, as equal. The point is virtually definitive; it is not that favouritism and relative rejection do not occur, but that they are always, regardless of circumstances, recognised categorically as faults. This concedes that the rule is inviolable. . . . The familial model is all the more useful because it is a working one. . . . Families know that talents must be developed, deficiencies compensated for, mediocrities tolerated or acted on as the occasion suggests . . . and that the principle that gives form and unity of purpose to all this diversity of practical decisions is a principle of equal value, and cannot be anything else. . . . In sum, the principle has these characteristics:
> – It is inviolable, universal and definitive.
> – It operates in a flexible and complex way.

In the same passage I set out what I believed, and still believe, to be the inadequacies of the notion of 'equal opportunity' when compared to that of equal value. Yet I would not want to give the impression that equal opportunity is not a useful, indeed essential, objective. The promotion of it, and also of 'fair systems', are ways in which the equal-value principle presents itself in practice. The distinction and relation between equal opportunity and fair systems is also important. There may be in the courts a reliable operation of 'equality before the law' (fair system) but for financial reasons there may not always be an equal opportunity to avail oneself of this. Alternatively, someone may benefit from equality of opportunity in attaining a job, only to find that he or she is discriminated against (say in conditions of work or promotion chances) after that because the system itself is unfair. The distinction here is similar to that between 'positive action' (or 'positive discrimination') and the elimination of 'negative discrimination' which was made in the 1986 Recommendation on Employment and which, somewhat laborious though it is, I believe we need to adhere to if confusion about the meaning of discrimination is to be avoided. It is as a rule positive discrimination which creates equality of opportunity, and the elimination of negative discrimination which enables us to have fair systems.

Equality of opportunity and fair systems are two of the means by which the principle of equal value is then expressed in practice. More of its operational implications will become clear when shortly we look at the guiding concepts of relativity and individualization. Before that there are several further points which need to be made about the principle itself.

The first is that it asserts an intention and not a fact. If we proclaim the equal-value principle we are declaring that we choose to value people in a certain way. It is evident that others may choose not to value people in this way, but to reject the principle by attributing more fundamental value to some individuals in society than to others. Even more commonly, I suspect people may wish to dodge the issues which the principle raises altogether. I believe that differences of choice of this kind may underlie many bitter disagreements whose foundation remains hidden.

Secondly, although I do not for a moment consider that adherence to the principle is dependent on the holding of any given set of religious or ideological beliefs, it does seem to be evident that for those who believe that all men are the children of God the familial model applies in a quite literal sense and the choice of rejecting the equal-value principle would not seem to be available. Nor, on the other hand, is the principle an isolated, one-off thing; it finds its home in the movement of universalism as I described that in 1974.[8]

It has been argued that every moral assertion contains descriptive as well as prescriptive elements.[9] The assertion that we should operate on the basis of an equal-value principle is, as I see it, a predictive one, based on the belief that this is necessary for the future welfare, even survival, of mankind. Its verification would depend therefore on the presentation of evidence that other approaches are detrimental or actually dangerous. (It should be observed that the equal-value principle might help to throw light on some very difficult issues such as abortion and post-natal non-intervention, though it is not of course one of the purposes of this book to go into these.)

Lastly, there are two particular advantages which I believe follow if we adopt the principle of equal value. The first is that we are released from the egalitarian dilemma: we are not either saying that all people need the same resources (which is ridiculous), or that primary resources should be distributed according to merit (which is to prescribe injustice).

There is also hope that the equal-value principle will help us to solve the problem of how people who are and are not disabled are to speak of each other and relate to each other. If someone were to say 'There is no such problem; we have only to treat each other as equals' they would I believe be right about the approach but wrong about the fact. It seems to me quite obvious that there is in fact a problem: many disabled people are still looked down on, at best with benevolent patronage but quite often with something much worse than that. There is a force in society which makes people need to believe in the existence of inferiors, and it is that force which we have to combat. The equal-value principle is a strong weapon in this contest simply because it applies to everyone, and therefore to disabled people not because they are disabled but because they are people.

Relativity

The need to apply relativity as one of our guiding concepts follows from the principle of equal value and can be described very simply. All that is meant is that the value of any measure taken, and of every individual act of progress, in the direction of the aim is relative to the circumstances in which it is set.

This means, for example, that for a profoundly mentally handicapped person to make some simple choice about his everyday life is intrinsically of the same order of significance as for an intelligent motor disabled person to win an outstanding post.

This must be so, or the principle of equal value would not be operating at all. The same applies on a wider scale than the individual: the introduction of long canes for blind people into a poor country, for example, could be as significant as that of reading machines into a rich one.

We need this guide if we are to avoid the dangers of elitism in the choice of those measures and investments to which to give priority.

Individualization

The equal-value principle reinforces the imperative, indicated a number of times in this book, that all measures and services should be designed so as to respond as closely as possible to individual needs. In this sense individualization has nothing of course to do with individualism; it applies nevertheless over all the policy sectors which are relevant to the promotion of a good quality of life for disabled people — employment, education and training, transport, public access, housing and assistance in the home, financial benefits.

I have said 'as closely as possible'. It is sometimes maintained that qualifications of that kind are meaningless, but I would argue against that. On the one hand it is unrealistic to suppose that everyone's individual needs can be met immediately; and this being so, it is merely dishonest not to admit it. On the other hand it must be stressed that the existence of (for example) currently insuperable financial difficulties is never more than a contingent fact which does not in any way affect the objective.

The point is important simply because it is always tempting to promote a quantitative problem into a qualitative one. If an individual service or aid is much more expensive than the available resources can meet, there is an inclination to conclude, quite illogically, that the idea of providing it is wrong in principle, whereas in reality it merely happens to be very difficult (as distinct, let us say, from rather difficult) in practice. The difference is important, because while what is too difficult to achieve in practice may have to go on the back boiler or even into the fridge, an idea we have once thought of as excluded 'on principle' goes in the dustbin and cannot be retrieved.

THE PRIMACY OF EDUCATION

Having discussed the aim of our endeavours and the principles on which I believe they should be founded, I can finish by returning to the topic of education in order to draw some implications about the nature of school experience and to underline the primacy which we should afford to education in relation to the other life functions and policy sectors which I have discussed.

Social integration in school

If we believe that social integration is one of the most important elements of a good quality of life, then we must believe that this is true for children as well as for anyone else. It follows too from what I have argued about the limits which should be set to the view of life in school as a preparation (Chapter 6, p. 140) that the social integration of disabled children is desirable primarily for the sake of their quality of life during childhood itself, and only secondarily as a preparation for social integration as adults. Since as it happens school plays a substantial and sometimes even dominant part in the social life of children, school mainstreaming is correctly seen as an essential means for promoting a better quality of life for children with special needs.

All this might appear to be educational, or at least academic, heresy, since it starts from the point of view of social integration; a correct educational view (it might be argued), and certainly the one more often taken, starts from the need for educational ('functional') integration and then proceeds to consider the social integration of the disabled child in the school as a second, albeit important, consideration.

I see this as a false analysis, which ignores the interaction of the formal and informal curricula in the school. If we think of the school first as a society or community, we perceive at once that it is a society with one dominant purpose — it is a learning society. This helps us to reject the normal but quite incorrect distinction between the functional (learning) life of the children and their in-school social life. This separation is incorrect for the obvious reason that the social and functional elements of life are interwoven or, more accurately, the formally functional elements (that is, the time spent in the classroom) are a part, possibly the most important part, of the child's social life in school. It is absurd to suppose that children only exist socially when they are outside the classroom, in the playground and so on, as if in the classroom they ceased to be social animals and were reduced to being some sort of isolated learning machines or receptacles into which chunks of knowledge can be inserted.

Education (in the sense of organized learning) for children, independence and employment for adults and care for the elderly — these, for all their great importance, must not be allowed to usurp the aim, which is the attainment of a good quality of life, of which these are important components, as is social integration.

True integration

Integration in school, mainstreaming, should be available and encouraged for all children with special needs whatever the nature or severity of their disability. Of course this may only be attainable by stages, both in the sense that some individual children may need to be introduced to integration gradually, and in the sense that it will take time to adapt the regular schools and to transfer or produce resources in such a way as to ensure that mainstreaming is successful.

All progress in the systems which is in the direction of integration is useful, and under the principle of relativity just set out, quite rudimentary progress may in some situations be of very high value. Nonetheless, although we can describe the setting up of contacts between special and regular schools where these did not exist before as an example of an integrating process we cannot call that level of development in itself true integration or anything like it.

On the other hand, it would be wrong in my view to assert that the full-time presence of a child with special needs in a mainstream class is the only pattern which can be called true integration. The practice of occasionally taking out a child with learning problems in order to give special educational support is not in itself a breach of true integration; this is evident from the fact that this service might be helpful for a child with a short-term specific learning difficulty as well as for one with a permanent disability. But also the existence in a regular school of a special unit operating as a learning base and resource centre for children with a particular impairment can be consistent with and indeed a vital support to true integration. This pattern may even be the best possible solution for deaf children, given their need to develop high levels of communication with each other. It may also be the only practical way of meeting the problem of children with severe or profound mental handicaps, including those with multiple handicaps. Provided the concept of individualization is respected by means of personal programmes which promote the time spent by each child in mainstream situations, the integrated special unit model need not be thought of merely as a stage in the development of true integration but as a possible and perhaps essential component of true integration in its completed form.

For further and higher education, too, the specialized unit within or alongside the mainstream institution could be one of the most successful models for the future. The examples of the Higher National Institute for the Deaf in Rochester, New York and of the Royal National Institute for the Blind's Vocational College in Loughborough (see pp. 74–5) are ones which could be followed in other countries and for other disabilities, even also at the European level.

The school community leading the way

The primacy of education in the whole endeavour to promote a better quality of life for disabled people depends on the notion of a school community ('communauté scolaire'). The school community consists obviously of the children, parents and other members of their families, the teachers, and the others who work regularly in the school building; it also comprises the members of the governing council, the inspectors or advisers from the educational authority, employers, and the representatives of the health, social and employment and other educational services in contact with the school. If the school has developed additional services for the local community, on the lines of the village colleges invented by Henry Morris in Cambridgeshire or other community schools in the United Kingdom, then the school community will be extended to include those who use a public library or play-group or who avail themselves of adult education provision or of facilities for clubs and social functions.

Now the point is that a school, if given the chance and some encouragement, is very much better at carrying through a major social development than is society at large, and is therefore in a unique position for influencing society by means of example. This applies particularly well in the matter of the promotion of a good quality of life for children with special needs and their social integration. Nor is it simply a matter of the successfully mainstreaming school establishing a working model which the local population might wish to apply in society at large if it were to come to their notice. The disabled children, of all kinds, in the school are the future disabled adults in the open society. Equally important, the children without disabilities in the school are the future non-disabled adults in the local community;

successful mainstreaming will have depended on them as much as on anyone else, and they will make the transition to adult life with the expectation that they will play the same part there.

Both disabled and non-disabled young people will therefore leave school with not merely positive attitudes of a theoretical kind towards such ideas as equality and integration but with habits based on everyday contact which enable them to take these ideas virtually for granted, and with skills in coping with all the practical or attitudinal problems which can arise from one side or another of the 'disability divide'.

Moreover, it is not only the children who will have been closely involved in the success, but also the parents, both those of the children with special needs and the others. The impact on the local society at large of new attitudes, habits of thought and social skills will therefore continually be made at two generational levels (at least) and could not fail to be extremely powerful.

It follows that as an agent of change in favour of equal opportunity, social integration and so a better quality of life for disabled people, school integration has more to contribute than any other set of measures or development that could be imagined. To this extent its primacy is therefore clear enough. But it depends of course on the degree to which the integration in the schools is successful in achieving the aim and the objectives we have identified, and this in turn will depend on the values which predominate within the educational system.

Paramount though the potential of educational integration therefore is, we must recognize its vulnerability, to political intervention above all. In so far as the preparatory role of the school is given the greatest stress, and its competitive, selective and summative functions fostered and rewarded, to that extent the mainstream will remain closed to all but a few children with disabilities and the contribution of the educational system to the overall aim will be insignificant if not actually negative. In so far as the equal-value principle is applied throughout the educational system, to that extent integration in the schools will make a unique and essential contribution to the best possible quality of life for 'Europeans with a disability'.

NOTES

1 Patricia Rock, 'Independence: what it means to six disabled people living in the community', *Disability, Handicap and Society* 3, No. 1, 1988. The article also bears on the concept of relativity, see p. 187 above.

2 Independence and integration are not to be conceived as incompatible but complementary.

3 It would be better for a Ministry for Disability not to be located within some larger Department (such as Employment, Health, Education or Social Affairs) as that associates its work too closely with one of the several sectors essential to disability policy. Solutions such as direct attachment to the Prime Minister's office would be worth exploring.

4 A favourite expression of British ministers.

5 For a useful discussion of rights, starting from the United Nations Declaration (see Reference below), see Hampden Inskip, *Resident Homes for the Physically Handicapped* (one of the Leonard Cheshire Foundation Handbooks of Care), London 1983.

6 By means of Catch-22 it was impossible for American airmen in the Second World War to be transferred from a certain dangerous base, because whereas the only accepted grounds

for transfer was mental disturbance it was evident that anyone with the good sense to apply for transfer could not be mentally disturbed.

7   For the equal-value principle, see Patrick Daunt, *Comprehensive Values*, London 1975, especially pp. 15–27.

8   Ibid., pp. 107–10.

9   Wendell Bell, 'Moral judgements, education and alternative futures', a paper read at the XIth World Conference of the World Futures Studies in Budapest, May 1990, quoting Keekok Lee, *A New Basis for Moral Philosophy*, London 1985.

REFERENCE

United Nations

Declaration of the Rights of Disabled Persons, New York 1975.

Chapter 9

Conclusions

AIMS AND PRINCIPLES

1. The *aim* of all policy and practice concerned with disability should be to promote the best possible quality of life for all disabled people. Determining factors include the individual's desires as well as his potential and environment (Chapter 8, p. 175).

   The *components of a good quality of life* include autonomy, independence, integration, respect, ownership, social involvement, activity and mobility, privacy and tranquillity. All such objectives are relevant to all disabled people, but their relative importance will vary according to the individual's situation (age, capacities, cultural setting, etc.) and choice of life-style (Chapter 8, pp. 175–7).

2. There are two *principles* on which policy and practice should be based. The first is that all measures should be founded on the explicit recognition of the *rights* of disabled people. The second is the recognition that all people, including therefore all disabled people, should be regarded as of *equal value* in the society and for the society (Chapter 8, pp. 184–7).

   These principles should be applied in practice with the aid of two guiding concepts, one of *relativity* and the other of *individualization*. All progress should be perceived as relative to the potential and possibilities of individuals in their particular circumstances; priority should at all times be given to the provision of services designed to meet individual needs (Chapter 8, p. 178 and pp. 187–8).

3. While policy needs to cover all life functions, primacy should be given to *basic education*, since positive attitudes towards disability practised in the school community affect two generations at once and so contribute more than any other development can do to the evolution of an adult society in which the rights of disabled people are recognized and the principle of equal value implemented (Chapter 8, pp. 188–91).

REPRESENTATION AND PARTICIPATION

National level

1. We should campaign for the establishment in all countries of a *Ministry for Disabled People* responsible for the design and implementation of a *national plan* to ensure a good quality of life for people with disabilities. The Minister should command his or her own civil service, be independent of other Ministries and be empowered to co-ordinate the initiatives of all other departments whose responsibilities touch on the needs of disabled people (Chapter 8, p. 180).
2. In each country, rights of consultation and of participation in the implementation of measures should be statutorily established in favour of a *National Council of Disabled People*. The members of the Council should be disabled people representing all the principal national associations of people with disabilities; at all meetings each Council member would have the right to be accompanied by a friend or assistant. The Council would elect its own chairman by rotation (Chapter 8, pp. 179–80).

The National Council should be represented on all *boards of national funds, institutes or services* concerned with disability, and on other national bodies in the economic, health, social or educational fields whose responsibilities extend beyond disability but are relevant to it (Chapter 8, pp. 179–80).

3. The principles and practice for representation and participation at national level should be repeated also at the regional and local levels (Chapter 8, p. 180).

European level

4. European associations of disabled people should be represented on the formal *Advisory Committee* which works with the European Commission on the implementation of its disability action programme (Chapter 8, p. 181).
5. The European Parliament should be persuaded to establish a *Forum of Disabled People*, made up of representatives of European associations of people with disabilities (Chapter 8, pp. 180–1).
6. Representation under (4) and (5) above should be derived from an independent *European Council of Disabled People*, established from European associations on the same lines as the National Councils in (2) above, and financed by the European Commission (p. 180).

EMPLOYMENT AND VOCATIONAL TRAINING

National level

1. In all member states of the Community *comprehensive and coherent national plans* should be established for the promotion of the employment of disabled people, as far as possible within the open labour market.

These plans should, as a minimum requirement, satisfy all the provisions of the 1986 Recommendation of the Council on the employment of disabled people in the European Community, and take into full consideration also all elements of the Model Code of Positive Action annexed to it (Chapter 4, pp. 79–80).

European level

2. The European Commission should be encouraged to bring forward shortly a draft Directive on the employment of disabled people in the European Community (Chapter 7, pp. 151–3 and Chapter 8, pp. 183–4).
   The Directive should include a proposal for a European scheme of quotas for the employment of disabled people, based on the latest models and offering to employers both a number of options and substantive incentives and supports.
3. All disabled people engaged in sheltered or supported employment, whether of a traditional or innovatory kind, should be explicitly recognized as workers by the European Community for all purposes, including the operation of the European Social Fund and the implementation of the 1989 Social Charter (Chapter 8, pp. 182–3).

THE ENVIRONMENT FOR INDEPENDENT LIVING

Mobility and transport

National level

1. All member states should develop *comprehensive and coherent plans* for the promotion of the mobility of disabled people.
   These plans should cover *public transport (accessibility and concessions), special transport systems, private vehicles, access and mobility in the street* and the necessary supporting actions of training, information, public awareness and research, and should take into full consideration all the elements of the *European Code of Good Practice to Promote the Mobility of Disabled People* contained in the Commission's 1989 study 'Moving to Independence' (Chapter 5, esp. pp. 90, 92, 95, 98 and 100; Chapter 7, p. 157).

European level

2. The European Commission should be encouraged to bring forward a series of *Directives or other policy instruments* on mobility and transport for disabled people, so as to cover all the ground of the 1989 Code of Good Practice mentioned in (1) above. These initiatives should include a proposal for the institution of a *European Travel Card for Disabled People* (Chapter 7, pp. 155–6).

Housing and access to public buildings and facilities

National level

1. *National regulations* in all member states should ensure that all new buildings for public use are fully accessible to disabled people, and that new housing is built so as to be easily adaptable. *Comprehensive schemes* should also be instituted to provide assistance to disabled people living independently (Chapter 5, esp. pp. 106–8 and 108–11).

European level

2. The European Commission should be encouraged to proceed as quickly as is reasonable with the preparation of *Community policy instruments* to promote on behalf of disabled people the accessibility of public buildings and facilities, the provision of accessible housing and the offer of assistance in the home, in accordance with the commitments already made (Chapter 7, pp. 157–8).

EDUCATION

National level

1. Each member state should establish a national plan or strategy for the development of integrated (mainstream) education for children and young people with disabilities (Chapter 6, pp. 135–6). Such plans should be implemented only in so far as the priorities and values being promoted by government in the regular schools are consistent with a programme of radical mainstreaming (Chapter 8, pp. 190–1).

   National plans should allow for the provision of specialized units or services within schools as one of the long-term components of a fully integrated system (Chapter 8, pp. 189–90).

European level

2. Arising from the experience of its action programmes, the European Commission should be encouraged to develop a common European Community policy for the educational integration of children and young people with disabilities between now and the end of the century (Chapter 6, p. 141).

Appendix 1

List of Abbreviations

AEH	Action européenne des handicapés [European Action by Disabled People]
AFPA	Association nationale pour la formation professionnelle des adultes (France) [National Association for Adult Vocational Training]
AIAS	Associazione italiana assistenza spastici [Italian Association for Assistance to People with Cerebral Palsy]
ANAPH	Association nationale d'assistance aux personnes handicapées (Belgium) [National Association for Assistance to Disabled People]
ATEE	Association for Teacher Education in Europe
BECIPH	Bureau européen de coordination et d'information pour les personnes handicapées [European Co-ordination and Information Bureau for Disabled People]
CEDEFOP	Centre européen pour le développement de la formation professionnelle [European Centre for the Development of Vocational Training]
CEFES	Centre d'étude et de formation pour l'éducation specialisée (Belgium) [Centre for Research and Training on Special Education]
CERI	Centre for Educational Research and Innovation
CNFLRH	Comité national français de liaison pour la réadaptation des personnes handicapées [French National Liaison Committee for the Rehabilitation of Disabled People]
COFACE	Confédération des organisations familiales de la Communauté européenne [Confederation of Family Organizations in the European Community]
COLITRAH	Comité de liaison pour le transport des personnes handicapées (France) [Liaison Committee on Transport for Disabled People]
DG	Directorate-General
DPI	Disabled People's International
EASE	European Association for Special Education
EBU	European Blind Union
ECRS	European Community Regional Secretariat (of WFD)

ECSOC	Economic and Social Committee
ENAIP	Ente nazionale ACLI per la inserzione professionale [National Organization ACLI for Vocational Integration]
ERC	Employment Rehabilitation Centre (UK)
ERICA	European Research into Consumer Affairs
ESF	European Social Fund
EUCREA	Association européenne pour la créativité des personnes handicapées [European Association for the Creativity of Disabled People]
FAS	An Foras Aiseanna Saothair (Ireland) [Training and Employment Authority]
FNRSH	Fonds national de reclassement social des handicapés (Belgium) [National Fund for the Social Resettlement of Disabled People]
GIHP	Groupement pour l'insertion des personnes handicapées physiques [Society for the Integration of People with Physical Disabilities]
GIRPEH	Groupements interprofessionnels régionaux de l'emploi des personnes handicapées [Regional Interprofessional Societies for the Employment of Disabled People]
ICIDH	International Classification of Impairments, Disabilities and Handicaps
ICTA	International Commission on Technical Aids
IL	Independent Living
ILO	International Labour Organization
ILSMH	International League of Societies for Persons with Mental Handicap
INSERSO	Instituto nacional de servicios sociales (Spain) [National Institute for Social Services]
ISO	International Organization for Standardization
Ligue HMC	Ligue luxembourgeoise pour le secours aux enfants, aux adolescents et aux adultes mentalement ou cérébralement handicapés [Luxembourg League for the Support of Children, Adolescents and Adults with Mental Handicaps or Brain Injuries]
LMA	Local Model Activity
NGO	Non-governmental Organization
NRB	National Rehabilitation Board (Ireland)
OAED	Employment Manpower Organization (Greece)
OECD	Organization for Economic Co-operation and Development
ONCE	Organización nacional de ciegos (Spain) [National Association of the Blind]
RADAR	Royal Association for Disability and Rehabilitation (UK)
RI	Rehabilitation International
SAHVA	Samfundet og Hjemmet for Vanfoere (Denmark) [Society and Home for the Physically Disabled]
SIVA	Servizio informazione e valutazione ausili (Italy) [Information and Evaluation Service on Technical Aids]
SNR	Secretariado nacional de rehabilitação (Portugal) [National Rehabilitation Secretariat]

UNESCO	United Nations Educational, Scientific and Cultural Organization
USL	Unità sanitaria locale (Italy) [Local Health District]
WBU	World Blind Union
WFD	World Federation of the Deaf
WFMH	World Federation for Mental Health
WHO	World Health Organization

Appendix 2

Commission Networks

A. THE DIALOGUE GROUP OF NON-GOVERNMENTAL ORGANIZATIONS

Action européenne des handicapés (AEH) [European Action by Disabled People]

Alliance européenne de sclérose en plaques (AESP) [European Multiple Sclerosis Alliance]

Association européenne pour la créativité des personnes handicapées (EUCREA) [European Association for the Creativity of Disabled People]

Association européenne d'étude des traumatisés craniens (EBIS) [European Research Association for People with Brain Damage]

Association internationale autisme Europe (AIAE) [International Association 'Autism Europe']

Confédération européenne des laryngectomisés (CEL) [European Confederation of People with Laryngotomy]

Confédération des organisations familiales de la Communauté européenne (COFACE) [Confederation of Family Organizations in the European Community]

Disabled People's International (DPI)

Eurolink Age

European Alliance of Muscular Dystrophy Associations (EAMDA)

European Association for Special Education (EASE)

European Blind Union (EBU)

European Communities Deaf–blind Secretariat (ECDBS)

European Dyslexia Association (EDA)

European Lupus Erythematosus Federation (ELEF)

European Parents Association (EPA)

European Stuttering Self-help Organization (ESSHO)

Fédération internationale mutilés invalides de travail et invalides civils (FIMITIC) [International Federation of Disabled Workers and Civilian Handicapped]

International Bureau for Epilepsy (IBE)

International Cerebral Palsy Society (ICPS)

International Federation of the Hard of Hearing (IFHOH)

International Fund Sports Disabled (IFSD)

International League of Societies for Persons with Mental Handicap (ILSMH)

Mobility International (MI)

Rehabilitation International, European Community Association (RI/ECA)

Union européenne des associations de spina bifida et d'hydrocéphalie (UEASBH) [European Union of Associations for Spina Bifida and Hydrocephalus]

Volonteurope

World Federation of the Deaf, European Community Regional Secretariat (WFD/ECRS)

World Federation for Mental Health (WFMH)

World Veterans Federation (WVF)

B. LOCAL PROJECTS AND ACTIVITIES

Note: DP = district project in the first action programme. Others are local model activities (LMAs) in the second action programme (Helios), specified as follows: ED = education, EM = employment, IL = independent living.

Belgium	DP —	Liège, Genk-Hasselt
	ED —	Leuven, Brussels (CEFES)
	IL —	Dendermonde, Jalhay
	EM —	Hasselt, Liège
Denmark	DP —	Aarhus
	ED —	Hinnerup
	IL —	Nykobing Falster
	EM —	Vejle
Germany	DP —	Berlin (Spandau), Gelsenkirchen
	ED —	Bonn, Reutlingen
	IL —	Gelsenkirchen, Peissenberg, Stuttgart, Nuremberg
	EM —	Hanover, Abensberg, Offenburg
Greece	DP —	Ahaia province
	ED —	Marousi (Attiki), Thessaloniki
	IL —	Thessaloniki, Rodos
	EM —	Athens, Patras
Spain	DP —	Salamanca, Mostoles
	ED —	Oviedo, Valladolid
	IL —	Salamanca, Vitoria (Alava), Mostoles
	EM —	Murcia, Badajoz
France	DP —	Dijon, Montpellier
	ED —	Nanterre, Suresnes
	IL —	St Quentin en Yvelines, Bordeaux, Macon Champigny-sur-Marne
	EM —	Caudun, Wasquehal, Dijon
Ireland	DP —	Midlands
	ED —	Cork

	IL	— Dublin, Kilkenny
	EM	— Tullamore, Dublin
Italy	DP	— Piacenza, North Basilicata
	ED	— Cagliari, Siena
	IL	— Villa Rosa, Giugliano, Bologna, Belluno
	EM	— Rieti, Bologna, Roma
Luxembourg	DP	— Luxembourg
	ED	— Luxembourg
	IL	— Esch-sur-Alzette
	EM	— Dudelange
Netherlands	DP	— Dordrecht, North Limburg
	ED	— Rotterdam, Tholen
	IL	— Spijkenisse, Arnhem
	EM	— Amsterdam, Dordrecht
Portugal	DP	— Coimbra
	ED	— Lisbon
	IL	— Coimbra, Portalegre
	EM	— Lisbon (two projects)
UK	DP	— Lambeth, West Berkshire
	ED	— Morpeth, Swansea
	IL	— Brighton, Llanelli, Banff, Walthamstow
	EM	— Newtownabbey (Antrim), Bradford, Balham

C. REHABILITATION CENTRES

Note 'I' indicates centres participating in the first action programme only, and 'II' centres involved for the first time in the second action programme (Helios). Centres marked 'I+II' have taken part as network members in both programmes.

Belgium I — Centre national de formation et d'études pédagogiques, Brussels [National Centre for Pedagogic Training and Research]; Centre de réadaptation fonctionnelle Clinique Reine Fabiola, Charleroi [Functional Rehabilitation Centre in the Queen Fabiola Clinic]
    I+II — Dienst voor begeleiding en opleiding van minder-validen, Ghent [Service for the Guidance and Training of Disabled People]; Centre de réadaptation au travail, Tinlot [Vocational Rehabilitation Centre].
    II — Expériences de formation professionnelle FNRSH, Brussels [Vocational Training Activities of the FNSRH]; Brailleliga–Ligue Braille, Brussels [Braille League].

Denmark I+II — Handvaerkskolen (SAHVA), Copenhagen [Technical Training School]; Optraening Instituttet Rijshospitalet/Revacentrett, Copenhagen [Retraining Institute, State Hospital]/Rehabcentre; Handelskole, Skive [Commercial Training Centre].

Germany I — Josefs-Gesellschaft, Cologne [Josefs Society].
    I+II — Berufsförderungswerk, Bad Vilbel, Frankfurt [Vocational Retraining Centre]; Neurologisches Rehabilitationszentrum Godeshöhe, Bonn [Neurological Rehabilitation Centre]; Werkstatt für Behinderte, Hamburg [Workshop for the Handicapped].
    II — Niedersächsisches Landeskrankhaus, Osnabrück [Regional Hospital, Lower Saxony]; Berufsbildungswerk, Worms [Vocational Training Centre]; Kinderzentrum, Munich [Centre for Children].

Greece I+II — National Institute for the Rehabilitation of Disabled Persons, Athens; Theotokos Foundation, Athens.
    II — Psychiatric Hospital, Thessaloniki.

Spain I+II — Centro de reabilitación de minusválidos físicos 'San Fernando', Cadiz [Rehabilitation Centre for Physically Disabled People]; Centro de Promi, Cabra (Cordoba) [Promi Centre]; Centro ocupacional 'Juan de Austria', Madrid [Occupational Centre]; Centro de recursos educativos para deficientes visuales 'Joán Amades', Barcelona [Educational Resource Centre for those with Visual Disabilities].

II — Instituto valenciano de audio-fonología, Valencia [Valencia Centre for the Education of the Deaf].

France I — Centre de rééducation et de perfectionnement professionnel Suzanne Masson, Paris [Centre for Retraining and Vocational Development]; Centre de réadaptation professionnelle et fonctionnelle, Nanteau-sur-Lunain (Nemours) [Functional and Vocational Rehabilitation Centre]; Centre de réadaptation, Mulhouse [Rehabilitation Centre].

I+II — Association nationale pour la formation professionnelle des adultes (AFPA), Montreuil [National Association for Adult Vocational Training].

II — Centre de la Tour de Gassies, Bruges [Tour de Gassies Centre]; Centre de rééducation professionnelle, St Etienne [Vocational Retraining Centre]; Centre de rééducation pour aveugles récents, Marly le Roi [Retraining Centre for the Recently Blind]; Promofaf, Paris; Centre de réinsertion de Celleneuve, Montpellier [Resettlement Centre].

Ireland I+II — Rehabilitation Institute, Dublin; FAS, Dublin; COPE Institute (formerly Cork Polio and General Aftercare Association), Cork.

Italy I — Centro di addestramento, Bologna [Training Centre]; Centro di formazione professionale ENAIP, Reggio Emilia [ENAIP Vocational Training Centre]; Centro di formazione professionale, Melfi [Vocational Training Centre].

I+II — Centro di formazione professionale 'Don Calabria', Verona [Don Calabria Vocational Training Centre]; Centro comunitario 'Gesù risorto', Comunità di Capodarco, Rome [Jesus Risen Community Centre]; Fondazione pro juventute 'Don Carlo Gnocchi', Milan [Don Carlo Gnocchi Youth Foundation].

II — Centro di formazione professionale ENAIP, Cagliari [ENAIP Vocational Training Centre]; Centro studi Tirrenia (Unione italiana ciechi), Rome [Study Centre of the Italian Blind Union]; Associazione 'Nostra Famiglia' and Istituto Eugenio Media, Ponte Lambro (Como) ['Our Family' Association and Eugenio Media Institute].

Luxembourg I+II — Centre de réadaptation Ligue HMC, Capellen [Rehabilitation Centre of the League HMC].

Netherlands I — Lucasstichting voor revalidatie, Hoensbroek [Lucas Foundation for Rehabilitation]; Stichting revalidatie, Instituut Muiderpoort, Amsterdam [Rehabilitation Foundation of the Muiderpoort Institute].

II — Revalidatiecentrum 'Het Roessingh', Enschede ['Het Roessingh' Rehabilitation Centre]; Stichting beroepsopleiding 'Werkenrode', Groesbeek ['Werkenrode' Vocational Training Foundation]; Pameyer Stichting, Rotterdam [Pameyer Foundation]; Stichting Nieuwe Werkvormen, Maastricht [Foundation for New Forms of Work].

Portugal I+II — Centro de educação e formação profissional integrada, Porto [Centre for Integrated Education and Vocational Training]; Centro de reabilitação profissional de Alcoitão, Sintra [Centre for Vocational Rehabilitation]; Centro de reabilitação de paralisia cerebral 'Calouste Gulbenkian', Lisbon [Gulbenkian Centre for the Rehabilitation of Cerebral Palsy].

UK I — Employment Rehabilitation Centre, Birmingham; Finchale Training College for the Disabled, Durham; Training Services Agency Skillcentre, Plymouth.

II — Employment Rehabilitation Centre, Billingham; Enham Industries, Andover; Pengwern Hall, Clwyd; Queen Alexandra College, Birmingham; Court Grange, Newton Abbot, Devon; Atlantic House, Edinburgh.

D. REHABILITATION INTERNATIONAL SECRETARIATS

Belgium Association nationale d'assistance aux personnes handicapées (ANAPH) [National Association for the Assistance of Disabled People]

Denmark Samfundet og Hjemmet for Vanfoere (SAHVA Foundation) [Society and Home for the Physically Disabled]

Germany Bundesarbeitsgemeinschaft für Rehabilitation [Federal Rehabilitation Council]

Greece Hellenic Society for Disabled Children

Spain Instituto nacional de servicios sociales (INSERSO) [National Institute for Social Services]

France Comité national français de liaison pour la réadaptation des personnes handicapées (CNFLRH) [French National Liaison Committee for the Rehabilitation of Disabled People]

Ireland National Rehabilitation Board (NRB)

Italy Associazione italiana assistenza spastici (AIAS) [Italian Association for Assistance to People with Cerebral Palsy]

Luxembourg Ligue luxembourgeoise pour le secours aux enfants, aux adolescents et aux adultes mentalement ou cérébralement handicapés (Ligue HMC) [Luxembourg League for the Support of Children, Adolescents and Adults with Mental Handicaps or Brain Injuries]

Netherlands Stichting Nederlandse Gehandicaptenraad [Dutch Council of the Disabled]

Portugal Secretariado nacional de rehabilitação (SNR) [National Rehabilitation Secretariat]

United Kingdom Royal Association for Disability and Rehabilitation (RADAR)

E. HANDYNET: NATIONAL DATA COLLECTION CENTRES

Belgium Handynet belgique, ministère de la prévoyance sociale [Handynet Belgium, Ministry for Social Security]

Denmark Sozialministeriet [Ministry of Social Affairs]

Germany Institut der Deutschen Wirtschaft, Cologne [Institute for German Economics]

Greece Foundation of Research and Technology of Computer Science

Spain Centro de autonomía personal y ayudas técnicas del INSERSO [Centre for Personal Autonomy and Technical Aids of INSERSO]

France Handynet France, Comité national français de liaison pour la réadaptation des personnes handicapées (CNFLRH) [French National Liaison Committee for the Rehabilitation of Disabled People]

Ireland National Rehabilitation Board (NRB)

Italy Servizio informazione e valutazione ausili (SIVA), Fondazione pro juventute 'Don Carlo Gnocchi', Milan [Information and Evaluation Service on Technical Aids, Don Carlo Gnocchi Youth Foundation]

Luxembourg Ministère de la famille et de la solidarité [Ministry for the Family and for Solidarity]

Netherlands Stichting Handynet Nederland, Informatievoorziening Gehandicapten, Utrecht [Dutch Handynet Foundation, Information Service for the Handicapped]

Portugal Centro de reabilitação de paralisia cerebral 'Calouste Gulbenkian' [Gulbenkian Centre for the Rehabilitation of Cerebral Palsy]

United Kingdom Disabled Living Foundation

Community Decision-Making

THE INSTITUTIONS

The Council of Ministers is responsible for decisions, on the basis of proposals from the Commission. It consists of the ministers of the member states responsible for the matters on the agenda. For a General Council this is the Foreign Ministers; for an Education Council, the Ministers of Education, for a Social Council, the Ministers of Social Affairs and/or Employment, and so on. Legally decisions made by any of these are equally simply decisions of *the* Council. Every six months heads of governments meet in a 'European Council'; this however has no legal status and cannot make decisions.

The presidency of the Council changes every six months, rotating by alphabetical order of member state as follows: Belgium, Denmark, Germany (Deutschland), Greece (Ellas), Spain (España), France, Ireland, Italy, Luxembourg, Netherlands, Portugal, United Kingdom.

The Council has its own secretariat in Brussels. Council meetings are prepared first by special committees (e.g. Education Committee, Social Questions Group), finally by the Committee of Permanent Representatives (COREPER).

The Council normally meets in Brussels, but during two months of the year in Luxembourg.

The European Parliament is directly elected every five years by universal suffrage. There are 518 members, representation of countries ranging from 81 each for Germany, France, Italy and the United Kingdom to 6 for Luxembourg. Members sit in the Assembly by political parties, in a semicircle from left to right. The two largest parties are the Socialists and the Christian Democrats ('European People's Party').

The Parliament gives advice on all important Commission proposals and decides on budget allocation over many areas, including all those directly affecting disability. It may adopt Resolutions on its own initiative calling on the Council or the Commission to act in a certain way; these invitations have no binding force. It also has the power to dismiss the Commission.

Parliament elects its own President, currently the Spanish MEP Enrique Baron Crespo.

Parliamentary business is prepared by specific committees (for example, Committee on Education, Training and Youth; Committee on Social Affairs). There are also informal forums — for example, the All-Party Group on Disablement.

The Assembly, the committees and the political groups have separate secretariats. The Assembly meets in Strasbourg, the committees in Brussels. The headquarters of the secretariat is in Luxembourg.

The European Commission exists at two levels, the political (the members of the Commission) and the administrative (the services of the Commission). The Commission bears no resemblance to the secretariat of an International Organization.

The Commission is responsible both for making all formal proposals for the implementation of the Treaties, and for carrying out all decisions once made by the Council. The members of the Commission are politicians appointed by their own governments, but to serve the Community, not the national interest. There are at present 17 Commissioners, two each from Germany, Spain, France, Italy and the United Kingdom, and one each from Belgium, Denmark, Greece, Ireland, Luxembourg, Netherlands and Portugal. The President of the Commission (at present Jacques Delors) is appointed by the Council. He is responsible for the allocation of portfolios among his colleagues; currently the Greek Commissioner, Vasso Papandreou, is responsible for both education and social affairs, including employment.

The services of the Commission operate much like any civil service. In principle there is a rational distribution of senior posts (director-general, director, head of division) among nationals. There are 23 directorates-general, a secretariat-general, a legal service and a number of other units. For disabled people the most important departments are the Directorate-General for Employment, Industrial Relations and Social Affairs (DG V) and the Task Force Human Resources — Education, Training and Youth. The latter and most directorates of the former are in Brussels, the Commission's headquarters; one directorate of DG V, together with a few other departments of the Commission, is in Luxembourg.

The directorates in DG V are as follows:

1. Employment, including equality for women.
2. Living and working conditions and social protection, including the divisions responsible for the problems of poverty and the elderly, for migrants, and for measures in favour of disabled people.
3. The European Social Fund.
4. Health and Safety (in Luxembourg).

The process

The stages by which a decision is reached are typically these:

1. *The Commission makes a proposal*. This could be for a policy instrument (a Directive or Regulation, which are legally binding; or a Recommendation, which is not), or for the establishment or review of a fund, a research programme, an exchange scheme, an action programme made up of several elements, or the like.

    The proposal is prepared in the relevant service under the political direction of the responsible Commissioner and his or her cabinet. It is then agreed by the Commission as a whole and submitted formally to the Council.
2. *The Council refers the proposal to the Parliament*. The relevant parliamentary committee appoints a rapporteur who prepares a draft Resolution; this, once amended, goes to the Assembly for adoption.
3. If all goes well, *the Council adopts the proposal*. This will be in a form more or less modified, both in the light of the Parliament's response, and as a result of discussion in the Council committee and COREPER (see above).
4. *The Commission carries out what has been decided*. In the case of a policy instrument, this will mean monitoring and reporting on its implementation in the member states. In the case of a fund or programme, this will involve overall management, including the financial aspects.

    The same basic procedure applies for the whole of the Community's annual budget, apart from the right of the Parliament to have the last word on the allocation of resources on a number of items including the action programme on disability.

Appendix 4

Date Chart

Jan. 1974 Adoption of the Community Social Action Programme

June 1974 Adoption of the initial action programme for the vocational rehabilitation of handicapped persons

July 1975 Commission's Communication on the elimination of architectural barriers; launching of the scheme of grants to housing projects

Oct. 1975 Launching of the network of rehabilitation centres

Oct. 1979 Commission's report on the initial programme

Sept. 1980 Commission report on the housing grant scheme

1981 UN International Year of Disabled People

Mar. 1981 European Parliament Resolution on the economic, social and vocational integration of disabled persons

Nov. 1981 Commission's Communication on the social integration of disabled people (first action programme proposal)

Dec. 1981 Council Resolution adopting the first action programme

May 1982 Establishment in the Commission's services of the Bureau for Action in Favour of Disabled People

Feb. 1983 Launching of the network of district projects

Mar. 1984 Commission workshop on employment

June 1984 Council Conclusions on the integration of disabled children into ordinary schools

Sept. 1984 Milan conference launching the Handynet project

July 1986 Council Recommendation on the employment of disabled people

Oct. 1986 District project seminar on independent living, Piacenza

Oct. 1986 Commission report on progress in implementation of educational integration

Jan. 1987 Commission workshop on mobility and transport

Mar. 1987 Commission proposal for a programme on educational integration

May 1987 Council Conclusions concerning co-operation on educational integration

July 1987 Commission proposal for a second action programme on social and economic integration

Sept. 1987 European Parliament Resolution on transport for elderly and handicapped persons

Sept. 1987 Commission workshop on public access

Apr. 1988 Council Decision adopting a second action programme (Helios)

Dec. 1988 Commission report on the implementation of the Recommendation on employment

May 1989 Commission workshop on housing

June 1989 Council Conclusions on the employment of disabled people

Sept. 1989 Council Conclusions on a global policy for disability

Sept. 1989 Commission report on the progress of the Handynet project

Dec. 1989 Council Decision on the development of the Handynet project

May 1990 Council Resolution on educational integration

Feb. 1991 Commission interim report on the progress of the Helios programme

Feb. 1991 Commission draft Directive on mobility of disabled workers

Name Index

Country Index

General Index